T0327729

ON COMPANY TIME

Modernist Latitudes

MODERNIST LATITUDES

Jessica Berman and Paul Saint-Amour, Editors

Modernist Latitudes aims to capture the energy and ferment of modernist studies by continuing to open up the range of forms, locations, temporalities, and theoretical approaches encompassed by the field. The series celebrates the growing latitude ("scope for freedom of action or thought") that this broadening affords scholars of modernism, whether they are investigating little-known works or revisiting canonical ones. Modernist Latitudes will pay particular attention to the texts and contexts of those latitudes (Africa, Latin America, Australia, Asia, Southern Europe, and even the rural United States) that have long been misrecognized as ancillary to the canonical modernisms of the global North.

On Company Time

AMERICAN MODERNISM

IN THE BIG MAGAZINES

Donal Harris

COLUMBIA UNIVERSITY PRESS   NEW YORK

COLUMBIA UNIVERSITY PRESS

Publishers Since 1893

NEW YORK   CHICHESTER, WEST SUSSEX

cup.columbia.edu

Library of Congress Cataloging-in-Publication Data

Names: Harris, Donal, author.

Title: On company time : American modernism in the big magazines /
   Donal Harris.

Description: New York : Columbia University Press, [2016] |
   Series: Modernist latitudes | Includes bibliographical references and index.

Identifiers: LCCN 2016013380 (print) | LCCN 2016024427 (ebook) |
   ISBN 9780231177726 (cloth : alk. paper) | ISBN 9780231541343 (e-book)

Subjects: LCSH: American literature—20th century—History and criticism. |
   Modernism (Literature)—United States. | Periodicals—Publishing—United States—
   History—20th century. | Authors and publishers—United States—History—
   20th century. | Popular literature—United States—History and criticism. |
   Literature and society—United States—History—20th century

Classification: LCC PS228.M63 H37 2016 (print) | LCC PS228.M63 (ebook) |
   DDC 810.9/112—dc23

LC record available at https://lccn.loc.gov/2016013380

c 10 9 8 7 6 5 4 3 2 1

Cover design: Philip Pascuzzo

CONTENTS

ACKNOWLEDGMENTS

I N THE DAILY HUSTLE OF OFFICE LIFE, IT'S EASY TO
take for granted how edifying it can be to lean on one's colleagues
and coworkers. This book makes a case for the central role such
moments of institutional affiliation play in the history of American modernism, so it seems only fitting to begin by acknowledging my own
debts. Foremost on this list is the University of Memphis, which has
provided the support—financial, intellectual, temporal, moral—to complete the research and writing of this book. Eric Link and Josh Phillips
have been ideal department chairs, full of advice and encouragement
that made life much easier. Conversations with Kathy Lou Schultz, Carey
Mickalites, Shelby Crosby, Terrence Tucker, and Theron Britt have all
made their way into this book, and Will Duffy, Darryl Domingo, and
Ron Fuentes have made Memphis a wonderful place to live and work.
Philip Leventhal and Columbia University Press have shown me invaluable support, and I've been lucky to have them on my side in bringing
this project to fruition.

Much of the research and writing of this book began in the basement
of the English Department at the University of California, Los Angeles,
where I was provided ample time and generous resources. Mark McGurl

and Michael North have guided this project at every stage, have been unfailing in their support, and have struck models for rigorous, generous, and stylish scholarship that will stay with me long after this book is put to bed. Richard Yarborough taught me to say what I mean, and he made the things I say far more interesting. He also instilled in me a healthy fear of scare quotes, for which I will be forever grateful. Yogita Goyal made crucial suggestions to several chapters at a key moment of the revision process. At an early moment, Michael Szalay reminded me to write about what I like—advice that went along way. Aaron Jaffe, Stuart Burrows, Loren Glass, Jeff Allred, Matthew Levay, Evan Kindley, and Merve Emre are only some of the far-flung readers who have left a mark on this project over the years.

Portions of two of these chapters benefited from the perennially insightful feedback of the Americanist Research Colloquium and the M/ELT research group at UCLA. Chris Looby, Michael Cohen, Sarah Mesle, Christopher Mott, and Brian Kim Stefans always asked the right questions. Jackie Ardam, Jeremy Schmidt, Jack Caughey, Christian Reed, Tara Fickle, and Justine Pizzo were inspiring fellow travelers in grad life. I always write with the goal of impressing Brendan O'Kelly and Ian Newman. Kate Marshall modeled for me good scholarship and good citizenship, and I'm honored to call her a friend. Sam See was and is incomparable. The world is a less inspiring place without him.

Finally, I owe my deepest debts to my family. My parents, my brothers, and the Winn family have been unflagging in their faith in me. I cannot imagine where I'd be without Sarahbeth Winn, who is the best person I know. This book is dedicated to SB, Milo, and Theodore.

Portions of chapters 3 and 4 appeared in altered forms as "Finding Work: James Agee in the Office," *PMLA* 127, no. 4 (2012): 766–781; and "Understanding Eliot: Mass Media and Literary Modernism in the American Century," *Modern Language Quarterly* 76, no. 4 (2015): 491–514. The material in chapter 4 is reprinted here with the permission of Duke University Press.

ON COMPANY TIME

Making Modernism Big

F RESH ON THE HEELS OF COMPILING *FLAPPERS AND PHILOSOPHERS* (1920), a short-story collection mostly culled from fiction previously published in the *Saturday Evening Post*, F. Scott Fitzgerald momentarily paused to imagine how popular magazines might occupy themselves when no one is reading them. The resulting short play, "This Is a Magazine," published in *Vanity Fair*, drops the "familiar characters from the American Periodical World" into an empty theater, turns on the stage lights, and lets the reader see how they interact.

The scene is the vast and soggy interior of a magazine—not powder or pistol, but paper and popular. Over the outer curtain careens a lady on horseback in five colours. With one hand she raises a cup of tea to her glossy lips while with the other she follows through on a recent mashie shot, meanwhile keeping one rich-tinted, astounding eye upon the twist of her service and its mate on the volume of pleasant poetry in her other hand. The rising of the curtain reveals the back-drop as a patch-work of magazine covers. The furniture includes a table on which lies a single periodical, to convey the abstraction 'Magazine,' and around it your players sit on chairs plastered with advertisements. Each actor holds a placard bearing the name of the character represented. For example, the Edith Wharton Story holds a placard which reads "By Edith Wharton, in three parts."

Near (but not in!) the left hand stage box is stationed a gentleman in underwear holding a gigantic placard which announces that *"THIS IS A MAGAZINE."*[1]

It is a satire, to be sure, but not of the stock characters of popular fiction or the real-world personalities with whom they shared column space. Instead, Fitzgerald sends up the eccentric form of the magazines themselves. He lights on the physical texture of the magazine, its "glossy" curtain and the backdrop made of covers, which can pull together "pleasant poetry" and Edith Wharton stories, teatime rituals and faddish sports, and then flatten them all into a single "abstraction[,] 'Magazine.'" When the curtain draws back and the action begins, the aforementioned Edith Wharton Story rubs shoulders with The Baseball Yarn, The British Serial, The Detective Story, The Robert Chambers Story, and The Little Story Without a Family. They take part in something like a drawing-room comedy, trading pun-filled banter while two Love Poems "lean tenderly across a story" to whisper sweet nothings: "I adore your form," says the first; "You've got a good figure yourself—in your second line," the second responds (228). Though a little unwieldy, the shared physical material provides the opportunity to see this unlikely cast as involved in a single plotline, one centered on the relative aesthetic fitness of each character-story, even if that means smoothing out an awful lot of stylistic heterogeneity.

It's possible to glimpse a utopian edge to this paper-based world, where the aristocratic Wharton and the plebeian sports tale can walk hand-in-hand with the British spy story and where the cover girl can ingest her poetry and tea in one fell swoop, mental labor and physical exercise all at once. Neither class nor nation nor genre stands in the way of this group: the medium of the magazine encompasses all. Alas, all is not well. It turns out the stage is rather crowded, and when each character tries to take its place the sweet talk devolves into insults: "Your climax is crooked," The Robert Chambers Story warns The Edith Wharton Story; "At least, I'm not full of mixed metaphors!" she tells The Baseball Yarn (229). The argument explodes in a "contagious excitement" that finds "an Efficiency Article los[ing] its head" and the Baseball Yarn threatening the British Serial, "I'll kick you one in the conclusion!" which, we've been told, is not much of a conclusion at all. With the fight at full broil, the "large glossy eyes of the cover girl, on horseback in five colours," loom over the action as she rides across the stage, trailed by a single sentence that removes any doubt about the ultimate goal of the printed pandemonium: "The Circulation increases" (230).

When Fitzgerald pulls back the cover to see how a magazine acts on its own, he finds the content arguing about its form, and in doing so he enters an ongoing conversation about the popular periodicals' effect on the character of literary culture in the early twentieth century. In fact, his skepticism about the aesthetic possibilities of a medium defined by its stylistic variety echoes a fairly common sentiment for authors who were tempted by the seemingly endless number of massive, mass-market magazines that could offer a fledgling writer financial solvency in the form of an accepted story or an editorial position but were also wary of the long-term consequences for their writing and reputation. W. E. B. Du Bois, less playfully than Fitzgerald, referred to popular magazines as a "hodge-podge of lie, gossip, twaddle and caricature" that had transformed his contemporaries into a "magazine mad—a magazine-devouring nation."[2] Willa Cather, ever one to pour cold water on the popular press, argued that the generic variability of the magazines can be traced to the first general-interest magazines of the 1890s, and that variability made it nearly impossible for readers to evaluate any single published work. In "On the Art of Fiction," which appeared the same year as "This Is a Magazine," she claimed that "the greatest obstacles that writers today have to get over are the dazzling journalistic successes of twenty years ago. . . . They gave us, altogether, poor standards—taught us to multiply our ideas instead of to condense them." Where Fitzgerald imagines the stories fighting among one another for page space and Du Bois sees magazines producing pathological readers, Cather locates the battle in the individual author: she argues that every good story "must have in it the strength of a dozen fairly good stories that have been sacrificed to it."[3] This trade in quantity for aesthetic quality in turn might remind one of the sacrificial compression espoused in Ernest Hemingway's theory of writing, which, as legend has it, he learned in the editorial offices of the *Kansas City Star* and applied to his early *transition* stories. Each of these writers understands differently the problem of periodical overabundance for literary production, but taken together they attest to the imaginative energies that early twentieth-century authors in the United States dedicated to, in Fitzgerald's words, the "abstraction 'Magazine.'"

That Du Bois edited magazines for roughly fifty years, that Willa Cather started as a cub reporter in Red Cloud, Nebraska, before publishing her critiques of journalism in major periodicals, and that Hemingway tied his massively influential literary style to time spent in editorial offices suggest that the interlocking questions of periodical and literary form were most potent in those writers who in various ways strapped themselves to the mastheads of the very journals they spoke down to. In this vein, one of the many ironies in Fitzgerald's mockery of the flabby, frenetic material inside mass-market magazines is that they are the very ones that provided him with his foothold in the literary market. With a slightly updated character list, one could easily imagine The Fitzgerald Flapper Tale right in the middle of the battle royal, explaining the wonders of bobbed hair and the Jazz Age in the lyrical prose that he would practice in early short stories and perfect in *The Great Gatsby* (1925). For although he contributed to "smart" journals such as *Vanity Fair* and *The Smart Set*, he more often and far more lucratively sent material to glossies such as the *Saturday Evening Post*, the ostensible target of "This Is a Magazine." In fact, he sold more than half a dozen stories to the *Post* in the year leading up to his parody, and his one-hundred-plus publications in that journal over the course of his career made him for many reviewers synonymous with the figure of a "*Post* writer."[4] Placing fiction at the *Post, Collier's, Scribner's*, and *Century*, among others, provided him the financial freedom to move back to New York from Minnesota, where he had holed up to write *This Side of Paradise*, and finally marry his sweetheart, Zelda; however, his new fame brought other section editors calling, too, as his extravagant personal life became the topic of gossip columns and society pages. Much like the editorial content of his satire, his own contributions ended up spilling out of the fiction section and into other departments of the magazine. In June 1920, he complained to the editor of *Movie Weekly*, "I have unearthed so many esoteric facts about myself lately for magazines etc that I blush to continue to send out colorful sentences about a rather colorless life."[5] That is, magazines fund the escapades that turn him into the editorial content contained in other, less prestigious areas of the table of contents, which, if "This Is a Magazine" is to be believed, is doing a poor job of keeping everything in its place.

This book takes Fitzgerald's, Du Bois's, and Cather's ambivalence toward the role of popular magazines in literary culture and their transformation of that ambivalence into formal innovations in their own work as a representative feature of American modernism. It argues that American modernism's long, conflicted history on the pages and inside the editorial ranks of mass-market magazines provides a crucial yet understudied catalyst for some of the movement's key authors and texts. A surprising number of American novelists and poets associated with modernism found financial sustenance in the expanding mass-market-magazine market of the twentieth century, and this book combs through a motley archive of publication prospectuses, editorial mastheads, glossy (as well as matte-finished) pages, newsrooms and production offices, and personal and corporate biographies, as well as a bevy of novels, short stories, and poetry in order to account for the influence of commercial periodical production on their literary output. In their roles as founders, editors, reporters, and columnists, as well as their inclusion as editorial content, a wide range of modernist writers came into close and sustained contact with big magazines, and this institutional setting indelibly marks the literary work produced both under the magazine's mantle and in the writer's ostensibly free time outside of the office. The authors I discuss—Cather, Du Bois, Jessie Fauset, James Agee, T. S. Eliot, and Ernest Hemingway, among others—are mostly remembered as exceptional innovators of literary form and standout theorists of literary culture and authorship as it relates to the marketplace. But they often did their innovating and theorizing from inside the editorial offices of groundbreaking popular magazines— *McClure's, The Crisis, Time, Life, Esquire*—while influencing the editorial mission statements and house styles that made these periodicals thrive. The relationship works in the other direction as well. That is, "modernism" as a loose, often tacit set of ideas about the relationship between aesthetics and the literary market, as well as a malleable set of tropes, provided a useful cultural formation against which popular magazines could leverage their own ideas about and experiments in the print marketplace. So, along with reading these "big magazines" into modernism, this book also turns the focus around to see how modernism influenced the look and feel of those magazines from both within the editorial office and outside of it.

During the period covered here—roughly from the professionalization of magazine production in the 1890s to the mass adoption of television in the mid-1950s—the interactions between modernism and big magazines expand in scope and change in tone from general hostility to mutual appreciation. The 1940s found modernist writers like

T. S. Eliot, Gertrude Stein, Ernest Hemingway, and William Faulkner becoming popular, to some degree, and it is also when "modernism" became an increasingly well-defined and widely visible category in the United States. Midcentury art critics and intellectuals such as Clement Greenberg, Dwight MacDonald, and Paul Goodman interpreted both the popularity of individual artists and the consolidation of formerly disparate avant-gardes as a decline narrative: the subsumption of art by kitsch, or of genuine experimentation by the highly mannered middlebrow, or of aristocratic taste by popular demand.[6] Yet a decline narrative depends on some original purity of cultural fields that was later mongrelized, and this book complicates that position by detailing the prevalence of writers who participated in and often outright depended on brazenly market-oriented big magazines. This does not replace the decline narrative with one of triumph. Instead, *On Company Time* describes the deep affiliations of mass-market magazines and literary modernism as a mundane fact of everyday life, offering a literary-historical interpretation of this institutional overlap rather than an opinion on whether it is good for literature. And when one emphasizes the structural connection between mass-market and modernist print culture, it becomes clear that the story of twentieth-century American literature is not just one of modernism becoming mainstream—which isn't really all that surprising—but also one of the mainstream reimagining itself as modernist.

Throughout, I use the term "big magazine" to draw together examples from an eclectic range of periodical genres: the muckraking journal, the African American monthly, the newsmagazine, the photomagazine, and the men's fashion monthly. What they have in common, beyond the necessary qualification of being unapologetically commercial, is a conscious effort to expand their readerships by way of their textual and visual styles rather than their content. This style-driven approach was not normally the case in the popular periodical market. In the late nineteenth century, Edward Munsey of *Munsey's*, Edward Bok of *Ladies Home Journal*, and George Horace Lorimer of the *Saturday Evening Post* were only the most prominent pioneers of a hybrid magazine genre alternately titled the general-interest or "family home" magazine that brought together the high tone of older "quality" magazines such as *The Atlantic Monthly* and *Harper's* and the economic model of the penny press. Spurred on by advertising revenues—which were tied to circulation numbers—and new marketing strategies, these magazines took part in "selling culture" to as many people as possible, and they understood the path to more readers as content driven.[7] This content-based approach is embedded in the etymology of "magazine," which comes from the French "*magasin*," for storehouse, an architectural metaphor that would be reimagined by Edward Bok as analogous first to a general store and then to the middle-class home. The different "departments" within the table of contents were like a house's functionally divided living and work spaces. Fiction for the easy chair, recipes for the kitchen, gossip for the parlor, advice columns, sporting news, celebrity profiles, travel articles, political stories, advertisements, questionnaires: all between two covers, all under one roof.

This is the overstuffed, content-driven magazine that "This Is a Magazine" says could benefit from a little attention to craft. The titles I group under "big magazine" agree with Fitzgerald, and they experiment with the formal possibilities of the periodical, particularly with editorial voice and visual patterns, while still keeping commercial success and enormous readerships at the center of their business model. By manipulating distinct aspects of the editorial and aesthetic production of periodicals, they set standards for what today we take for granted as a journal's "house style," a notion of aesthetic uniformity that develops over the first half of the twentieth century alongside the transformation of magazines into professional endeavors. I discuss a distinct aesthetic preoccupation for each magazine—a preoccupation always intrinsically tied to the magazine's perceived audience—and argue that each responds to a unique issue in the print market at a given moment in its development: in the 1890s, the omniscient gentlemanly voice of *McClure's* plays to its gendered notion of middle-class readership; in the 1910s, *The Crisis* literalizes racialized intellectual work in its attention to page color; and in the 1920s, the impersonally corporate voice of "*Time* style" develops out of the fear of information overload. The path traced is not a teleology, but it does have a logic internal to the periodical market, and we will see how over the course of the twentieth century the field of popular periodicals evolves into a highly complex, diverse, well-organized, self-conscious, and aesthetically rich field of cultural production.

In describing these particular titles as big magazines, I am not claiming that they are the only ones that respond to commercial demands with formal solutions, nor is this book an encyclopedic account of every connection between a mass-market magazine and a modernist writer.

Instead, I see each offering an exemplary case of how at specific historical moments, publishers and editors answered the felt need for product differentiation by reimagining how a magazine could produce, store, and distribute information to the largest readership possible. And, in addition to employing and publishing so many masscult-phobic novelists and poets whom we now consider modernist, these magazines' experiments with the limitations and possibilities of their medium echo the very formal tenets of modernism that popular magazines are often placed in opposition to.

This book has three major goals: first, to bring modernist studies to bear on commercial magazines and vice versa; second, to show that a cluster of questions regarding office culture and periodical design can help us discuss magazines that are not often grouped together; and, finally, to trace how the organizational and aesthetic developments in specific magazine offices feed forward into the literary writing of key figures in American literary modernism. To address these goals best, each chapter takes up a different possible relationship between authors and magazines: Willa Cather as managing editor, W. E. B. Du Bois as founder and publisher, James Agee as reporter, and T. S. Eliot and Ernest Hemingway as editorial content—the former unintentionally becoming a symbol of American culture's mobility at midcentury, the latter all too active in transforming his famously terse prose into a widely circulating affective posture. To be sure, there is a long paper trail of complaints against and apologies for journalism's effect on literature; it's a genre that dates back to the eighteenth century and reaches its apex in the early 1900s.[8] A major impetus behind *On Company Time*, though, is to refrain from proscriptive judgments about economic and aesthetic arrangements, either pro or con, between artists and their periodical patrons. And when one looks at modernism and big magazines together, one finds a fraught network of writers, editors, publishers, and media conglomerates, as well as their various printed artifacts, that is conflicted over American print culture's proper book or periodical form but also deeply invested in print's primacy in shaping the cultural landscape. So, by acknowledging the fundamental role of big magazines in modernist literary production, this book first describes and then interprets American modernism as evolving within rather than against the mass print culture of its moment.

For instance, I could simply note how often commercial magazines turn up as thematically weighty props within American modernist literature.

F. Scott Fitzgerald uses the "Town Tattle" and a movie magazine in *The Great Gatsby* to accentuate Myrtle's social difference from Tom and Daisy, though he also portrays the East and West Egg–ers congregating around a *Saturday Evening Post*, which Jordan Baker reads aloud. Popular magazines are strewn throughout William Faulkner's *Light in August*, and T. S. Eliot acerbically refers to the readers of the *Boston Evening Transcript*, who "sway in the wind like ripe corn." Theodore Dreiser's *Sister Carrie*, which, as much as anything else is a warning against the siren's song of the popular press, finds a melancholic Hurstwood confining himself to his rocking chair as he pathologically rereads news coverage of the same labor unrest that he witnessed firsthand moments before. Ernest Hemingway's "Banal Story" correlates the language of self-promotion in an American magazine to the profanation of a bullfighter's memory in the full-length colored pictures that Andalusian newspapers sell after his death. A similar image gets picked up by Professor Godfrey St. Peter, the protagonist of Willa Cather's *The Professor's House*, who laments that "whenever he wrote for popular periodicals it got him into trouble."[9] No matter the individual attitude toward mass-market periodicals—and over the course of this book we will encounter many different shades of ambivalence—I take the basic literary-historical situation as worthy of interpretation: many authors made their money in the magazines, they were expected to have an opinion about the value of such an arrangement, and their attitude toward such employment arrangements bleeds into their literary output.

In its focus on the medial and institutional axes of modernist literary production, this book contributes to a growing number of studies energized by book history, print-culture studies, and a loosely sociological approach to the public and private institutions that establish and normalize literary value. Most obviously, this study contributes to what Robert Scholes and Sean Latham call "the rise of periodical studies," which has found special traction among modernist scholars interested in the coterie of literature and arts magazines produced in the 1910s and 1920s.[10] After all, to quote a recent introduction to the field, "modernism began in the magazines,"[11] and the little magazines produced by and for a consciously insulated readership were key venues for circulating experimental writing and visual art. From *The Little Review*'s twenty-three-part serialization of James Joyce's *Ulysses* (1918–1920) to Ernest Hemingway's early submissions to *transition* to *The Waste Land*'s initial publications in *The Dial* and *The Criterion* to Jean Toomer's compiling *Cane* from pieces previously published in *Broom, The Nomad, The Modern Review, The Little Review, S4N*, and elsewhere, the growing consensus that little magazines provide, in Mark Morrisson's words, the "public face of modernism" can seem long overdue.[12] In this light, the recent emphasis on the modernist little magazine can be seen as an extension of the critical trajectory inaugurated by Lawrence Rainey's field-defining *Institutions of Modernism*, which countered the long tail of New Critical assumptions about the autotelic text by focusing on modernism's material and institutional contexts. "Modernism," Rainey writes,

> poised at the cusp of th[e] transformation of the public sphere, responded with a tactical retreat into a divided world of patronage, collecting, speculation, and investment, a retreat that entailed the construction of an institutional counterspace, securing a momentary respite from a public realm increasingly degraded, even as it entailed a fatal compromise with precisely that degradation.[13]

Self-consciously modern writers, in Rainey's telling, establish independent cultural institutions that rely on the technological and medial forms of the print revolution but not its content. Or, in his own words and borrowing a phrase from T. S. Eliot, he shows "how modernism negotiated its way among the 'contrived corridors' of its own production."[14]

On Company Time retains Rainey's insights into the complex inner workings of modernist cultural capital, but it turns his focus inside-out and instead surveys how modernism grows out of the innovations taking place within mass print culture—and, importantly, how specific modernist writers and the idea of modernism as an artistic movement played fundamental roles in the development of commercial periodicals over the course of the twentieth century. When one looks at modernism from the point of view of well-funded and massively popular titles like *McClure's, The Crisis, Time, Life*, and *Esquire*, the "contrived corridors" of coterie groups can look rather narrow. The exponential increases in mass print culture between 1890 and 1905 saw the total newspaper circulation in the United States rise from 36 million to 57 million. During the same period magazine circulations tripled, leading periodical historians to claim the magazine as America's "first national mass media."[15] The new methods that people such as S. S. McClure, W. E. B. Du Bois, Henry Luce and Britton Hadden, and others develop to finance, staff, advertise, and distribute these magazines bring into the fold many novelists and poets who would prefer to remain outside. And the influence of these affiliations on the development of modernism is nearly impossible to measure from the little magazines, which, in Rainey's telling, had more or less free rein to define and publicize their literary endeavors, with very little connection to the other writers, magazines, publishing houses, or cultural institutions that constitute the overwhelming majority of the literary field and that might want to define the relationship between modern literature and modern mass print culture differently.[16] So by turning from the self-consciously little to the unapologetically big magazines, *On Company Time* takes account of the institutional and aesthetic feedback between modernist and periodical forms as they help define each other over the first half of the twentieth century.

The category of the "big magazines," then, offers an alternative model to that of the little magazines of modernism, but it also speaks to other, less aggressively insular periodical forms, such as the nineteenth-century "quality" magazines and the "general-interest" or "family home" magazines that emerged in the 1890s and early 1900s. The scalar categories "big" and "little" may seem incompatible with one of "quality," but in truth the big magazine is the outlying term. This is because "quality" and "little" work as meaningful generic descriptions of specific types of magazines insofar as they refer to restrictive attitudes toward readership rather than to size or content. Part of this has to do with cost. As the historian Frank Luther Mott has documented, quality journals such as *The Atlantic* and *Harper's*, both founded in the 1850s as venues for and about an elite audience, marketed themselves to a socially elevated readership centered in American metropolises. In addition, they purposefully priced themselves out of the average reader's budget (usually, around thirty-five cents), thus ensuring that their brilliant ideas would not fall into the hands of the impressionable, irrational masses.[17] A central quality of "quality" entails the geographic and economic restriction of the magazine's circulation.

The method of such restriction is quite different from that of the little magazines, though "little," like "quality," is also a misleading adjective. As Ezra Pound outlines in his 1930 essay "Small Magazines," size—either the size of readership or size of the actual document—matters much less than "motivation," which is far more difficult to quantify:

> The significance of the small magazine has, obviously, nothing to do with format. The significance of any work of art or literature is a root significance that goes down into its original motivation. When this motivation is merely a desire for money or publicity, or when this motivation is in great part such a desire for money directly or publicity as a means indirectly of getting money, there occurs a pervasive monotony in the product corresponding to the underlying monotony in the motivation.[18]

Pound explicitly compares experimental journals like *Broom*, *The Little Review*, and *The Dial* to the same "somnolent" titles that Mott categorizes as quality: *The Atlantic* and *Harper's* of the older stock, *Century* and *Scribner's* of the newer. Small magazines, Pound surmises, distinguish themselves by a "pure intention" that "makes them worthwhile," one thoroughly aligned with the notion of autonomy intrinsic to modernist aesthetics, which here expands its range to include the publication sites of modernist art, too (699). He says that there is "a vast and impassable . . . gulf" (694) between the truly intelligent audience who appreciates pure artistic intention and the evaluative capabilities of the general population. Though the material contained in these magazines usually bears little resemblance to that of *The Atlantic* or *Century*, Pound's summation of their attitude toward most readers places them in ironic proximity to the qualities.

So the quality magazines and the little magazines both imagine restrictiveness as constitutive of their periodical projects, but it serves a different purpose for each market. The end goal of the little magazines for Pound is no less than literary history. "The work of writers who have emerged in or via such magazines outweighs in permanent value the work of the writers who have not emerged in this manner," he writes, and the front line of literary history takes places in these journals.

> The history of contemporary letters has, to a very manifest extent, been written in such magazines. The commercial magazines have been content and are still more than content to take derivative products ten or twenty years after the germ has appeared in the free magazines. . . . The heavier the "overhead" in a publishing business the less that business can afford to deal in experiment. This purely sordid and eminently practical

consideration will obviously affect all magazines save those that are either subsidized (as chemical research is subsidized) or else very cheaply produced (as the penniless inventor produced in his barn or his attic).

(702)

Without explicitly naming it, Pound sets up the "purely sordid and eminently practical" matter of an economics of cultural capital. The artists' showy turn away from financial success insulates them from the demands of a large and obtuse reading public.

The big magazines I consider in *On Company Time* take these competing economies of capital and attention as their motivating force, but toward both contemporary circulation and lasting literary value, they take the opposite approach of the quality and little magazines. Instead of tying literary value to restricted circulation, they seek a form that differentiates the magazine from the masses of overly abundant print culture but that also can reach the widest and most diverse readership possible. For example, S. S. McClure envisioned the style of his new ten-cent magazine as replicating that of a "gentleman" on a social visit to the readers' homes, bridging the content of the quality magazines with "ordinary conversation in the family gathering." *McClure's*, unlike either *The Atlantic* or *The Little Review*—the latter bore the phrase "making no compromise with the public taste" on its cover—sought to be "representative of many people's interests," always aiming to be "still more representative."[19]

In various ways, the big magazines attempted to expand their reading publics beyond class-based or regional designations, and what is most interesting about this process, from the perspective of a literary scholar, is how often this expansion is figured as a formal project in dialogue with that of modernism. This notion, that a popular and commercial enterprise would place priority on prose and visual style, is anathema to some of the most well-traveled definitions of what makes literature "literary" during the early twentieth century. These definitions often specifically contrasted serious literary writing with journalism. "Literature is news that STAYS news," Pound pronounced in *ABC of Reading*. A similar sentiment can be found in the 1918 Dada manifesto, which opens by regretting that the very term "DADA" has "brought journalists to the gates of a world unforeseen" and then goes on to claim that "a comprehensible work is the product of a journalist."[20] Tzara's image of journalists at the gates of a forbidden world, attempting and failing to write about an approach to cultural production that simply cannot be translated outside of its place of origin, can help us extend the foregoing discussion of periodical content and form to the issue of writing itself. Tzara's insistence that literature and journalism are separated by their attitudes toward comprehensibility finds a more elaborate form in T. S. Eliot's introduction to Djuna Barnes's *Nightwood*. Eliot contends the novel's formal innovations are its greatest assets and favorably compares them to the standard prose of mass print culture. "Most contemporary novels are not really 'written,'" he explains, because their content consists of "an accurate rendering of the noises that human beings make in their daily simple needs of communication."[21] Transcribing common life isn't just insufficient art, though: it sinks down all the way to journalism, settling at the cultural bottom alongside "a prose which is no more alive than that of a competent newspaper writer or a government official." The "ordinary novel-reader," whose taste and threshold for complexity have been thoroughly stripped away by the news (and novels that strive for newslike reflection of the world), simply can't meet the intellectual demands of *Nightwood*. The equation of the reporter and government official is telling, as it emphasizes a feeling of dry, rote, bureaucratic standardization associated with popular periodicals.

The great trouble with Eliot's insistence on the novel's verbal purity, though, is that Barnes was a respected newspaper and magazine writer, and before writing *Nightwood* she worked the "freak beat" in New York for a number of American periodicals, reporting on the burgeoning bohemian scene in Greenwich Village, the political tribulations of New York Wobblies, and the cultural life of Coney Island. In what was perhaps her most famous piece of experiential journalism, she followed a suffragette and documented what it felt like to be force-fed. That is, Barnes's journalism not only recorded an "accurate rendering of the noises that human beings make" for consumption by readers of the *New York Press* and *Brooklyn Daily Eagle*, but her job entailed making the latest activities of political, cultural, and artistic outsiders comprehensible for "ordinary novel-reader" types. From this angle, *Nightwood* lies on a continuum with her exposé journalism as it reports back on the eccentric philosophies and affiliations of an increasingly prominent social type: the postwar expat. More telling for the interaction between big magazines and modernism, though, is that she first traveled to London and Paris on assignment for *McCall's*—a popular women's magazine—and met Eliot, Pound, and James Joyce because both *McCall's* and *Vanity Fair* asked her to conduct interviews.

So it isn't just that Eliot may overstate the literary limitations of the journalist or that ordinary novel readers, reporters, and bureaucrats might have more interest in innovative literary works than he assumes but also that those newspapers and magazines invest resources in bringing eccentric cultural practices into the fold of mainstream print culture, both by hiring people like Barnes and by reporting on the cluster of artists she comes to be identified with.

Viewing the relationship between American literary modernism and popular magazines through the critical lens made available by Barnes's career and Fitzgerald's "This Is a Magazine" allows us to step back from Eliot's and Fitzgerald's evaluative claims about the practice of journalism and the role of the "Magazine" in American print culture, on the one hand, and their relationship to the writing practices and material circulation of American modernism, on the other, and track the patterns of affiliation between big magazines and modernism as an increasingly normalized arrangement over the first half of the twentieth century. Although "This Is a Magazine" does not make for particularly compelling theater, Fitzgerald's speculations on the complicated inner life of mass-market magazines, and particularly his attention to the aesthetic questions that those stories seem to be asking themselves about literary form and print media, capture a number of ways in which, as both collaborators and competitors, each contributed to the other's success. Commercial magazines acted as financial, imaginative, and institutional incubators for a number of literary experiments over the first half of the twentieth century. It is not just that Fitzgerald and other authors turned to popular periodicals when they needed money in support of their literary endeavors—though many certainly did this—or that a surprising number of authors worked at some of the most successful magazines in history, or even that these writers and their work often turned up as the editorial content filling the pages of mass-market publications. The very existence of "This Is a Magazine," its surprising weirdness, and the fact that it found a home in a slightly more upscale magazine than the one it satirizes evince how magazines could spark literary innovations among the many who took them seriously, even for a moment, and even when not being paid directly for the product of such works.

By focusing closely on one prominent site where these modernists earned a living and by defining big magazines as those that base their plans for commercial success and wider readership in formal experiments,

I open a dialogue between a strand of canonical modernism and a professional industry that often set themselves against each other. Each author I take up in the following chapters comes into contact with big magazines in a unique way, and by examining this contact I trace a strand of modernist writing and literary experimentation fundamentally indebted to the double life of literary author and magazine writer. While I refrain from establishing a prescriptive set of qualifiers for modernism, I do contend that the attributes of each author's output that align with a common "modernist" technique emerge from the intersection of their periodical and literary endeavors. Whether it is Willa Cather's insistence on the fiction of aesthetic autonomy, W. E. B. Du Bois's preoccupation with the materiality of language, James Agee's sometimes crippling formal reflexivity, or Jessie Fauset's narrative experiments with interiority, I show how each of these modernist techniques are indebted to work at the big magazines.

Alfred Kazin, himself a former staff writer for *Fortune*, goes so far as to claim the "poet-reporter" as one of the dominant figures of twentieth-century American authorship.[22] I'll trace the development of this figure back to the 1890s, when, according to Christopher Wilson, a new "character" of writer emerged alongside the expansion of mass media, one based on "strenuosity, political activism, and outdoor life."[23] This figure is opposed to the amateurish nineteenth-century "man of letters," for whom writing is a supplementary skill to some other occupation. Writing, both journalistic and literary, becomes *work* in this period, with its own set of professional standards. Both journalistic and literary writing share a model of masculine publicity, of investigation, an "ethos of exposure" and "the ideal of *reportage*."[24] Hence, according to Wilson, we find naturalist literature written by individuals (almost exclusively male) who also have served an apprenticeship in the news industry.[25] Creating literary professionalism entails writing one's cultural work into the public sphere; it conjoins literary work with mass-cultural writing, which simultaneously democratizes access to the world of ideas and extends the influence of the market into the field of letters.

As the first two chapters of this study make clear, the competences of writing literature and mass-market journalism begin to differentiate in the twentieth century for reasons related to their unique paths toward professionalization.[26] First, these decades saw both fields enter the realm of higher education, first with university-level journalism programs and then later with creative-writing programs, which separately institutionalized the skills associated with each. The Wharton School of Business at the University of Pennsylvania offered the first journalism classes in 1893; the University of Illinois offered the first four-year program in journalism in 1904; the University of Missouri founded the first standalone school of journalism in 1908; and in 1912 Columbia University opened its journalism school, with the help of a two-million-dollar endowment by Joseph Pulitzer, the publisher of the *New York World* and the *St. Louis Post-Dispatch*. Pulitzer's decision to fund journalism education became a flashpoint in a debate over the nature of reportorial and editorial work.[27] Pulitzer and other backers of journalism schools saw them as incubators for future reporters and editors, where students could systematically learn the skills of reporting, editing, and writing from journalist-professors— along with the relatively recent invention of a code of conduct known as journalistic ethics.[28] But others, such as Frederic Hudson of the *New York Herald*, claimed that the newsroom was "the true college for newspaper students" because journalism was, at the most basic level, a trade rather than a profession, meaning that one could only learn it by doing it and that fledgling reporters and editors must take up apprenticeships.[29] The question of whether writing can be taught resurfaced in similar terms when the University of Iowa established the first creative-writing program to train apprentice poets and novelists in the 1930s, though, tellingly, those debates have left the field of journalism behind.[30]

John Macy's entry on "Journalism" in Harold E. Stearns's *Civilization in the United States* (1922) offers a different cause for the professional differentiation between journalism and literary writing. For Macy, the serious writer's newfound disrespect for the work of news gathering can be seen as an unexpected symptom of the same methods of standardization that produce a nationalized, relatively independent press—that is, the things that helped make journalism respectable in the first place. According to Macy, the form and function of newspaper writing is taken for granted because of its national uniformity: "From Portland, Maine, to Portland, Oregon . . . you cannot tell from the general aspect of the newspaper you pick up what city you are in. . . . Editors, except those in charge of local news, move with perfect ease from one city to another: it is the same job at a different desk."[31] Aesthetic form replicates bureaucratic form in this situation. The model of newswriting, based on a masculine ethos of investigative writing—on uncovering "the new" and bringing it to public light—lost its luster because of its association with repeatability, with the doldrums of routinization; in the most pejorative sense, newspapers became information factories. As Archibald MacLeish says, his generation was told through the pages of magazines like *The Paris Review* to "avoid the practice of journalism as they would wet sox and gin before break-fast."[32] That is, the work associated with writing copy or reporting was positioned as antithetical to that of "serious" writing.

Literary writing, then, distinguishes itself from the standardization of journalistic writing and its mechanic work by insisting that artistic writing is idiosyncratic, nonstandardized, unprofessional, unteachable— that is, until all those characteristics are questioned when it enters the realm of higher education in the 1930s. Yet even though the protocols for journalism and literary authorship differentiate into competing com-petences, one considered low and the other high, modernism's social and aesthetic function can still be explained through a culture of profes-sionalism; one simply needs a more accurate definition of "professional-ism." The term, for Thomas Strychacz, entails "having status based on the possession of symbolic capital," and the coordination of modern-ist authorship with the organization and institutionalization of literary criticism aligned the bulk of symbolic capital with literary rather than journalistic activities.[33] High and low writing, or modernist and mass, define themselves in opposition to each other, and though the debates surrounding what truly constitutes either term often take place within mass-media forums, the debate reinforces the difference between the two types of cultural work.

This theory of literary professionalism might be described as a theory of limitation. It focuses on boundaries, on both the physical discipline and aesthetic protocols that define one type of work against another— professional mental labor against professional manual labor—and, sub-sequently, one type of writing as work against another. As the move from Wilson to Strychacz makes clear, the teleology of professionalism entails increased subdivisions based on specialization. First, all writing is defined by what it is not (it is work, it is not leisure); then different types of writing as work branch out like a family tree (literature is a fine art, it is not journalism; journalism is objective, it is not fictionalized). Yet there is an equally vocal argument among historians that the devel-opment of literary work in the twentieth century follows a process of expansion. Michael Denning's *The Cultural Front* (1996), for example, characterizes the "laboring" of the arts, especially writing, from the late

1920s until the end of World War II. Rather than read the protocols of writing as a method of cultural distinction, Denning argues that in "the age of the CIO" we find an appeal to the commonalities of work, not the differentiation of specific types. Along with rhetorical strategies, there is also an attempt among writers to replicate the organizational institutions of manual labor, which draws attention to the work of cultural production within the "cultural apparatus" or "culture industry," depending on which terminology one prefers.[34] Denning tracks the rhetorical markers of industrial work on cultural artifacts as well as the expansion of what constitutes work in this period. There is a migration of cultural work's "front" from a specific set of disciplines to all sorts of attitudes and position taking. Kenneth Burke's controversial 1935 address to the American Writers Congress becomes representative of this expansion of what counts as work, especially writerly work, when Burke compels each writer to think of himself or herself as a "total propagandist." Artistic production, for the propagandist, entails "a process of broadly and generally associating his political alignment with cultural awareness in general." In place of limitation, Burke and Denning after him seek an expanded vision of writing; cultural workers should "take an interest in as many imaginative, aesthetic and speculative fields as he can handle."[35]

Limitation or expansion, distinction or amalgamation: these are the two dominant ways that literary work in the twentieth century has been theorized. I want to consolidate these approaches into a unified argument about the position of writing in the first half of the twentieth century as it is imagined both as cultural work—how meaning attaches to art objects as they circulate through the social field—and as disciplined activity—the value and competences associated with the task of setting pen to paper. Though the limitation and expansion theories approach from different angles, both models establish a fundamental antagonism between an elitist minority culture—the limited definition of high culture—and a comprehensive version of culture, either mass or popular. I do not want to do away with the experiential reality of that antagonism; indeed, I hope to draw attention to a number of literary-historical issues during the first half of the twentieth century concerning writing, print form, and audience that produce an enormous amount of intellectual grist from the "great divide." Even after the work associated with mass-cultural and literary work began to splinter into structurally parallel yet internally differentiated practices, there were many writers who, for a number of reasons, found themselves plying their trade as staff writers or editors for large-circulation, mass-market magazines. They hoped to make use of their most salable skill set—the ability to write well—and so entered the field of commercial periodicals, and especially mass-market magazines, just as it fundamentally changed in size, scope, revenue sources, design, distribution, and, perhaps most importantly, operational organization.

Unlike newspapers, magazines were largely and self-consciously amateur affairs until the late nineteenth century. They were imagined to be and in some cases largely were "ideally to be constituted *by* contributions from readers" and in turn were considered "the natural outgrowth of readers who had been summoned by the periodical to become contributors themselves."[36] But as magazines became larger, more profitable, more diverse in their offerings, and more competitive with one another for an audience, their content also began to be produced by a more stable set of contributors increasingly hired on salary rather than paid per contribution. As George Jean Nathan explains in a 1911 *Bookman* article, this competition for audience attention caused publishers to seek a more stable body of editorial production. Thus, the "staff system" matriculated from the newspapers to the magazines, replacing freelanced content with contracted articles and bringing a wide array of writers from the outside to the inside of the modern magazine office. The impact of the staff system in magazine offices rippled out into many aspects of journalistic and literary practice in the period. The most important point at the moment is that, counterintuitively, the staff system brought with it a novel approach to market distinction. I say counterintuitive because processes of professionalization and institutional standardization usually are taken as the first steps toward homogeneity; indeed, for critics of mass-market magazines from F. R. Leavis to Ezra Pound to Dwight MacDonald, who will denounce the bland "masscult" magazines of the 1930s and 1940s, the shared economic models and standardized editorial practices of new magazines signal their sameness. At a certain level this is true, but the staff system also brought with it an extraordinary preoccupation for editors with the "personality," or house style, of specific magazines—or, with a more literary bent, what I'll take to calling the periodical voice. In short, as the magazine market became more competitive and more profitable and as individual magazines became more professionalized and regimented in the way they produced content, the savviest publishers and editors sought to distinguish themselves not by content but by style.

At the end of his memoir about the interwar expatriates, *Exile's Return*, Malcolm Cowley describes how the Great Depression upended the artistic communities of the 1920s and focused attention for the returning exiles on a much more prosaic task: getting a job. "Modestly, they were rebelling once more," he writes, but "they hadn't time to be very unhappy" because "most of their hours were given over to the simple business of earning a living." There is an "end of an era" tone in Cowley's memoir, but he also seems to find these writers' "simple business" of getting a job to be utterly prosaic.[37] Archibald MacLeish was one such job seeker. He spent time on the Left Bank with Ernest Hemingway in the mid-1920s, but then in 1929 he faced financial insolvency and moved back to the United States to serve as the education editor at *Time*. He would work at Time Inc. off and on for the next twenty years, and in a speech given in the 1950s he referred to the juxtaposition of his poetic writing and the work he did to fund it as the "two ends of the typewriter keyboard," suggesting that because his journalistic and artistic activities share so much *materially*— they require the same tools, so to speak—it is difficult to cordon off one from the other cleanly.[38] In a glowing essay on his Time Inc. years, he gushes, "Henry Luce's [founder of Time Inc. and publisher of *Time*, *Fortune*, and *Life*] offer of a job was one of the luckiest things that happened to me in a fairly lucky life," and "I got more of my own work done in my years at *Fortune* than in any other comparable period in my life."[39] MacLeish is more sanguine than most about the synergy between the two ends of the typewriter, but he is not alone in his attempt to make sense of how literary writing relates to the editorial work that often pays the bills. He came into the big-magazine fold during the Great Depression, when there were few obvious paths to financial solvency for a fledgling author other than working for the magazines.[40]

To make sense of the occupational overlap between journalism and literature that Wilson traces to the 1890s and that Cowley and MacLeish reiterate in the 1930s, I borrow from the French sociologist Bernard Lahire. Lahire's central insight into employment-based identity is that while professional fields develop by distinguishing themselves from one another, an individual's position in one field often depends on its relationship to and overlapping identification with other fields. Lahire calls this state of being "the plural actor," a condition he finds to be particularly intense for artists in the twentieth century, who more often than not must subsidize their "serious" work by making money somewhere else.[41]

This situation produces what he refers to as "the double life of writers," and by setting up shop in the border zones between social fields, he emphasizes the productive friction when two fields come into contact through an individual's double life:

> The sociologist who is interested in variations in intraindividual behavior and in individuals' patrimonies of dispositions cannot help but wonder what "kind of man" (in the Weberian sense) society is shaping when it considers the more or less schizophrenic *double life* of the writer to be a regular social phenomenon. . . . Unlike those people who experience their profession as a central and permanent part of their personality, writers who, for economic reasons, work a "day job" have a cultural and "personal" foot in literature and a material (and sometimes also "personal") foot outside of literature (the second foot freeing the first from dependence on market constraints).[42]

Whereas sociological field theory, developed most prominently by Pierre Bourdieu, is largely interested in explaining how specific fields develop distinctions, Lahire turns his attention to the ways that individuals experience social fields simultaneously. Lahire may overestimate the amount of personal fulfillment achieved through a nonartist's professional work, but it serves us well to investigate the implications of his argument for the literary history of modernism. First, Lahire's argument provides a powerful description of the paired economic and aesthetic condition of modernist authors who, for the very reason that they did not seek financial success and popular audiences, had to find other ways to pay the bills. Second, it refrains from proscriptive judgments about economic and aesthetic arrangements and instead opens up the space for a historically grounded interpretation of the effect of such an arrangement on definitions of literature.

In this vein, I take a Lahire-inspired approach to defining the modernist text as one that reconstitutes the epistemological concerns of its "double life"—it enters one field as an ostensibly original work of art and another as a collectively produced mass-cultural artifact—as thematic and formal concerns. This definition is beholden to those favored by practitioners of "New Modernist Studies," for whom modernism gains the most traction when theorized in relation to those features of modernity that it attempts to leave behind. It is worth nothing that this definition of modernism is anachronistic, even if it is rhetorically helpful; in fact, from the perspective of the magazine editors, authors, and poets I write about, defining "modernism" by way of literature makes little sense as the term was much more likely to refer to theological debates than artistic ones in the first two decades of the twentieth century. Even though *Time*'s first issue refers to Clive Bell as an "English critic and pontiff of modernism"[43] and *Vanity Fair* sometimes used the term in the 1920s in reference to visual art,[44] modernism usually is contrasted with religious orthodoxy, such as in a 1923 *Time* article that contrasts Catholic "Fundamentalists" with "Liberals or Modernists, who believe they are more fundamental than the Fundamentalists."[45] When the term does describe literature, it often turns up when a writer fears that an artist or type of formal experimentation has become too staid: the invocation of Clive Bell above claims that cubism's daring break with realistic representation "has served its purpose . . . and is in danger of becoming itself a mere convention"; likewise, a 1930 article entitled "Sterile Modernism" assumes that the "multitudes of laymen" are familiar "at least by name with Matisse, Picasso, Zuloaga, Augustus John, Rockwell Kent," even if they are not enamored with their work.[46] Modernism, as it applies to a literary movement, most often happens after the fact.

In the spirit of reading American modernism's development in tandem with the generic differentiation of mass-market periodicals, I open with chapter-length studies of the formal and thematic repercussions on literary form of three distinct periodical types: the muckraking journal, the African American monthly, and the newsmagazine. Chapter 1, "Willa Cather's Promiscuous Fiction," finds that Cather's ideal of the "unfurnished novel" emerges directly out of her editorial work for *McClure's*, where she became managing editor at a key moment in the magazine's evolution. At the same time that she reimagines the perfect editor as one whose work goes undetected, she also theorizes a version of authorship in which true artistry consists of what a writer leaves off the page. She thematizes the link between two kinds of unseen work as a productive tension between an overabundant, feminized, "promiscuous" mass print media and a version of literature that is singular, autonomous, and abstinent. This happens through the central objects in her novels: the overburdened bridge in *Alexander's Bridge*, the cracking "vessel of one's throat" in *The Song of the Lark*, the sewing room in *The Professor's House*, and even the character of S. S. McClure in her ghostwritten autobiography of him.

Chapter 2, "Printing the Color Line in *The Crisis*," moves from the formal and thematic confluence of editorial and authorial work to the materiality of magazine production, discussing W. E. B. Du Bois's, Jessie Fauset's, and Frank Walts's long tenures at *The Crisis*, by far the most popular African American monthly of the early twentieth century. This chapter tracks how Du Bois's and Fauset's interest in new printing technologies—multigraphs, linotypes, and halftone reproduction—influenced the magazine's portrayal of racialized bodies and racialized intellectual work in everything from its news coverage to its cover designs to its serialized fiction. Du Bois's essays in the magazine repeatedly focus on the material preconditions of racial representation, and Fauset's serialized magazine stories depict racialized bodies as medialike in their capacity to archive and transmit but also hide information. In their various attentions to the material texture of racial representation, Du Bois, Fauset, and other prominent contributors to *The Crisis* ultimately are imagining both the technological and political roadblocks to establishing a popular, nationally distributed African American magazine.

Chapter 3, "On the Clock: Rewriting Literary Work at Time Inc.," triangulates the feminized work of editing at muckraking magazines and the racialized print technologies of the black monthlies with the overtly masculine newsmagazine of the 1920s, particularly *Time*. Time Inc., at one time the largest media conglomerate in the world, strategically hired poets and novelists to develop a uniformly stylish periodical voice, and in different ways James Agee and Walker Evans's *Let Us Now Praise Famous Men* and Kenneth Fearing's *The Big Clock* formalize the felt erasure between personal writing and salaried corporate work. Taken together, these authors and periodicals exemplify how the generic differentiation of twentieth-century big magazines is integrally related to the institutionalization of American modernism and, related to this, how the most vitriolic attacks on an overabundant mass culture are increasingly waged from the inside of mass print media.

The recovery and popularity of Agee's texts in the 1960s signal a shift in the cultural status of the outsider artist, a figure that William Whyte's *The Organization Man*—also originally a Time Inc. essay—paradoxically describes as the epitome of postwar corporate life. Chapters 4 and 5 pick up this theme of the outsider on the inside, but they do so by looking at how big magazines appropriate canonical modernist writers such as T. S. Eliot and Ernest Hemingway as editorial content rather than as contributors after World War II. By turning from life inside offices to representations of authors in the pages of mass-market periodicals, the second half of the book theorizes an emerging postwar *mass modernism*, where the tropes of modernist exile and alienation become part of the "vital center" of U.S. postwar culture. The final two chapters use T. S. Eliot and Ernest Hemingway as paired case studies to track how modernism's stylized alienation informs mainstream postwar ennui. Chapter 4, "Our Eliot: Mass Modernism and the American Century," studies the midcentury explosion of articles about and reproductions of T. S. Eliot's work in the pages of *Time*, *Life*, and *The Atlantic*. These magazines repatriate Eliot as a Howellsian realist and read his poetry, especially *The Waste Land* and "The Hollow Men," not as opaque and cosmopolitan but as realistic accounts of the complexity of an overly baroque continental culture. Chapter 5, "Hemingway's Disappearing Style," takes two encounters between Ernest Hemingway and the big magazines as touchstones for the cultural style of a new mass modernism: a little-known legal skirmish with *Esquire* over republication rights in 1958, which effectively ended his two-decade association with the magazine, and the 1952 appearance of *The Old Man and the Sea* in *Life*, which sold five million copies in two days. Hemingway's ambivalence about the literary influence of his characteristically sparse, flat prose is well documented, and this chapter establishes a conceptual bridge between Hemingway's late style, his resurgent popularity in postwar magazines, and his increasing preoccupation with specific time frames of print-media forms—that is, the singularity and historical weight of the book versus the serial newness but short shelf life of the magazine. These two chapters offer complementary accounts of modernist writers as the content of popular periodicals, but, more importantly, they argue that a number of big magazines remap Eliot's and Hemingway's exilic authorial personas as versions of a conflicted postwar nationalism. Chapter 5 concludes by briefly looking forward to a moment in the 1960s when the big magazines will provide grist for a new generation of writers influenced by literary modernism who must cope with the fear of print culture's demise. Norman Mailer's *Armies of the Night* and Robert Coover's *The Public Burning*, both of which are narrated in part from the point of view of *Time*, contrast their own abrasive, idiosyncratic styles with an overabundant and overly familiar mass print media. Yet, after the rise of television, these nostalgic representations of the big magazines can be seen to fantasize a moment of informational totality based in print, metonymically reduced to a single, ubiquitous magazine.

Eliot's and Hemingway's postwar literary output resided at the center of midcentury debates about middlebrow culture, the "tepid ooze" that "is spreading everywhere," according to Dwight Macdonald.[47] Macdonald's "Masscult and Midcult" and Clement Greenberg's "Avant-Garde and Kitsch" are two of the most trenchant critiques of the postwar culture industry. Both first appeared in *The Partisan Review*, a journal that Lionel Trilling called out as a spiritual descendent of the modernist little magazine. For Macdonald, masscult's open embrace of the market makes it far less insidious than midcult or middlebrow, which is "a peculiar hybrid" of high and low because it steals the tone and style of high culture but adopts the inoffensive content and cheap production standards of masscult. Though much could be written on the relationship between big magazines and the middlebrow—Macdonald's essay catalogues the midcult journals of record, from *Life* to *The New Yorker* to newer titles such as *Horizon: A Magazine of the Arts*—I have less to say about the specifics of Macdonald's theory than I might, if only because I find him more interesting as an example of a writer who begins in big magazines only to make his reputation by denouncing them. Though he is better known for his editorship of *The Partisan Review*, Macdonald spent most of the Great Depression filing stories for Time Inc. magazines, and "Masscult and Midcult" was originally commissioned by the *Saturday Evening Post* as part of its "Adventures in the Mind" series, which featured essays by Clement Greenberg, Randall Jarrell, and C. P. Snow, among others.[48] And, according to Macdonald's footnote to "Masscult and Midcult" when it was republished in an essay collection, the *Post* did not reject the essay because of Macdonald's stubborn refusal to take popular magazines seriously; instead, the editors turned it down because they felt that he was not critical enough of *The New Yorker*, where he was an employee.

Macdonald's affiliation with big magazines does not discount his sense of cultural decline any more than Cather's work at *McClure's* invalidates her feelings about the detrimental effects of the machine-made novel, but it does help locate his theory within a tradition of writers who make a career out of denouncing the institutions that fund their positions as public intellectuals. Tellingly, he locates midcult's "special threat" to be that "it exploits the discoveries of the avant-garde," therefore sullying the legacy of modernism. Even more damningly, "lapsed avant-gardists" such as Hemingway, Eliot, and MacLeish are the most prominent middlebrow authors because they "know how to use the modern idiom in the service of the banal."[49] And in this correlation of Macdonald's employment history with his ideas about the unhealthy appropriation of modernist form,

I find it more productive to consider Macdonald's theory of the middle-brow as symptomatic rather than explanatory of the changes in literary and periodical culture after World War II.

Macdonald's correlation of cultural decline with changes to print media seems especially relevant right now, as a similar sentiment regarding the possibility of a postprint culture is common among those that make their livings by writing, publishing, and teaching literature and other print-based objects. In some ways, the midcentury lament epitomized by Macdonald foreshadows one of the uncomfortable ironies at the heart of periodical scholarship today, this book included: at the same time that new technologies and research tools make it possible to study several centuries of newspapers, magazines, and other print materials as a comprehensive field, there has been a severe disinvestment in periodicals as a living cultural form and professional practice. Because of herculean efforts on the part of both public and private institutions, it has never been easier to access virtually archival print material previously holed up in special collections or far-flung libraries; an unprecedented number of full print runs of previously hard-to-find periodicals—both newspapers and magazines—have been scanned, uploaded, and made readily available to anyone with a university proxy server.[50] Yet while the advent of digitization has made new research projects possible on print and literary history that could not even have been dreamed of twenty years ago, actually to start a print magazine right now with the goal of making money, or to try to make a living by writing for one, seems like an antiquated dream. The very print-based periodical culture that is now opening its doors to scholars as an object of *historical* study is collectively shuttering its offices and laying off its writers. According to many in the commercial periodical industry, we are in the age of "the last magazine," to quote the title of a recent roman à clef by a former *Newsweek* staffer.

The general constriction of the periodical market has certainly given birth to a number of revivalists, *McSweeney's* in San Francisco and *n+1* in New York among the most prominent, and in quite different ways they are attempting to keep the periodical form alive by producing sophisticated content and innovative designs. But they do so at nowhere near the circulation, not to mention the profitability, of those journals that defined the golden age of magazine culture—and do not even intend to reach such an audience. That isn't to say there is a dearth of reading material, of course, just that the "information anxiety" that for the first half of the twentieth century grew out of the overwhelming amount of paper-based writing now originates in the digital quarters of the media industry. Additionally, at the same time that print magazines are going belly up, the editorial work and professional practices that congealed in the large, commercially successful periodicals of the twentieth century are also changing. Many have noticed the widespread amateurization of journalism, especially in its digital manifestations. The need for web content and the seemingly endless ability of a group whom the journalist Dan Gillmor refers to as the "former audience" to write for free has found a wider and more diverse demographic taking an active role in filling virtual column space.[51] This has had an immense effect on the relationship among contemporary readers, writers, and the media forms that bring them together, one that quite often is taken to be unprecedented in terms of its disruption of writing as a profession.

The recent proliferation of eulogies for print's demise, coupled with myriad new approaches to understanding print as a historical medium, make the time seem ripe to look back on modernism's life in the magazines. While the terms of the debates regarding new technologies, augmented professional practices, and media forms have altered in the twenty-first-century media environment, the conversations have a long history, and they look remarkably familiar to the set of economic, aesthetic, and disciplinary concerns that accompanied the rise of the "big magazines" a century ago. In intriguing ways, the debates both within big magazines and between those magazines and modernism echo forward into the institutional, disciplinary, and economic debates taking place within literary studies and commercial periodicals today.

CHAPTER I

Willa Cather's Promiscuous Fiction

The best magazine executive I know is Miss Cather.
—s. s. MCCLURE, in Peter Lyon,
Success Story: The Life and Times of S. S. McClure

Some of the figures of my old life seemed to be waiting for me in the new.
—WILLA CATHER, *My Ántonia*

Personifying Periodicals

Halfway into Willa Cather's *The Professor's House* (1925), Tom Outland enters the plot by way of a magazine. "I just got in this morning, and your name was the only one here I knew. I read an article by you in a magazine, about Fray Marcos. Father Duchene said it was the only thing with any truth in it he'd read about our country down there," he tells Godfrey St. Peter, the titular professor who holds serious reservations about the types of companionship that result from such paper-based introductions. "Whenever he wrote for popular periodicals it got him into trouble," St. Peter ruminates.[1] And he's right, at least in this case, because even though Tom's entrance into "The Family" (St. Peter's family, and the title of the novel's opening section) gives the book its pulse, it also sets off the chain of events that will leave Tom dead in Europe and the professor near-dead on his workroom floor, pining for his lost youth. In the meantime, Tom wants to attend the university where St. Peter teaches, and after gleaning Tom's intelligence and maturity, the Professor accepts this new pupil. Thus begins what could have been an aspirational comedy along the lines of Shaw's *Pygmalion*: the refined, socially awkward academic reshapes Tom, the underclass cowboy, in his own image. The Professor will open the university doors and its attendant social mobility: Tom's friend tells him that college is "some kind of hocus pocus that enabled a man to live without work" (188). And Tom will provide St. Peter with an intellectual spark and a good story: "Tom Outland's Story," to be exact, the middle section of the novel that in both style and setting leaves behind the Professor's house and family, which Cather famously declared to be purposefully "crowded and stuffy . . . rather stifled," so as to "open the square window and let in the fresh air that blew off the Blue Mesa."[2]

The novel is still best known for its purposefully claustrophobic narrative and St. Peter's academic hermeticism—what Leon Edel early on called "the dilemma of St. Peter's isolation in his attic."[3] St. Peter romanticizes the singularity of his intellectual work: he imagines his desk as "a hole one can crawl into," and he delights in the fact that his massive, eight-volume *Spanish Adventurers in North America* was ignored so thoroughly that he "might as well have dropped them into Lake Michigan" (32). But the magazine's openness to many different publics and its ability to forge the connection between St. Peter and Tom suggests the possibility of a different relationship between writers and readers. Unlike the Professor's weighty tome, which was born anchored to a small readership, his periodical article circulates freely and can connect ideas and people across vast amounts of space. In this way it looks like a better version of the train that carries Tom to Hamilton and repeatedly shuttles St. Peter and his family to the metropolis of Chicago and beyond. The periodical press and the railroad system have long been credited by historians as agents of modernization—in developing the nation-state, particularly— as they link local experiences with national and global concerns and vice versa.[4] To be sure, Cather makes this connection, showing how both the train and the magazine puncture the claustrophobic bubble of Hamilton, a paradigmatic regionalist town described as "flat and heavy . . . small and tight and airless" (131). In *The Professor's House*, though, these technologies of modernity work at opposite purposes: the train takes people to the city, which is even more crowded and stuffy than the small town, while the magazine brings the invigorating "fresh air" of the West to Hamilton. In fact, the magazine seems to conflate those spatial registers: instead of bridging distant places it erases the distance between them, so that one can open a window in Michigan and feel the breeze from New Mexico.

The magazine as a cultural form, then, does what neither the university in Hamilton nor the Professor's heavy monographs can manage: it widely distributes the intellectual work produced in cloistered outposts to a dispersed and unschooled public. Put another way, it allows the professor to hide behind his desk and lets the West come to him.

Magazines get the Professor into trouble, for sure, but the exact meaning of that trouble is unclear. There is no *Spanish Adventurers* without Tom, and there is no *The Professor's House* without the magazine that connects the two main characters. In this way, the role of periodicals within the novel neatly reiterates Cather's own long, ambivalent relationship with popular magazines. In fact, *The Professor's House* is emblematic of the overlapping periodical and literary histories that this project examines as well as of some of the formal and thematic repercussions of reading modernist literature through the lens of the big magazines. St. Peter's and Outland's affiliation, which begins with their mutual participation in popular-magazine culture yet retroactively gets figured by St. Peter as being the only thing insulated from being "commonplace like everything else" (61), allegorizes the often overlooked productive friction between early twentieth-century writers' visions of aesthetic autonomy and the massively popular, unapologetically successful economic and institutional worlds in which that autonomy is formulated. For this reason the novel, and Cather's career more generally, offer a starting point for examining the emergence of an intellectual and artistic autonomy theorized from within the confines of a market-oriented periodical culture, a situation that one can trace in widely divergent ways from Cather to W. E. B. Du Bois to James Agee and that can also be read into the post–World War II appropriations of writers like T. S. Eliot and Ernest Hemingway by American magazines.

By excavating the deep institutional, economic, and aesthetic affiliations that bridge the golden days of modernism and American magazine culture, the ensuing chapters explore how the idea of literary modernism's aesthetic and social insularity often originated in the work authors did in commercial magazine offices. This chapter will look at the connections between bureaucratic and literary form in Cather's double life as editor and author, and it will parse out her various attempts to keep her two lives distinct. Although she published her first novel at the age of thirty-eight, she had been a professional journalist since she was a kid, submitting articles to the local paper in Red Cloud, Nebraska, at the age of fourteen.

As an undergraduate at the University of Nebraska, Cather wrote for and edited three different periodicals, and the recognition of her talent by increasingly prominent magazines brought her from the Great Plains to Pittsburgh and later New York, where she moved in 1906 to work at *McClure's*. Cather became managing editor in 1909, placing her in charge of the daily operations of a magazine so innovative and successful that it was described as "standing out like Gulliver among the Lilliputians."[5] All of this occurred before she ever wrote a novel, making it easy to figure her journalistic career as a purgatorial way station that preceded entrance into long-form fiction. This is certainly her longtime companion Edith Lewis's summation of that work: she says it was "to be sure, a kind of practice—but practice in the wrong direction, in doing over and over the kind of thing most destructive to talent."[6] Cather uses similar language to describe her editorial work, claiming that even "the first important piece of work [she] did for the magazines," a ghostwritten essay on Mary Baker G. Eddy and Christian Science, was merely "a sort of discipline, an exercise."[7] Practice as destructive to talent and discipline as the opposite of creativity: these are the oppositions that guide Cather's distinction between editorial work and writing novels. And in her fiction, Cather incessantly thematizes this as a gendered tension between an overabundant, feminized, "promiscuous" periodical culture and a vision of the book, and particularly the novel, as singular, autonomous, and abstinent. By this chapter's end, we will see how the impetus toward an unfurnished, isolated, and self-reproducing book form—an ideal that the Professor's scholarship exemplifies and one that finds its thematic corollary in Cather's nostalgia for the cloistered lives of pioneers, precocious children, immigrant farmers, self-consciously single women, and antisocial artists—is born out of the messy, collaborative social relations instantiated by the magazines where she first developed, and later rejected, an idiosyncratic notion about how authors and their works should circulate in public.

Between 1893 and 1902 Cather penned upward of 560 articles, essays, and reviews, which her biographer estimates to be "more copy than appears in all of her collected works of the following thirty five years."[8] Yet to suggest that *Professor*, in both its publication history and plot, presents mass-circulation magazines as at least ambivalently necessary and maybe even a positive force in the creative lives of those that it comes into contact with is to contradict baldly the many, many negative statements that Willa Cather lobbed against periodicals and journalists and even more broadly against mass culture at large. Her novels all operate with a similar disdain for the messiness of modern cities and the work that happens there. *O Pioneers!* (1913), *The Song of the Lark* (1915), *My Ántonia* (1918), *One of Ours* (1922), and *The Professor's House* center on the isolated pioneer towns of Cather's youth and emphasize the dignity and artisanal craft of agrarian individualism. These settings and locations reflect Cather's rural upbringing in Nebraska as well as her indebtedness to the realist tradition, what she called "a long apprenticeship to Henry James and Ms. Wharton."[9] However, Cather's apologias for the simple life also depend on their opposite: Alexandra's new farming technologies in *O Pioneers!*, Thea's protracted and intense vocal training in Chicago in *The Song of the Lark*, Jim Burden's engineering classes in *My Ántonia*, mechanized war and modern military planning in *One of Ours*. In Cather's novels, these competing thematic concerns are most legible when they are in close proximity, which is particularly true of *The Professor's House*. When the magazines and trains bring together competing spatial and stylistic registers—rural and urban, empty and overstuffed, the city's "orgy of acquisition" and the hamlet's isolated intellectual work—we see the watermark of her formative years in modern editorial offices alongside her attempt to erase that history.

Until the early 1900s editorial work was closely tied to the professionalization of literary authorship. During the Progressive Era of the 1890s, fiction became associated with the masculine task of reportage: venturing out into the world, flipping over its seedy underbelly, and documenting the results.[10] No cultural outlet more epitomized the conflation of literary, journalistic, and gendered work than *McClure's*, where under the editorship of Lincoln Steffens the long-form muckraking exposé became codified as a genre, with Ida Tarbell's serialized "The History of the Standard Oil Company" (1902–1903) providing the paradigmatic example. As many have noted, the era's implicit and even sometimes explicit gendering of authorship papered over the experiences of women writers who produced journalism, short stories, and serialized novels in popular magazines; further, the masculinization argument is complicated by the major contributions to muckraking journalism and its fictional relative—the naturalist novel—by female journalists and authors. Still, the dominant discourse at the time figures men as the producers of culture while "the monthly-magazine-made American female," to borrow Henry Adams's phrase, passively reads anything that the masculinized reporters write.[11]

Willa Cather entered this gendered authorial space and internalized its assumptions: like many female writers she wrote under dozens of male pseudonyms and took potshots at women as both hyperbolic writers and overinvested readers. She referred to sentimental fiction, which she associated with women writers and readers, as the "novel of amusements" and denounced both its popularity as well as its style, which she found overwritten. Yet Cather blamed this aesthetic flabbiness and overabundance on the false equivalence of literary and journalistic writing and reading rather than on the actual sexual difference of authors and audience. In 1937, she would recount how reporters at *McClure's*, while compiling material on the Standard Oil Company or Chicago machine politics, often "apologetically explained that they were making these investigations 'to collect material for fiction.' I couldn't believe that any honest welfare worker, or any honest novelist, went to work in this way."[12] For Cather, the feminized "novel of amusements" resembles the masculinized muckraking story in that both prioritize sensational content over attention to form. Both are "manufactured to entertain great multitudes," and she claims that the "machine-made novels" are the descendants of "the dazzling journalistic successes of twenty years ago, stories that surprised and delighted by their sharp photographic detail and that were really nothing more than lively pieces of reporting."[13] What she does not say about the "dazzling successes" of twenty years ago that have hamstrung innovation is that she was a key player in manufacturing them and that her editorial work shaped her vision of literature's social and artistic function.

Just when Cather was reimagining herself as a novelist rather than a journalist and developing a theory of writing in which those two tasks could be clearly distinguished from each other, the magazine she worked for, *McClure's*, was working out a parallel project to differentiate its periodical identity from its competitors. These distinct processes—that is, *McClure's* differentiation from older magazine models and Cather's differentiation from older ideas of literary production tied to reportage—are deeply intertwined, and they tell one part of a larger story about how mass-market magazines and literary modernism interact in the early decades of the twentieth century. A closer look at *The Professor's House* makes clear that this is more than just an isolated story of one writer and one magazine. The first and third sections of *Professor*, "The Family" and "The Professor," roughly take their plots from Cather's 1902 short story "The Professor's Commencement," published in *New England Magazine*.

And during the summer of 1925 before Knopf published *Professor* as a book, *Collier's Weekly*—which maintained a circulation of slightly over one million—paid Cather ten thousand dollars to serialize the novel. If the letters sent both to Cather and to *Collier's* are any indication, the long middle section, "Tom Outland's Story," was understood as a stand-alone short story by *Collier's* readers, too. Cather took pride from reports that "the railroad boys were saying that the book was the best picture of the old railroad days that they'd ever read"—which slyly rewords Tom's appreciation of St. Peter's magazine article with Cather in the professor's knowing position. And, with a little interpretive stretch, it suggests that Tom's vouching for the authenticity of the Professor's article informs how readers of the serialization in *Collier's* interpreted *Professor* as well.[14]

Editorial work entails discipline, repetition, practice, routine—all the traits that begin to mark it as an organized profession in the late nineteenth century. If this practice isn't helpful for creative work, in Cather's opinion, then presumably artistic writing requires a different standard of accomplishment. For her, an author's "good intentions and praiseworthy industry *don't count a damn.*"[15] Or, as she put it in her most succinct theory of fiction, "The Novel Démeublé," an author "must learn to write, and then he must unlearn it" if he wants "the novel [to] develop into anything more varied and perfect than all the many novels that have gone before." Writing as a skill that must be "unlearn[ed]," a faculty that one must possess and then hide, redescribes what elsewhere she refers to as the distinctive *effect* of the "varied and perfect" novel, but with an emphasis on compositional technique. In what surely must be her most famous statement about writing, Cather theorizes a version of composition that consists of not writing:

> Whatever is felt upon the page without being specifically named there—that, one might say is created. It is the inexplicable presence of the thing not named, of the overtone divined by the ear but not heard by it, the verbal mood, the emotional aura of the fact or the thing or the deed, that gives high quality to the novel or the drama, as well as to poetry itself.[16]

Scholars have found fertile interpretive ground in the discrepancy between her insistence on not naming the content of this stimulus and the litany of names that she does provide for the form of its aftereffect: an overtone, a verbal mood, an emotional aura. Notably, feminist and queer approaches to Cather's oeuvre have produced powerful accounts of "the inexplicable presence of the thing not named" as the open secret of her sexuality—the Wildean love that dare not speak its name. In this mode, Cather's characteristic narrative withdrawal, as well as her way of repeatedly drawing attention to it, formally manifests her conflicted, maybe closeted, sexual desire. What follows will build off this line of inquiry while pursuing a different argument about what Cather doesn't want to talk about: rather than sexuality, it attends to the magazine work that was just as much an open secret in her literary life. More specifically, it details how the professional protocols of Cather's career as a magazine editor can be read into her ideas about authorship, specifically her insistence that authorial work is something that constantly must be effaced.

The editorial work that Cather was almost preternaturally talented at entailed taking other people's writing (or talking) and silently giving it style and shape. That is, she gave good form to lively content. Edith Lewis, who also worked at *McClure's* during Cather's tenure, describes how "often some article of unusual journalistic interest would come into the office, but so badly put together, so buried in a jungle of obscuring words, that it took great divination even to recognize that there was anything there."[17] It was Cather's job to work that "great divination" and cut back the "jungle of obscuring words" into a well-organized and pleasantly written magazine article. Cather, then, provides a different model of editorship than other prominent nineteenth- and early twentieth-century editors, such as William Dean Howells, Henry James, or later Ezra Pound.[18] Both Howells and James exemplify the highly visible editor-as-tastemaker that develops in the second half of the nineteenth century. Howells pontificated about the state of American letters from "The Editor's Study" and "The Editor's Easy Chair," columns he wrote for *Harper's Monthly*.[19] James, especially in the New York Edition of his collected works (1907–1909), framed his revision as the difficult work of editing someone else's lesser material. In the process he produced the editor as interpretive master: by drawing attention to all of his emendations in the prefaces, he articulated the proper way to read his work (which is always to reread it) and by extension provided a model for the art novel (something that one only ever rereads).[20] Unlike the eminently visible version of editing in these two figures, both of whom influence Cather's ideal of authorial work, Cather's editor is a self-canceling one who invisibly purifies literary production. This can apply to her own writing, in the case of her novels, but also the work of others—such as S. S. McClure, for whom she ghostwrote an autobiography. It also informs her fiction in both theme and style in a way that runs parallel to the authorial impersonality of other modernist authors. She repeatedly represents the perfect artistic act as either self-erasure (as opposed to self-expression) or passive acceptance of a preexisting artifact. As "The Novel Démeublé" alludes, the distinctive quality of artistic production for Cather does not actually produce anything: it works invisibly, behind the scenes or under the face of the page, unavailable for study in the final product other than as an "overtone" or "mood."

This editorial allegory, that perfect work contains no trace of work, surfaces in a number of ways in Cather's fiction, and in what follows I'll explore how it grows out of her editorial jobs that culminate as a manager of *McClure's*. For Cather, to erase work is also to erase the worker, and as such the project to make writing invisible prefigures her attempt, late in life, to close off her reputation as a novelist, as well as the world inside her novels, from her biography. She actively avoided talking about her editorial work after 1912 when she left *McClure's*, except to say it didn't matter. She burned many of her letters and asked her friends to do the same. She made stipulations in her will that forbade biographers and scholars from quoting her unpublished work that have only recently been lifted. The insistence on the autonomy of her identity as a novelist from outside factors also inflects her ideas about adaptations. She refused to anthologize her books, license them for other media (theater, radio play, film), or even reprint them as trade paperbacks (a decision her executor later overturned).[21] As Lise Jaillant has shown, Cather's preference for her novels to be published as expensive hardcovers rather than as cheaper, widely available paperbacks negatively affected her reputation in the 1930s among critics such as Granville Hicks, and it also hindered her entrance into the canon of modern literature as it was being constructed in midcentury American universities and high-school English classes.[22] Taken together, these insistences on the material specificity of her books as artisanal objects and the attempt to erase their connections to other types of cultural mediation can be seen as retroactive attempts to insulate her fiction from the taint of popularity: specifically the popular periodical work that defined her early life. Yet her life in editorial offices provided her with the platform and professional skill with which to circulate her theory of noncirculation to an enormous readership, a situation central to the codevelopment of literature and journalism and, relatedly, literary modernism and mass print culture over the twentieth century.

Gentlemen, Mobs, Magazines

In Lewis's memoir about living and working with Cather, she summarizes the kind of company one kept at *McClure's*:

> A continuous stream of people flowed through the McClure offices; most of them are now forgotten names. I remember William Dean Howells visiting the place my first year there. He came over to my desk and asked me what I was doing. When I told him, he said in his beautiful voice: "I was a proof-reader, too." Ezra Pound stopped in once, on his way, he told me, from Idaho to Italy. He had with him a suitcase full of poems, one or two of which he read aloud to me.[23]

The social world of New York magazines in miniature: a place that collects the "beautiful voice" of Howells's realism in the past tense, on its way out, and the ascension of the Pound Era, perfectly captured in the poem-filled suitcase that he's shopping to the magazines that pay. In the office of *McClure's*, gathered around the desk of a proofreader who happens to live with Willa Cather, we find a bridge between two literary movements and their overarching attitudes toward the work that happens in an editorial office: that is, the broadly conceived realist association of literary writing with journalism as an attempt to professionalize intellectual work and the modernist attempt to differentiate artistic production from journalistic naivety about the transparency of representation. And despite the clear differences in Howells's and Pound's aesthetic programs, their shared stance over the desk of the proofreader—Howells cozying up, Pound standing back and orating—points to a lineage of masculinized literary tastemaking that overlooks the work of female bodies.

It's fitting that Cather remains offstage in the anecdote above—that Howells and Pound are connected by someone close to her, but without her participation—because, however metaphorically, it epitomizes her difference from the models they struck. As an editor, she perfected the craft of directing attention to others, even though she largely steered the editorial style of the magazine.[24] In this way, Cather provides an early model of "editing as carework" that Mary Kay-Wilmers of the *London Review of Books* describes as one of the "ventriloqual occupations," like translation, because it means "speaking through other people."[25] Cather arrived at a similar definition of editing, partially from her working conditions at *McClure's*. S. S. McClure founded the magazine in 1893 with seed money from his profitable news syndication business, which was buoyed by a rapidly expanding periodical market. McClure's genius, according to magazine historians, lies in combining the syndicate system—distributing the same copyrighted editorial material to different publications—with the advertising-revenue model of the general-interest magazine. However, McClure also distinguished his magazine from the increasingly standardized content of other periodicals by focusing on original, in-depth reporting that would only appear in his own magazine. His staff—Ida Tarbell, Lincoln Steffens, Ralph Stannard Baker, and others—pioneered the genre of muckraking. One distinguishing feature of their journalism was the time spent writing it. McClure said that "A man spends as much time writing an article for *McClure's* as he would to produce a book," a sentiment echoed by Ralph Stannard Baker, who gushed, "What a boon to the writer! . . . To be able to really take his time, saturate himself with the subject, assure accuracy . . . and then, above all, to be able to write and re-write."[26]

Thus, *McClure's* combined the standardization of the press syndicate with an approach to reporting that strove for booklike depth. In addition, it attempted to create a seamless link between the social world and the periodical's formal structure. McClure claimed that his magazine succeeded by insinuating itself into the common life of readers and by projecting a unified worldview: he wanted a magazine that "people read from cover to cover" rather than piecemeal.[27] This holistic approach to readerly attention is quite different than the miscellany of newspapers, which had to cover an array of topics quickly and be legible to an audience that only read particular sections. *McClure's* defined its wholeness more by contemporaneity than by genre or field; the first issue claims that it will only present "articles of timely interest," including "the newest book, the latest important political event, the most recent discovery or invention—in fact, what is newest or most important in every department of human activity."[28]

McClure's holds together "every department of human activity" by embracing the magazine's position in the hierarchy of news distribution.

McClure sees the unique qualities of his print form, which publishes less frequently than the newspaper but more regularly than a book, to be "the ability to analyze events and reconstruct them in perspective."[29] For this reason Lincoln Steffens, who preceded Cather as managing editor, saw the magazine as the perfect medium for in-depth, time-sensitive investigations of corporate and governmental malfeasance, "which ran so long that the newspaper readers lost track of them." A magazine like *McClure's* could "tell the whole completed story all over again, and bring out the meaning of it all with comment."[30] In this, Steffens highlights the increasingly specific cultural missions of books, magazines, and newspapers as well as the difference in writerly stance between newspapers and magazines. That is, while newspaper journalism in this period created and then strove for objectivity, magazine journalism came with "comment," or a writer's individual interpretation, which usually followed the general politics of the magazine.[31] The differentiation of style and tone among print forms depended in part on the standardization of journalistic practices but also on what a 1900 article in *The Atlantic Monthly* called the "gettableness" of different periodicals and books. A more reliable postal system made it just as easy to access books, magazines, and newspapers across the United States, and the relative flattening of distribution networks set in motion "a process of delimitation . . . defining more exactly the proper sphere of each." "In the process of delimitation, [the magazine] surrendered to the newspaper certain classes of article which in the development of the newspaper fall to it naturally, for example, the article simply descriptive, the old 'travel' article, so familiar in magazine pages twenty-five years ago." In this functionally differentiated world of print, "the office" of magazines like *McClure's* was to "interpret the significance of life as it is being lived, after it is mirrored, *en passant,* in the press, but before its perpetuation in the book."[32] The magazine combines the functions of the observer and the cultural interpreter, a perfect fit for the mixture of in-depth reporting and populist outrage that *McClure's* popularized.

Though now primarily remembered for muckraking, *McClure's* also had a strong literary component. As the anecdote about Howells and Pound signals, the journal walked a line between nineteenth-century realism and early twentieth-century modernism in the literature it featured. It published poems by Yeats, Kipling, A. E. Housman, and Louise Imogen Guiney; reprints of Whitman and translations of Verlaine; short and serialized fiction by Conrad, Stevenson, Ford Madox Ford, Hardy, Crane,

O. Henry, London, Twain, and Conan Doyle. Though it mixed politics and the arts and nineteenth-century classics along with current authors, the magazine also sought to achieve "a certain consistency of voice"[33] across its editorial material, one that it personified as a universally knowledgeable yet slightly bemused aristocrat. McClure described the magazine's style as replicating that of a "gentleman" on a social visit to the readers' homes, maintaining a level of propriety and loose intimacy that would ingratiate rather than shock its metaphoric hosts—and that would be equally comfortable in public and domestic situations. The language, topics, and images would be those found "in ordinary conversation in the family gathering" because a gentleman would not enter someone else's house "with oaths on his lips, or with words that violate the universal canon of good breeding." *McClure's* was to be "representative of many people's interests," always aiming to be "still more representative."[34]

This figuration of the magazine as a polite gentleman who works his way into the houses of every reader brings together the conflicted ideas of reading, gender, and class associated with magazines in this period. This is because the advent of new sales strategies upset the clearly striated market of women's journals or "family house" magazines, "qualities" or "genteel" magazines, and the penny press.[35] *McClure's* offered a similar content as the upmarket "qualities" such as *The Atlantic* and *Harper's* at a fraction of the price, selling for ten cents rather than thirty-five cents per issue. An 1895 editorial in the *Independent* counsels the older magazines against following the lead of *McClure's* into the lower-class market:

> It may not be easy to foresee; but it seems probable that they will not find it wise to reduce their price to a like figure. . . . The reason is that they will wish to maintain that higher, purer literary standard which succeeds in securing the best but not the most numerous readers. . . . They cannot change their constituency beyond the comparatively cultivated class which appreciates them. They cannot, half a dozen of them, secure half a million purchasers apiece, for there are not so many families of their sort in the country. . . . The rest may or may not be sturdy citizens, may count in the militia and the population and the lower schools; but they are not the ones who delight to seek the instruction they need most.[36]

Such attacks project a vision of the lower classes to whom *McClure's* sells its version of gentlemanliness as simply unfit for the type of reading that actual gentlemen must do. The above column, in light of *McClure's* goal to make a uniformly "quality" house style become representative of the American reading public, forecasts an odd conclusion. That is, it argues that the "higher, purer literary standard" will be victimized by the popularization of high literary taste. Or put another way, that the routinization of literary taste will bring an end to literary taste as such. The assumption here is that restrictiveness is an inherent characteristic of quality; big magazines such as *McClure's* upend this assumption by selling genteel culture to a more economically diverse reading public. By making a house style out of gentlemanliness and then disseminating it to those hoping for access to restricted literary and social circles, *McClure's* opens up fashionable elitism to a new crowd who can now replicate the voice of the gentleman. In effect, the magazine exposes the insider game of elitism to those that are kept outside.

Office Lives and Office Wives

McClure rarely stopped to oversee this organizational system as he frequently traveled to round up new subscribers for his syndicate and story ideas for his magazine. He advised his staff to do the same: Steffens recounts being told that he would never learn how either to write or edit in the office, that instead he should "Get out of here, travel, go—somewhere. Go out in the advertising department. Ask them where they have transportation credit. Buy a railroad ticket, get on a train, and there, where it lands you, there you will learn to edit a magazine."[37] Because of *McClure's* penchant for getting out, the task of actually managing the production of each issue fell to other, more sedentary souls. After Lincoln Steffens left the magazine with Ida Tarbell and others to found *The American*, it was Willa Cather's job to standardize *McClure's* gentlemanly voice across its content and to do so without either alienating the name-brand journalists and authors who supplied *McClure's* with content or upsetting S. S. McClure. And she did extraordinarily well: in the first year of her management the magazine increased its circulation by an average of sixty thousand copies per issue.

By all accounts, it was not a particularly pleasant job. According to Edith Lewis, it was "like working in a high wind, sometimes of cyclone magnitude; and of course S. S. McClure was the storm center." "Some of his ideas were journalistic inspirations, some, of course, were very impracticable," she writes. "He did not bother to sort them out, he expected his staff to do that." As managing editor, Cather was the head idea sorter in charge of making sure that the writers, editors, and advertising offices all ran smoothly. Unlike McClure, who was often out of the office for weeks on end, and unlike Howells and Pound, who spent large amounts of time forging and maintaining their reputations at the center of literary networks, Cather mostly stayed put in the office and separated the good from the bad. She specialized in "taking a mass of turgid, incoherent material and clarifying it, giving it a sequence and form."[38] This vision of Cather as head administrator runs in the face of her own characterization of how writers should interact with their world; in fact, Cather's ideal novelist looks something like the antimanager. In language that would make her the perfect straw man for 1930s Popular Front critics, Cather claims that the best writers "were valuable, like powerful stimulants, only when they were left out of the social and industrial routine which goes on every day all over the world." Most exemplars of true literary talent, she insists, "have managed their own budget and their social relations so unsuccessfully that I wouldn't want them for my landlords, or my bankers, or my neighbors."[39] Cather might have been a bad neighbor, but her work at *McClure's* proves she would have made an excellent landlord. And the way she did so, in contrast to her statement about the artist's shelter from the social world, was to meld the magazine's house style to the rhythm of "social and industrial routine."

Cather's rise at *McClure's* occurs during a transitional period in the makeup of editorial staffs more broadly. Though still more likely to occupy clerical positions, an increasing number of women were entering magazine offices as editors and copy readers. As Helen Gruber Garvey summarizes, editing was widely thought of as an extension of reading rather than of writing, and because of the long association of women with novel reading, editorial work provided an occupational space for the growing number of college-educated, unmarried women entering the job market.[40] Magazine offices were in particular need of bodies to fill their expanding staffs because, as I addressed in the introduction, the period also witnessed the migration of the "staff system" from newspapers to magazines: article assignments traveled from editors to in-house staff rather than being submitted ad hoc by amateur correspondents. Edwin L. Schuman's industry handbook, *Practical Journalism* (1910), signals the drastic shift in editorial power this change brings with it. Brand-name writers matter less than a strong office manager who can ensure the editorial team stays on track. "The greatest rewards no longer fall to the powerful editorial writer, but to the business-like managing editor, who rarely writes a line."[41]

From the beginning, *McClure's* was innovative because of the ways that it tied editorial style to the economics of circulation, but under Cather it also pioneered a standardized method for producing content: George Jean Nathan's "The Magazine in the Making" (1911), which coins the term "the staff system," lists *McClure's* by name. Cather's job as a female editor, then, entailed shaping the work of a large staff of writers into the magazine's gentlemanly voice, which could be circulated among the aspiring middle class, but she was to do so without letting her presence be felt on the page. She was roundly successful, and at least in part it is because from an early age she worried over how authorial style provided an especially useful tool for pairing texts and social types. For example, in 1895, on the cusp of striking out for Pittsburgh to take a position running *The Home Monthly*, she dedicated a column in the Lincoln *Courier* called "The Passing Show" to the strange ways that books and people can move:

> The other day I saw an elevator boy intently perusing a work of literature. I glanced at it and saw that it was Ouida's *Under Two Flags*. I could remember when I first met that book and read it quite as intently as the elevator boy was doing, and I was inclined to be patient with him when he took me to the wrong floor, for I knew that he was envying Bertie Cecil his beautiful boots or that he was pondering upon the peaches of great price that Bertie used to throw at the swans to please his sweetheart, and it struck me that it is rather tragic that one of the brightest minds of the last generation should descend to become food for elevator boys.[42]

In a rather neat symbolic logic, Ouida's novel experiences a double descent in social standing and physical space: it travels in time and between classes, from "one of the brightest minds of the last generation" to a lowly elevator boy (and indirectly to a childhood Cather). This decline in social distinction mirrors its path up and down the height of the building while the young man reads it. Cather moves into and out of the mind of the elevator boy, identifying with his reading experience across gender, class, and time by waxing nostalgic for her own childhood encounter with Ouida. As she does so she begins to overstuff her prose: when she imagines what he likes, which is what she liked when she was a child, she starts writing with obvious flourishes, like the bouncy consonance of "Bertie Cecil his beautiful boots," "pondering upon the peaches of great price," and "swans to please his sweetheart." Heightened sentiment, which originates in affective identification with another person over a novel, is rendered as heightened style. The passage finds Cather, her prose, and the book that sparks the anecdote ending up in places they were not supposed to go: Cather on the wrong floor mimicking bad writing; Ouida in the hands of the workers who initiate such uncomfortable social and spatial crossings.

Cather catches herself and blames this little gush on the contagiousness of *Under Two Flags*'s poor form, which she sees as a general symptom of poorly crafted and overly emotional writing. As she recounts, Ouida's "greatest sins are technical errors, as palpable as bad grammar or bad construction, sins of form and sense. Adjectives and sentimentality ran away with her, as they do with most women's pens." The technical flaw here looks like a surface phenomenon whose origin can be traced to a lack of emotional restraint, the inability of a writer to cordon off her "sentimentality" from creating fiction. What's worse, though, is that this unchecked sentimentality can quickly move from the author to the form of writing on the page and then from the page to the reader. All of this excess—of words, of feelings, of movement—leaves Cather to "wonder why God ever trusts talent in the hands of women, they usually make such an infernal mess of it. I think he must do it as a sort of ghastly joke."[43] Whereas the gentlemanly voice of *McClure's* prioritizes class mobility as a way to distinguish itself among its competitors, Cather's article insists that novels—especially those written by women—should stay quiet and closer to home.

For Cather, the overabundant "adjectives and sentimentality" that mar women writers' work produce the bad reading practices that she associates with the working class. But they also follow from a tendency among both writers and readers to mix novels and work more generally. The elevator boy cannot *read* and do his job at the same time, for sure, but in other places she insists that to *write* and work cannot happen simultaneously either. She puts it most succinctly in a preface to the collected stories of Sarah Orne Jewett: "A reporter can write equally well about everything that is presented to his view," Cather argues, "but a creative writer can do his best only with what lies within the range and character of his talent."[44] Unlike journalism, which expands outward and can convey any information in equally compelling prose, fiction must insulate itself from this desire to impinge on the world. "To note an artist's limitations is but to define his talent," she asserts, which leads her to the counterintuitive claim that journalism is by far the more imaginative mode of writing. Reporters, rightly, mold the story into the most compelling framework, but a novelist "who tries to improve upon his subject-matter with his 'imagination' can at best produce a brilliant sham."[45] Or, as she writes elsewhere, journalism "gave us, altogether, poor standards—taught us to multiply our ideas instead of condense them."[46]

When ideas multiply, according to Cather, so do the number of half-baked books that house them, and this strains a reader's ability to stay abreast of the market. "Really, it's terrible to think of, the mass of fiction that is thrust upon us every year," she laments. "Nowadays if one pretends to half way keep up with current fiction he has absolutely no time for anything else. If you did a thorough job on it you would not have time to sleep."[47] The ease with which texts circulate between people and with which styles move between writers and print forms—from the novelist Ouida to the young elevator operator to the periodical writer Cather—provides a different way of thinking about the criticism of female writers that Cather makes above. The problem, it would seem, is that their writing travels too freely from one place to another and from one person to another. This is not a problem solely for women: she decries the "bewildering productiveness" of writers whom she at one time admired, such as Sinclair Lewis, as part and parcel with what she feels to be a general decline in contemporary fiction. Instead, it seems that overproduction follows from too few barriers to entering the literary market and the confusion of one kind of writing done for pay with another kind that should not be considered work. "It is a solemn and terrible thing to write a novel," she claimed. "I wish there was a tax levied on every novel published. There would be fewer ones, and better."[48]

These early comments are of a piece with the gendered conception of overabundant writing that Cather's own fiction faced. The stories in her first, *The Troll Garden* (1905), repeatedly hinge on the relationship between isolated artists, preciously constructed texts, and unreceptive audiences, and Cather's editor Witter Bynner hoped that Henry James would recognize a kindred spirit and provide a positive blurb. When Bynner followed up after a long silence, James crankily replied, "I not only haven't yet read it, but haven't even been meaning to." He refuses as a matter of policy, and he hopes it will stop a certain type of person from writing. James's hope is to register the sacred truth. The sacred truth is that, being now almost in my 100th year [he was sixty-eight], with a long and weary experience of such matters behind me, promiscuous fiction has become abhorrent to me, and I find it the hardest thing in the world to read almost *any* new novel. Any is hard enough, but the hardest from the innocent hands of young females, young American females perhaps above all.[49]

Cather's book, here, suffers a different fate than Ouida's; instead of falling prey to the lower classes, *The Troll Garden* fails to scale upmarket into the higher register of respectable readers. However, James makes the issue of improper movement that we find in Cather's column more explicitly about erotic affiliations; books can be promiscuous for James, and their quality of affiliation is located in the ways that they move among individuals other than the writer. Cather's book and her editor's decision to pass it along fit into a model of casual engagement that James describes in "The Future of the Novel" (1899), where he scathingly writes of the "immense public, if public be the name," that "subscribes, borrows, lends, that picks up in one way or another, sometimes even by purchase," one of the novels that collectively constitute a "a flood at present [that] swells and swells." That is, unconscionably, they treat novels exactly how McClure imagines the perfect magazine. All of this oversharing amounts to something like a reading orgy, and as books wantonly pass from reader to reader, the "public . . . grows and grows each year." In short, the overproliferation of books produces more readers rather than the more common understanding that higher literacy rates and mass education produce the market for more books. According to James, giving this public the title of "readers" might be going too far, though, because for all the "association" between people and books—they subscribe, borrow, lend, and grow—nowhere does James say that they actually *read* the stuff on the page.[50]

James's oracular "sacred truth" about Cather's promiscuous fiction articulates the different expectations for how books and magazines should circulate, which we'll see emerge in a slightly different way in W. E. B. Du Bois's attitudes about the relative intellectual heft of books and magazines, and yet again in Ernest Hemingway's various battles over the publication (and republication) rights of his work. Each example assumes that an increasingly diverse and crowded media culture should lead to the functional differentiation of print forms: magazines do this, novels do that. As such, James's attitude is of a piece with responses to mass print culture in general, which at the beginning of the twentieth century is overwhelmingly figured as too big and unorganized for its own good. Yet the truth James lays out is a strange one: it establishes an inverse relationship between the fidelity of books and their authors, who are in this case figured as women. Here the "innocent hands of young females" are the primary agents of "promiscuous fiction," so that the bodily abstinence of women translates into their ability to churn out new books. In some ways this echoes an old saw of the nineteenth century, most famously captured in Nathaniel Hawthorne's 1855 screed against the "damned mob of scribbling women" whose quantitative dominance in the literary market is at fault for killing the careers of better, more-deserving male writers. Cather's interest in models of textual affiliation, then, can look like a preemptive absolution of her sin of womanhood, a symbolic alignment with those illustrious male writers who, as figured here, are small in number but large in reputation.

The language of intellectual and writerly wantonness surfaces repeatedly in Cather's discussions of her own books, most strikingly when she literalizes James's invocation of promiscuous fiction by giving her books the power to choose their friends. "I wrote this book for myself," she says of O Pioneers!, and she hopes that it "would remain faithfully with me, and continue to be exclusively my property."[51] The filial capability that Cather expects of a novel—that it can and will reciprocate the author's monogamous, exclusive attention and not traipse off with other readers—also figures into the content of O Pioneers! When young Alexandra Bergson learns that Carl, her closest acquaintance, is moving to the city, the biggest problem appears to be that the bonds of friendship will loosen from a one-to-one correspondence to something more social. " 'We've liked the same things and we've liked them together, without anybody else knowing,' " she tells Carl. " 'We've never either of us had any other close friend. And now'—Alexandra wiped her eyes with the corner of her apron, 'and now I must remember that you are going where you will have many friends.' "[52] The circulation of books and young boys, here, is equally tragic because the faceless "many friends" threaten the singular quality of how Alexandra and Carl "liked the same things" and "liked them together." Their friendship allegorizes the ideal author-reader relationship, figured here as a two-person tastemaking coterie, one that is internally self-similar and outside of the public eye.

Put another way, Alexandra's and Cather's shared anxiety about the overcirculation of the things and people they love trades on the overlap between the adjectival and verbal uses of "like"—that is, two things being *a*like versus the aesthetic evaluation of favoring a particular object or person. There is a long history of suggesting that "the apprehension of similarity—what Walter Benjamin calls the mimetic faculty—is the condition of possibility for affective affiliation."[53] But, with our attention honed on the specifics of print publication, here we might also see that Cather's discomfort at least partially resides in the possibility that, despite their differences, magazines and novels are capable of being liked in similar ways. And, even worse, those readers might wrongly apply the criteria for evaluating the aesthetic success of one to the other. That is, though magazines and books are alike in their printedness, they must be liked according to different criteria. Though the dispassionate affect of liking as a mode of being seems particularly fit for late-capitalist social life, Cather clearly chafes at the homology between liking and likeness when it comes to her writing; even more, her insistence on the distinction between her books (singular and faithful) and her magazine editing allows her to buffer out their greatest similarity. In fact, the insular faithfulness of Alexandra to Carl and of Cather to *O Pioneers!*—a book that if it is to remain hers cannot circulate—refuses one of the primary facts of publishing that Cather learned, depended on, and excelled at as an editor. That is, she exponentially increased the number of exact copies of *McClure's* in circulation and inspired readers' affective attachment to the personality contained in its pages. The financial tenability of her aesthetic project—as well as her livelihood as a writer—relies upon this facet of print culture, which can reproduce many identical copies of the same text for other people to buy, read, enjoy, and otherwise affiliate with outside of the author's control.

Often Cather imagines that she can keep her books faithful by managing their circulation, but other times she removes books and magazines from writerly production altogether. In "Ardessa" (1918), one of Cather's few stories actually set in an editorial office, she imagines the perfect authorial creation as one that doesn't circulate because it never actually gets written. The title character serves as secretary to O'Mally, publisher of *The Outcry*, a thinly disguised version of S. S. McClure and his magazine. Ardessa ghostwrites O'Mally's correspondence, restrains the mass of bad writers who are looking for their big break, and looks after the currently popular writers who are all too engrossed in their single "line" of expertise to deal with the banalities of office life. Throughout she provides the calm, unmoving, unflustered center around which the office operates: she's the "being at the heart of things."[54] The repeated references to Ardessa's "contentment" and the general freedom to work at her own pace and delegate unpleasant tasks to her underlings quietly undoes the image of a frantic and male-dominated newsroom. Ardessa's serenity within the managerial milieu and, through her, the office's association with a properly functioning human body naturalizes administrative order. It also makes it feminine. Or, viewed differently, it makes a problem of the kind of production or reproduction that is natural for women to take part in. Whether extending nature into the office or questioning what is natural for an office worker, it's clear that Ardessa's comfort with management reworks Sarah Orne Jewett's call for Cather to give up editorial work and find a "quiet centre of life" where she can become a novelist. Jewett told Cather that dividing her attention will hobble her growth as a fiction writer, but the portrayal of Ardessa suggests that the office is precisely the place for quiet contemplation.

"Ardessa" presents the title character and O'Mally as opposite models of modern work that compete for dominance in the editorial office. O'Mally, the narrator makes clear, is perfectly attuned to the twentieth-century periodical market. Like Tom Outland in *The Professor's House*, he comes from the West and succeeds because, as an outsider, he can see the problems with periodicals that those on the inside cannot. He thrives because he can "manufacture celebrities" out of "cheap paper and cheap ink," though at first it is unclear whether the writers or the robber barons who fill their muckraking articles are the bigger draw for readers (169). To some extent, it does not matter; celebrity primarily is a matter of circulation without moralization, a function captured when one claims that any press is good press. The problem for O'Mally, though, is that he isn't in the office enough to manage his magazine-as-celebrity-machine when it starts feeding back on itself. The manufactured talent takes to "staring at their own faces on newsstands and billboards, [and] fell to venerating themselves," a situation that makes O'Mally "more or less constrained by these reputations that he had created" (168). The muckraking journalism that O'Mally (and McClure) make popular requires the writers to bring an ever-wider range of modern vice into the purview of the public, but in "Ardessa" the producers of this content quickly and self-reflexively become unable to see beyond themselves. The insularity of the office's staff system threatens to undo its organizational achievements.

Ardessa's genius is in balancing this inward looking self-satisfaction and outward expansion of the magazine. She does so by serving as its institutional memory, "the card catalogue" of the magazine's "ever-changing personal relations" (170). Rather than the pastoral artist outside of social relations—the image often associated with Cather—here we find a heroine who is the artist *of* social relations, whose craft precisely consists of administering networks of authors, editors, and publishers. And, in the story, this is a uniquely literary talent: O'Mally values Ardessa because she is "steeped in literary distinctions and the social distinctions" that the art world brings with it. Her mechanical efficiency, then, is not the absence of cultural knowledge but its greatest manifestation. While the division of labor here remains gendered—the quixotic, unaccountable male publisher; the organized, managerial female editor—it is the former who appears unfit for the strictures of the modern office. Unlike O'Mally, Ardessa's name never appears in the magazine, and her ability to disappear within the work of management comes off as its own kind of genius. Ardessa's problem, at the end of the story, is not that she fails at the work required of her; instead, she delegates and administers so successfully that she works herself out of having any work. Worse, she has turned her female subordinates into more perfect versions of herself. She teaches Becky, a new girl "who never ceased to tremble," how to be "impersonal, unreproachful, and fairly pan[t] for work," and the boss decides Becky is of "better material" because, unlike Ardessa, she looks like she is trying (180). At the end of "Ardessa," then, there is a new and improved Ardessa in Becky, which indirectly restates James's "sacred truth": female work reproduces itself—and, in Becky, produces a new generation of female workers—while remaining "innocent" of procreative coupling.

Another version of Ardessa's organizational promiscuity, one more specifically attuned to female authorship, turns up in "The Willing Muse" (1907), which trades the administrator of authors for the administrative author. The story follows the doomed marriage of Kenneth Gray, an unproductive male writer, to Bertha Torrence, a female writer deeply engrained in the "public consciousness" who publishes with unceasing regularity.[55] Bertha's skillful management of social and literary productivity in the story ends up cancelling out any objections one might have to her as a remnant of Hawthorne's scribbling woman: "She made a point of looking astonishingly well, of being indispensable in an appalling number of 'circles,' and of generally nullifying the traditional reproach attaching to clever women" (115). Her true art, it seems, is relentless circulation: she travels between an untold number of influential people and writes about it. Cather populates "The Willing Muse" with men of letters trying to make sense of Bertha Torrence and her productivity, and her new husband Kenneth Gray is the most pure version of their outdated idea about what writers should be. He "was born an anachronism," the narrator tells us, and he yearns for the idyllic life of Olympia, his hometown in Ohio, where he occupied the center of literary life by pure charisma (117). The fact that the reader never sees any of Gray's isolated, agonized, and deeply personal poetry—because, as the narrator says, he never wrote any of it down—ironically links him to a whole cast of failed male writers in the Cather canon, such as Thea Kronborg's early suitor Ray Kennedy in *The Song of the Lark*. Kennedy, a loud-talking railroad hand, shares Gray's big personality as well as his utter lack of writing skills, which *Song* clearly differentiates from storytelling. Kennedy tells harrowing tales from his past, but he fails at recording them because he "had the lamentable American belief that 'expression' is obligatory" when it comes time to set pen to page.[56] The pages of his notebook, "Impressions on First Viewing the Grand Canyon, Ray H. Kennedy," "were like a battlefield; the laboring author had fallen back from metaphor after metaphor, abandoned position after position. He would have admitted that the art of forging metals was nothing to this treacherous business of recording impressions, in which the material you were so full of vanished mysteriously under your striving hand" (128). Ray's insistence on treating writing as expression rather than as "recording impressions" makes the task impossible. If only he were a little more mechanical, a little more like Thea, who is described as "vibrating with excitement, as a machine vibrates from speed" (156).

Ray, Kenneth, and the other male writers in Cather's work who revel in the difficulties of recording their self-expression can learn something from Ardessa, Bertha, and Thea, who refuse to acknowledge that they are expressing anything about themselves at all. As the boyhood friend of Gray's who narrates "The Willing Muse" makes clear, he arranged for Kenneth to meet Bertha so that her productivity might rub off on him. But after the wedding, the opposite happens. Gray almost completely stops writing; he becomes so self-conscious about it that he cannot even finish a letter to one of Bertha's admirers. All the while, his wife's fiction comes out faster and faster. The narrator declares:

> I never picked up any American periodical that Bertha's name was not the first to greet my eye on the advertising page. She surpassed all legendary accounts of phenomenal productiveness, and I could feel no anxiety for the fortunes of the pair while Bertha's publishers thought her worth such a display of heavy type. There was scarcely a phase of colonial life left untouched by her, and her last, *The Maid of Domremy*, showed that she had fairly crowded herself out of her own field.
>
> (117)

Bertha's ability to touch on any "phase" of life and transform it into her own material would seem to align her with Cather's pejorative definition of a reporter. It is a trait that leaves her with the peculiar problem of her books getting in their own way, published so closely on one another's heels that they compete for readerly attention, "crowd[ing]" herself out of the market. Unlike bad journalism, though, the writing gets better the faster she produces it. "The real wonder was, that, making so many, she could make them so well—should make them, indeed, rather better and better" (117). In the case of Bertha quantity produces quality. Just like Ardessa, she so perfectly engineers the system that she ends up pushing herself out, a qualified success to be sure, but one quite different than the compositional underproduction of her male counterparts.

All of this systematic writing results in an author that is neither quite human nor fully present in her finished product. Bertha writes behind a partition in her home, and the narrator cannot separate her from "the sharp, regular click of the machine" (119).[57] At the end of the story, Kenneth leaves his wife and absconds to China because, according to the narrator, "His brain was beaten into torpidity by the mere hammer of her machine, as by so many tiny mallets." The affinity that Cather describes between Bertha and writing machines is not necessarily unique—"typewriter," of course, referred both to the machine and to the woman using it. In this way Cather's story can be read as one of many turn-of-the-century allegories of a gendered modernity, perhaps the most famous being Henry Adams's differentiation of the Virgin Mother and the

Dynamo, in which the fecundity of the female body gets replaced by the mechanical reproduction of modern industry.[58] And Cather's story seems to bear out Jennifer Fleissner's argument that Adams's model and others like it hinge on an anxiety that women's affinity for mechanical reproduction could subsume their role in biological reproduction. In other words, the "cold, metallic non-mothers" might stop making babies and, like the machinery that mediates their relationship to office work, start making just about everything else, including books.[59] Cather's version of the rising Dynamo subtly differs, though, in that the older, anachronistic model of organic production is associated with the men: virginal, unproductive men who are equally incapable of making books and babies. Rather than the disappearance of the Virgin Mother, in Cather's fiction we find belabored male expression replaced by the unseen, perfectly efficient work of women.

In this way, the central problem of the new public woman's mechanical productivity rests neither in the dearth of children nor in women's unfitness for industry, at least in "Ardessa" and "The Willing Muse." Instead, women possess a preternatural affinity for being productive in the regimented world of editorial offices. Their mechanicity creates a new model of authorship that brings with it a positively valued femininity, signaled here as mechanized and normalized mass circulation. As "The Willing Muse" closes, the narrator conjectures that Bertha "has passed all the limits of nature, not to speak of decorum. They come as certainly as the seasons, her new ones, each cleverer and more damnable than the last" (123). The "nature" of biological and ecological cycles is replaced here by the "seasons" of Bertha's books, so that print circulation fully eclipses any natural order. This upsets "decorum," but in the end Kenneth's disappearance is not an elegy for the unadulterated craftsman artist. As the narrator sits around with his friends pondering Bertha's success, they do not seem to think Kenneth is the real story. Instead, the last lines are devoted to Bertha. In their view her textual overabundance has not ruined literary culture; if anything, they are jealous: "Bertha is a wonderful woman—a woman of her time and people; and she has managed, in spite of her fatal facility, to be enough sight better than most of us" (123). What constitutes her "fatal facility" never comes to light, but the two differences between her and the "us" that identify it are her gender and her popularity.

The Social Life of the Unfurnished Novel

The proliferation of Berthas, or at least individuals just like Bertha, across the cultural landscape that occurs when she is declared "of her time and people" can be found in a slightly different form in the working-class figure of Augusta at the end of *The Professor's House*, who provides a counterweight to the claustrophobic insularity of the Professor's own writerly craft. With his family off exploring Europe, Godfrey St. Peter sits in his nearly empty house and attempts to edit and write an introduction for Tom Outland's journal. The journal contains Tom's notes about a life-changing experience on the Blue Mesa, where he and a friend discovered an ancient, long-abandoned Cliff City, and a catalog of every artifact he found there. However, like Kenneth Gray, St. Peter cannot write, and instead he sits "motionless, breathing unevenly, one dark hand lying clenched on his writing-table," thinking about "eternal solitude with gratefulness; as a release from every obligation" (274, 272). When a gust of wind through his office window blows out the flame on his old gas burner, St. Peter nearly asphyxiates. As the gas overtakes his senses, he decides that he does not, "being quite honest with himself, feel any obligations toward his family" (281). But just as he gives himself over to death, the family's seamstress, Augusta, bursts into the room and carries St. Peter to safety. Augusta's resourcefulness and strength in resuscitating St. Peter lead him to a newfound sense of purpose as he imagines his family returning to Hamilton. But more importantly, the event brings out an unexpected affection for Augusta. "He would rather have Augusta with him just now than anyone he could think of," he thinks, and as his family recedes from his frame of reference, he takes comfort in a strange image: "there was still Augusta, however; a world full of Augustas, with whom one was outward bound" (281). Many critics have addressed St. Peter's discomfort with the domestic, heterosexual model of affiliation, emphasizing how he replaces his legal and biological family with homosocial relationships, most prominently with Tom. And as the opening of this chapter pointed out, the homosocial bond between Tom and St. Peter rests upon both participating in a magazine culture that allows for special kinds of affiliation across economic and spatial boundaries. St. Peter's affection for Augusta, read alongside his relationship with Tom, exposes another version of periodical-centered affiliation. After all, when Augusta comes into the workroom and opens the window, she becomes another version of Outland: both let in the fresh air that rejuvenates the Professor. And the passage's insistence that St. Peter is "outward bound" subtly alludes to Outland's unstated presence in the scene in the form of his journal. Yet the connotations of Tom and Augusta for St. Peter point in opposite directions. St. Peter's relationship with Tom was marked by exclusion and possessiveness and, in this way, was much more like Cather's idea about the noncirculating book: in fact, it is St. Peter's inability to circulate Tom's work that leads to the final scene. In Augusta, though, he projects and identifies with an endlessly proliferating and endlessly self-similar other who represents an alternative model of circulation, one that is "a definite absence from the world of men and women" (279).

Augusta's "definite absence from the world of men and women" is different than Tom's physical absence from the world of the novel (he's dead before it begins) as well as the other absence he's associated with: the vacuum he invents, whose patent produces the money that causes so much strife among the St. Peter family. The source of this difference is alluded to early in the novel. St. Peter and Augusta share office space, and what we might call their respective archives end up getting intermixed in a large storage chest.

> At one end of the upholstered box were piles of notebooks and bundles of manuscript tied up in square packages with mason's cord. At the other end were many little rolls of patterns, cut out of newspapers and tied with bits of ribbon, gingham, silk, georgette; notched charts which followed the changing stature and figures of the Misses St. Peter from early childhood to womanhood. In the middle of the box, patterns and manuscripts interpenetrated. "I see we shall have some difficulty in separating our life work, Augusta. We've kept our papers together a long while now."
>
> (22)

One might read this mixing of St. Peter's and Augusta's "papers" as a more complex retelling of the gendered notions of authorial work in "Ardessa" and "The Willing Muse." The masculine intellectual work of writing here finds its twin in Augusta's "little rolls of patterns, cut out of newspapers," that link feminine domestic work with mass periodical circulation. The box is an archive of the familial life that St. Peter always keeps at arm's length, but it is also evidence that his elevation above or removal from that model of feminized, overabundant circulation covers over how they are "interpenetrated." Moreover, this image of their shared papers mixing together provides a counterexample to Tom's patent, which neglected to mention that he depended on someone else's laboratory space and hence cut his collaborator out of the profits.

This messy archive of fragments runs up against the much different vision that the Professor has of his own method of composition, one that brings us back to Cather's idea that real writing doesn't actually produce any writing. As St. Peter recalls, *Spanish Adventurers* simply descended from the heavens already complete. While lying on his back looking up into the sky, "the design of the book unfolded in the air above him . . . and the design was sound. He had accepted it as inevitable, had never meddled with it, and it had seen him through" (106). Likewise, he describes Tom's "plain account" of his expedition into the Cliff City and eventual betrayal by his partner as

> almost beautiful, because of the stupidities it avoided and the things it did not say. If words had cost money, Tom couldn't have used them more sparingly. The adjectives were purely descriptive, relating to form and color, and were used to present objects under consideration, not the young explorer's emotions. Yet through this austerity one felt the kindling imagination, the ardor and excitement of the boy.
>
> (238)

Tom's story is unadorned, unsentimental, immediate, austere. It lacks self-consciousness or stylistic flourish. It is much like the long-abandoned Cliff City that it so efficiently describes, which "seemed to have a kind of composition" of its own, like a sculpture that sits in "silence and stillness and repose"; at another point in the novel, it is described as organized by "convenience" and gives "unquestionably a distinct feeling for design" (179, 216). Simplicity, convenience, sparseness, stillness: all traits that characterize Cather's ideal novel. They also describe Jim Burden's memoir in *My Ántonia* (1918), which Jim only writes because of a deal he made with "Willa Cather": "It hasn't any form. It hasn't a title, either," he tells her.[60] Each of these instances of proper literary production share what, in her essay "On the Art of Fiction," Cather describes as a "composition which is so simple that it seems inevitable," both in terms of how much effort the author exerts on the form of the story and the streamlined path from pen to page and finally to print.[61] She applies this formula to her own work, as well. "In a single evening," *Death Comes for the Archbishop* "came to her essentially as she afterwards wrote it."[62] The structure and story of *O Pioneers!* arrived "as a sudden inner explosion and enlightenment" that took on "an inevitable shape that is not plotted but designs itself."[63] In each of these instances, the act of artistic production scrubs away the appearance of any actual effort or sustained attention that might have gone into the final product, severing any connection between author and the act of writing as well as between author and text-object itself. It's an especially telling erasure in *O Pioneers!* because, like *The Professor's House*, it began as three magazine stories: "The Bohemian Girl," "Alexandra," and "The White Mulberry Tree." Even the novel's epigraph, "Prairie Spring," with its stoic agrarian setting that is "rich and sombre and always silent," was first published as a standalone poem in *McClure's*.

What we see here is the *McClure's* editor, whose job entailed selecting and improving content without being noticed as the author of that content, reimagining authorial production as editorial work. Though she attempts to cordon off the editorial office from her career as a novelist and vision of artistic production, they end up looking almost identical. Thea Kronborg, the pianist-turned–opera singer in *Song of the Lark*, puts this in slightly different terms, arguing that for true artists there can be no division between one's work and one's life. In a thoroughly Jamesian parlor scene, a friend tells Thea that her life has come out of balance because she has sacrificed all of the pleasures of friendship and leisure to her artistic ascent. She responds that for a true artist, "your work becomes your personal life. You are not much good until it does. It's like being woven into a big web. You can't pull away, because all your little tendrils are woven into the picture. It takes you up, and uses you, and spins you out; and that is your life. Not much else can happen to you" (443). This vision of a "big web" of work that "takes you up, and uses you, and spins you out" would seem to bring together, at least metaphorically, the already "interpenetrated" work of St. Peter and Augusta as it uses the language of sewing to describe her own artistic production. When Thea sings in *The Song of the Lark*, the novel calls it "voice production," as if "a healthy and powerful organ has found its own method" (175). Or later, as "if her body were absolutely the instrument of her idea," which makes the gendered body of the artist a material on which some larger, more encompassing content is conveyed. This replicates the mechanical vision of female writing, yet it also transforms female writing into a kind of editing similar to that of the Professor, Tom Outland, and Jim Burden. Thea is not emotively creating when she performs; instead, she is simply the medium through which sound moves. At its best, then, the path of creative production looks a lot like the mechanized and heavily standardized models of mass print culture. Yet it takes Thea a lifetime of self-discipline to administer this restraint; after all, according to Cather, one must learn writing before unlearning it.

The awkward coupling of overabundance and self-enclosure, and of writing as mechanized work that erases the author's role in the creation, can also shed light on the overidentification of artists and their art objects in her works. In Cather's first novel, *Alexander's Bridge*, the narrator describes the title character, a bridge architect, as "look[ing] as a tamer of rivers ought to look," by which she means bridgelike: his shoulders are "strong enough in themselves to support a span of any one of his ten great bridges."[64] Thea Kronborg describes a sonata she is practicing as nonexistent unless in her presence: "it isn't here unless I have it—not for me. . . . Only what I hold in my two hands is there for me!"—which makes her musicality coterminous with her bodily presence. For Thea, this identification stretches beyond what she makes to include everything she likes. When she visits the Chicago Art Institute and sees the painting from which the novel takes its name, she thinks: "That was her picture. She imagined that nobody cared for it but herself, and that it waited for her. That was a picture indeed. She liked even the name of it, 'The Song of the Lark.' The flat country, the early morning light, the wet fields, the look in the girl's heavy face—well, they were all hers, anyhow, whatever was there."[65] *Alexander's Bridge* ends when one of Alexander's bridges collapses on him, which simultaneously ends the life of the architect, his architecture, and the narrative that constructs both of them. *The Song of the Lark* brings its main character into contact with "The Song of the Lark," a painting that anachronistically appears to be an image of the novel's own protagonist, enacting a similar collapse between the metaphoric and the literal within the narrative.

Cather's representational worlds, then, tend toward internal redundancy, where characters, aesthetic objects, and the books that contain them all become reiterations of one another. As we'll see in the next chapter, a group of editors, authors, and artists at *The Crisis* will experiment with the political implications of undermining the idea of a character's auton-omy and psychological depth. The burgeoning field of national African American magazines are especially well placed to investigate such matters. Here, though, what Eve Sedgwick refers to as the signature "viscosity" in Cather's prose makes it hard for these novels or the characters in them to move forward.[66] When Alexander becomes one with his broken bridge, or when Thea looks at the painting that inspired her own creation, Cather cancels out the plot that brought the man and his object together, in the first instance, and the possibility that an artist creates something new, in the second. It's a longstanding belief that literary modernism is modern-ist insofar as it makes a formal question of these almost claustrophobi-cally self-reflexive issues about the relationship between authors, texts, and audiences. And a novel interested in such questions—but also interested in maintaining the ruse of fictionality that defines it as a novel—must do so "by resisting the last degree of narrative self-consciousness that would simply collapse the world in which the titular object circulates, admit-ting that it's all just print, disabling the fictive dream."[67] In *Alexander's Bridge* and *The Song of the Lark*, a character, an object, and the narrative become so closely identified, so overly similar, that they give up that fic-tive dream and fall apart. *The Professor's House* follows the same pattern but then offers another option. In doing so, it provides one final way in which to read Cather's allegory of editing because it exposes the disabling effect of excising her periodical career from her authorial one: when her previous novels collapse, she is reduced to one of her own, impossibly self-conscious male writers. Yet *The Professor's House* succeeds in a way that these other novels do not because St. Peter's final revelation offers the possibility of another way to imagine the work of writing. *The Professor's House* stops looking inward only when St. Peter gives up trying to edit Tom's journal and begins to see all those Augustas as an identifiable, if still largely abstract, audience. The Professor and the novel that houses him have been outward bound to Augusta and her periodicals from the beginning.

CHAPTER 2

Printing the Color Line in *The Crisis*

W ILLA CATHER'S EDITORIAL WORK AT *MCCLURE'S* feeds forward into her theory of writing, which is most fully realized in her novels from the 1920s, the decade closely associated with the high point of modernism. It's also considered a turning point in the history of American magazines, as a generation of entrepreneurial businessmen and journalists will model what Theodore Greene calls the "cock-suredness" of publishers like S. S. McClure and Robert Underwood Johnson (of *Century*) and begin to rethink the size and scope of the big magazine. Until recently, though, the intervening decade of the 1910s was something of a forgotten era in terms of periodical innovation in the United States. Greene, describing the years around World War I, summarizes a widely held belief when he writes, "No enterprising publishers . . . broke through existing patterns to make their personal marks. No new young writers made an impact on the popular mind equal to that of" those in the 1890s.[1] Of course, such a statement ignores little magazines such as *Blast!* and *The Little Review*, which left their "personal marks" on the 1910s and, more recently, have sustained much scholarly attention. Yet these aren't the kinds of titles that Greene has in mind, as they often explicitly pitted themselves against unapologetically commercial magazines like *McClure's* and, precisely because of their smallness, went unread by the vast majority of the magazine-purchasing public. However, in 1910 another kind of magazine, the African American monthly, specifically *The Crisis*, emerged with the conscious desire to reshape the style, size, and color of commercial periodicals as well as the implicit race of the people who read and wrote them. Under the aegis of its founder, W. E. B. Du Bois, *The Crisis* played an integral but often overlooked part in the history of the big magazines, as its innovative methods for representing race and racialized intellectual work so successfully set a pattern for African American print culture that ironically, by the middle of the 1920s, Du Bois feared that *The Crisis* was obsolete.

As one of the most visible spokespersons for African American civil rights in the first half of the twentieth century, Du Bois's primary medium of promotion and argumentation was the periodical. He edited *The Moon* (1905–1906), *The Horizon* (1906–1910), *The Crisis* (1910–1934), and *Phylon* (1940–1944). He contributed articles to top-tier newspapers such as the *New York Times* and the New York *Post*; "smart" magazines such as H. L. Mencken's *Smart Set* and *American Mercury*; general-interest magazines such as *McClure's* and *Century*; older, genteel ones like *The Atlantic Monthly*, *The Nation*, and *The New Republic*; explicitly African American journals such as *The Independent* and Booker T. Washington's *New York Age*; and literary outlets such as *The Dial* and *North American Review*. Nearly two-thirds of the chapters in *The Souls of Black Folk* (1903), the book that propelled him to national recognition, began as essays in magazines and journals such as *The Atlantic Monthly*, *The Dial*, *The Worker's World*, and *The New World*. Fully betting on the power of periodicals was an active choice, too: Du Bois viewed his decision in 1910 to give up university work in Atlanta and move to New York for the NAACP as changing from "science to propaganda" in his quest for racial equality. Or, as David Levering Lewis puts it, as trading "the class room" for "the editorial desk."[2]

For at least the first thirty years of the twentieth century, then, Du Bois's contributions to the political battles over race in the United States, as well as his reputation regarding those fights, were indelibly tied to his career in magazines, and in what follows I'll make the case that Du Bois envisioned, and in *The Crisis* at least partially instantiated, the periodical as the ideal print form for wedding his political and aesthetic goals. Founding *The Crisis* is a turning point in Du Bois's career, and the time he spent building it fundamentally influences his ideas about how best to represent race in popular culture. Du Bois's editorship of the magazine is an equally integral turning point in the size and shape of African American print culture. His official title at the NAACP, which he helped cofound, was Director of Publicity and Research, but from 1910 until his resignation in 1934 he almost exclusively oversaw the production of *The Crisis*, his brainchild and the organization's official mouthpiece. The magazine's first editorial staff evidences his clout in journalistic circles, both in the older African American periodicals and in mainstream U.S. publications: it was composed of the *New York Times* staff writer Mary Dunlop Maclean, the New York *Evening Post* editor (and later owner of *The Nation*) Oswald Garrison Villard, the Boston *Transcript* poetry editor and anthologist William Stanley Braithwhaite, and the former *Voice of the Negro* editor J. Max Barber, among others. The magazine's relationship to the NAACP and Du Bois's single-minded control over its content caused significant political infighting at the parent organization. Du Bois imagined the magazine as semiautonomous, with its primary goal to round up a readership that could be converted into NAACP members and supporters. "What I am working for with the CRISIS is to make the N.A.A.C.P. *possible*. Today it is *not* possible," Du Bois wrote to Joel E. Springarn in 1913, defending the magazine's purposefully inflammatory editorial positions, which at times were at odds with the organization's official positions.[3] Villard, Spingarn, and other leaders, though, saw the relationship differently: for them, *The Crisis* was a fully embedded division of the NAACP; as such, its editorial policies and coverage should consistently reflect the interests of its parent organization. An even worse problem was that many feared that the magazine was more popular than the association and that it was more closely associated with Du Bois the man than with the organization he worked for. Mary Childs Nancy, secretary at the NAACP, protested that *The Crisis* served only as Du Bois's "personal machine," and apparently she was not alone in her fear that for much of the magazine's readership "Du Bois *was* the NAACP."[4] Du Bois's influence over *The Crisis*, then, becomes doubly damning; the time he spends overseeing it comes at the expense of organizational politicking, and as it succeeds, it inflames his relationship with key leaders of the NAACP. When Du Bois acrimoniously resigned as editor and renounced any connection with its parent company, the only specific feat *The Crisis* mentions him contributing to either the magazine or its parent company is that he increased the circulation to over one hundred thousand copies per month, which the unsigned editorial calls "an unprecedented achievement in American journalism."[5]

Du Bois's unprecedented achievement has as much to do with changing the style of the African American periodical as with raising its circulation, and his thorough understanding of the connection between form and expanded readership is, in part, what aligns *The Crisis* with the other big magazines in this book. Yet, despite Du Bois's clear investment in the content of American periodical culture, he was ambivalent about the social role magazines occupy. In 1907 he voiced his concern about the wide gap between the quantity and quality of magazines available, particularly regarding their ability to instill substantive intellectual discourse or political change. In an article for *The Horizon*, Du Bois lamented that "we are magazine mad—a magazine-devouring nation" and that magazines and newspapers are "festering abominations," a "hodge-podge of lie, gossip, twaddle, and caricature."[6] He was not the only one to say so. As he drew up plans for *The Crisis* in 1910, a skeptical acquaintance wrote to him, "Periodicals are as numerous and as pestilential nowadays as flies were in Egypt, and most of them meet with the very same reception."[7] F. H. M. Murray, Du Bois's coeditor at *The Horizon*, also complained about the floodtide of "Magazinelets," but he focused on how the physical form of magazines and especially how new technologies that help standardize and syndicate the content of magazines end up injuring readers and by extension the rational public sphere. Murray takes issue with the interchangeable, "regulation size" magazines that are nothing more than "big bundles of wood pulp with . . . garish covers," a formula that conjoins the rough materiality of these journals with their heavy-handed editorial style and undercooked intellectual work.[8] He goes further, specifying the print technology that brings periodicals into this situation:

> Strange it is that most people shun a large book but "dearly love" a big newspaper or a fat magazine. And so it come[s] about—paradoxically— that the most formidable enemy of truth in the world today is the linotype. It serves the couse [*sic*] of truth—not knowledge mark you, for the most that we know ain't so—in about the same degree that gunpowder fosters liberty.[9]

The linotype, which allowed a typesetter to arrange an entire line of type at once rather than set a page character by character, was one of several technological innovations that made printing both cheaper and faster in the late nineteenth century. Along with the stereotype, halftone printing, and new office technologies like the multigraph, the linotype fundamentally changed the quantity and quality of periodical culture. For the innovators of the 1890s, these changes were an unqualified good: they helped professionalize journalistic practice and expand magazines to an ever-wider audience. Magazines such as *McClure's*, which cheaply sold its "gentlemanly" voice to middle- and working-class readerships previously unable to afford quality journals, were unthinkable before the invention of printing methods and office machinery that drastically lowered production costs. These new magazines provided a vehicle for aspirational readers to look in on political and cultural conversations that, for most of the nineteenth century, were restricted to a more elevated demographic. The editorial office at *McClure's* also offered a place for fledgling authors to make a living by writing or editing; make connections with other journalists, authors, and publishers; and hone their compositional skills under the watchful eyes of more experienced writers. And, as in the case of Willa Cather, women quickly filled a number of professional roles in these rapidly expanding editorial offices while also shaping the form and content of that "gentlemanly" voice.

The story of Cather and *McClure's* is the print revolution as a success, even if Cather anguished over what that success would mean, on the one hand, for her career as a serious author and, on the other, for the relative cultural status and circulation of books and magazines. Du Bois and Murray are engaged with similar questions but for an entirely different set of reasons. *McClure's* mission statement—increase readership by selling more stylish and less expensive content than the competitor—speaks to a belief in the democratizing power of print culture. But for Murray to say that the linotype produces "truth" in the same way that "gunpowder fosters liberty" and for Du Bois to suggest that there is something "mad" about the magazine market suggests that the lowered entry cost for publishing and the subsequent proliferation of periodicals bring with them a dark side. An expanded print marketplace includes more people but not necessarily better ideas, and certainly not arranged as a meritocracy. That is, new technologies of print culture work by way of aggressive, violent coercion rather than positivist enlightenment and contemplative reflection. For Murray, this power struggle doesn't occur directly between people; instead, it happens within print itself: "dearly loved" magazines in competition with books. Du Bois would also rally behind books in *The Horizon*: "Buy books" was something of a refrain in his editorials. "Do not merely read them but buy them, own them, make them yours," he pleaded. "Do not simply use libraries, but buy books."[10]

In this appeal for the book over the periodical, we hear an echo of Willa Cather's distinction between the kinds of affiliations made available by different print forms, which is grounded in her epistemological separation of the work required for each. We might also read Du Bois's *Horizon* column as simply reinforcing a well-known story about the development of black print culture in the early twentieth century: that is, the emergence of a self-consciously African American reading public fostered by an increasingly organized black press, literary societies, reading groups, and church organizations.[11] It makes perfect sense that Du Bois would have in mind the networks and institutions that foster these "forgotten readers," to use Elizabeth McHenry's term—that, in 1907, they are not yet forgotten—because they are in many ways the same organizations that constitute the "Talented Tenth," a small subset of African Americans who guide intraracial discourse by sustaining the circulation and future work of magazines like *The Horizon*. However, the above quotation's unmistakable anxiety over the quality and quantity of intellectual work made available in magazines adds at least two new dimensions to this story: most obviously, his "Books" column indicates that from Du Bois's perspective, a self-conscious and organized black reading public may be immanent, but it does not quite exist yet, at least on a national level. Later in the same issue, Du Bois would matter-of-factly say that a national black monthly couldn't sustain itself financially. But, closer to the heart of this book, his column draws attention to the specific material forms of print culture and their unique capabilities for representing race. When Du Bois tells readers to buy books and "make them yours," he links the materiality of particular print media with their unique capabilities to impress content on a reader. That is, book ownership fosters a richer and deeper engagement with the text and, by some kind of magic specific to what Jessica Pressman would call its "bookishness," with the real world of politics and personhood represented therein.[12] It is easy enough to hypothesize this rationale for a hierarchy of print forms, especially if we keep in mind Cather's own preference for the felt uniqueness of a book. Bought books trump library books and doubly trump periodicals because the owned book's authorial singularity and self-completeness mirror the bourgeois individuality that Du Bois and other African American leaders who rose in the wake of Booker T. Washington would help extend to blacks. The privately owned book exudes the physical weightiness and focused authorial vision that allows for a deeper and lengthier investigation than the one-off magazine article, and purchasing a book entails a financial investment in the material that houses the content. The early twentieth-century book buyer—unlike the purchaser of the cheap and abundant periodicals that dominated print sales or the library patron who reads on a deadline—has the economic incentive as well as an open-ended timetable for serious reading, for mirroring the in-depth reflection that went into creating the book and leveling the balance between effort-in and effort-out for writing and reading. Thus, we might conjecture that, for Du Bois, book ownership—especially for an immanent black reading class—enacts between author and reader the ideal civic relationship, one guided by a communal respect for, as he would phrase it in the first issue of *The Crisis*, "the tremendous truth that it is impossible to judge the mind of a man by the color of his face."[13] The integration of African Americans into the public body, in this way, begins to look like a perfectly working print marketplace, one in which the quality of the content directly corresponds with its integration into the social world; put another way, the quality of its representations is on balance with the quantity of its representations in the ecology of printed texts.

The problem, of course, is that neither the print marketplace nor the enforcement of civil rights functions quite so smoothly, and the slipshod intellectual forum of periodicals rules the day. As Ann Ardis and others have shown, periodicals took "center-stage in the period's conversations about the possibility of radical democracy in a mass society, the function of the arts in a republic, and the intellectual 'health' of modern culture."[14] Du Bois's and Murray's discomfort with the utopian promise of the linotype and what Du Bois calls the "mental indigestion" of an overabundant magazine market forces us to pause and remember the obvious fact that not everyone experienced the same success as Cather and S. S. McClure. On one hand, the expansion and increased pace of periodical culture ushered in by better technology opened the door for a variety of new voices and the possibility of a more inclusive, representative public sphere. However, the vast majority of the new content during the print revolution either ignored the post-Reconstruction plight of African Americans or was explicitly hostile to political efforts promoting racial uplift. Many historians of journalism cite Robert E. Lee as the first advocate for tailoring university classes to journalists, which he did at Washington College (later Washington and Lee), which at least anecdotally corroborates Murray's and Du Bois's feelings that African Americans faced an uphill battle when entering into the field.[15] However, Lee and other Confederate holdovers were not the only roadblocks in the still fledgling world of black-owned periodicals. Up until the early years of the twentieth century, Booker T. Washington controlled virtually all of the race-oriented magazines and newspapers in the United States. Abby and Ronald Johnson have documented how Washington's influence in the publishing industry and journalistic circles made it nearly impossible to raise the funds for a periodical that didn't have his stamp of approval. When one emerged and even meagerly succeeded, like Pauline Hopkins's *Colored American*, Washington (through hidden channels) simply bought it, changed its editorial policy, and brought it in line with his own beliefs.[16] And even the most successful of these African American periodicals had minuscule readerships compared to white-owned presses. J. Max Barber's *Voice of the Negro*, for example, peaked at a paid subscription rate of 17,000.

The rising tide of the print revolution seemed to be lifting up everyone except the group that, for Du Bois, needed it the most. It is in this context that his investment in periodical culture and particularly in the material and technological form of magazines makes the most sense: to make a financially stable monthly journal entailed amassing as much of Murray's proverbial gunpowder as possible for African American political and cultural causes in the United States. More ambitiously, he hoped to establish what, to his mind, would be the first nationally circulated black periodical. To achieve this goal, Du Bois believed that the quantity of representations of African Americans could only go so far. As much as he wanted to provide "a record of the darker races," as the subtitle of *The Crisis* phrased it, he also thought that to do so would mean attending to the technological and material forms of racial representation. And it is through greater attention to the formal matters of black publications, for Du Bois, that one could expect greater parity in the content and quantity of images of African American life.

This chapter tracks several ways that Du Bois and his staff at *The Crisis* bring together a specific attention to the formal properties of their magazine's production and circulation with a wider desire for a national African American periodical culture. At its height, from 1918 to 1922, *The Crisis* was the most popular African American magazine in the United States, with a circulation around one hundred thousand copies per month.[17]

Admittedly, that number pales in comparison to the other magazines I discuss in this book. *McClure's* under Cather's editorship sold ten times that amount every month, and *Time* and *Life* in the 1930s would combine for a worldwide circulation close to three million every *week*.[18] Even though it was unprecedentedly popular for an African American periodical, when compared to these giants it's decidedly small. But Du Bois desperately *wanted* it to be big, to be what he called "one of the great journals of the world," even if the rest of the NAACP had less ambitious goals for the magazine.[19] For Du Bois and his hand-selected staff, style was the way to reach the widest circulation possible. *The Crisis* saw the pathway to both the individual and institutional success of African American magazines as deeply tied to their formal and stylistic innovation, and during the life of *The Crisis*, this nationalized network materialized. Later, when the market around *The Crisis* changed, he blamed the magazine's declining circulation—its new unpopularity—on the fact that everyone had copied its style. The overriding preoccupation for *The Crisis*, then, is *how* to represent racialized bodies and intellectual work most effectively.

Unlike the other magazines I discuss, *The Crisis's* target audience was explicitly raced, and its cover art and editorial content repeatedly drew attention to the implicit whiteness of popular print culture. More than this, it used its serial form to experiment with different versions of how to embed racialized authorship and editorship in the style of a magazine. The project of explicitly making a race magazine raises a number of questions about what, exactly, constitutes race for Du Bois and his staff. His attitudes toward the subject are notoriously hard to pin down, and they will be of less interest to me here than the representational strategies that *The Crisis* takes up to transmit on the page something that would be recognizable to its audience as "black" intellectual work.[20] I'll begin by laying out the many ways that Du Bois preoccupied himself with the material production of periodicals, showing how this attention to how a magazine gets made inflects his ideas about what a magazine—and specifically a race magazine—can include. The implicit two-pronged mission of *The Crisis* becomes quite clear here: first, it wants to aggregate information on African American achievements and circulate them to a national reading public so as to provide a counterhistory to racist mass culture, but it also wants to project a future when such work will not be necessary—that is, like the eponymous character in Cather's "Ardessa," a future in which it will have worked itself out of a job. These two tasks have competing temporalities as well as representational strategies. I'll illustrate how these two overarching goals come into contact in *The Crisis* by reading across many aspects of the magazine: its column titles, recurring visual motifs, individual essays, cover art, and serial fiction. To maintain some methodological order, I'll proceed by first presenting Du Bois's attitudes as represented in the magazine; then, I'll turn to several cover images, especially those by the artist Frank Walts, that visually represent the magazine's ambivalence over what black intellectual work should look like; and, finally, I'll use Jessie Fauset's serialized short story "The Sleeper Wakes" (August–September 1920) as an example of how *The Crisis* imagines both the medium-specific limitations of representing race as well as the magazine's own changing place in periodical culture.

As literary editor, Jessie Fauset shepherded Langston Hughes's first publication in the magazine, "The Negro Speaks of Rivers" (1921), an event that marks the first stage of the Harlem Renaissance. This chapter ends in late 1920, on the cusp of that shift in African American literary culture. On the horizon are the impending decline of *The Crisis* and the rise of a nationalized black periodical culture with Harlem at its imagined center. By cutting off the story in 1920, I offer less than I could on Du Bois's vexed role in the Harlem Renaissance and the competing black modernisms that Alain Locke collects in the issue of *Survey Graphic* dedicated to Harlem, which lays the foundation for the groundbreaking anthology *The New Negro*.[21] Instead, I provide a prehistory of the print networks that will be institutionalized in the early 1920s and the particular challenges that Du Bois and others faced in their attempts to create them. By emphasizing *The Crisis*'s interest in the specific medium in which it produces and immediately archives a racialized content—print, but more specifically the magazine—I join a conversation that foregrounds the materiality of cultural circulation in describing the work of writers from the African diaspora. As Brent Hayes Edwards, Katherine Biers, Madhu Dubhey, Mark Goble, and others have argued, a "phonocentrism" that stresses vernacular forms and tropes of orality has guided African Americanist criticism since the late 1970s.[22] And as George Hutchinson, Ann Ducille, and others have compellingly argued, such studies move "African American cultural studies out of the realm of the intellectual, where the written words of the literati have been privileged, into the world of the material, where other cultural forms such as the blues await analysis."[23] Yet, in Ducille's conceptualization of the field, we find a false division between the "written words of the literati" and "the world of the material," as if intellectual discourse existed outside of the constraints of physical media forms. As will become clear in the ensuing pages, Du Bois and others were long engaged with the media specificity of African American intellectual work and cultural practice. Theorizations of the racial "sound" of texts to which "we *listen*,"[24] along with tropes of the "Talking Book" and the "speakerly text,"[25] tend to sidestep how writers and artists account for the messy materiality of the print artifact, how the idiosyncrasies of different media shape their representational capabilities, and how the material characteristics of print media can supply their own thematics of African American artistic production.

It is striking how often magazines get singled out as the prime location for organizing these concerns about representation. For instance, Charles Chesnutt's turn-of-the-century novel *The Marrow of Tradition* (1901) figures post-Reconstruction life as being like a piece of magazine fiction. As two physicians—the white Dr. Burns and his African American former student, Dr. Miller—ride a train south from Philadelphia to the fictional town of Wellington, North Carolina, Burns explains to Miller his thoughts on the "race question":

> It is a tremendous problem, Miller, the future of your race . . . a tremendously interesting problem. It is a serial story which we are all reading, and which grows in vital interest with each successive installment. It is not only your problem, but ours. Your race must come up or drag ours down.[26]

Burns is not talking about a specific serialized story that takes racial discord as its theme; instead, he figures the "interesting problem" of African American integration into the political body of the United States as a serial story itself, something that develops in "successive installment[s]" and that one experiences collectively through the cultural practice of reading. Put another way, it is not just that what Richard Yarborough calls the period's "war over images" exists as a subset of a more expansive battle between a cultural and political movement for social equality and its attendant racist backlash.[27] Instead, Burns, through the limited perspective of a Northern white observer, interprets what W. E. B. Du Bois refers to as "the problem of the color line" quite literally as a problem instantiated in black and white on the pages of newspapers and magazines.

In a 1903 letter to Du Bois, Chesnutt claimed that though there are "many 'colored' papers," they are so poorly made that "most of them ought not brag about it." "What the Negro needs more than anything," Chesnutt argues, "is a medium through which he can present his case to thinking white people"—well-intentioned but generally ignorant people, like Burns.[28] *Marrow* makes establishing such a medium central to its plot and dramatizes how interracial periodical exchange can go terribly wrong. White racists read an article in a black-owned newspaper and then later reprint it in their own paper to stir up racial antagonism before an election, which ends in Chesnutt's fictionalized version of the Wilmington Race Riot of 1898. As Chesnutt traces the article's path across different periodicals and through the hands of many types of readerships, he highlights the uneven development of print-reading publics, particularly the sorry state of those "many 'colored' papers." The article at the center of *Marrow* begins in a regional African American weekly, "an eighteen by twenty-four sheet, poorly printed on cheap paper, with a 'patent' inside, a number of advertisements of proprietary medicines, quack doctors, and fortune-tellers," a document that the narrator describes as "not an impressive sheet in any respect, except when regarded as the first local effort of a struggling people to make public expression of their life and aspirations" (96–97). Its material cheapness, here, is part and parcel of its localness and the limited circulation intended for the paper and opinions expressed therein. When racist whites reprint the article, the material look of the article as well as the intentionally circumscribed audience change: the publisher, Carteret, is said to "represent the Associated Press," and "through [his] hands passes all the news of the state" (96). These two Southern positions are then triangulated with another: "Such an article in a Northern newspaper would have attracted no special attention, and might merely have furnished food to an occasional reader for serious thought upon a subject not exactly agreeable; but coming from a colored man, in a Southern city, it was an indictment of the laws and social system of the South that could not fail of creating a profound sensation" (97). Besides the material quality of each periodical, then, Chesnutt suggests that they differ in how successfully they delimit an intended public and speak to that group's concerns. More than this, he suggests that Carteret's connections to a national periodical network, the Associated Press, allow him to turn this antilynching article against its original intention. Content be damned: when the context of the editorial's publication changes, so does its meaning.

Du Bois even more directly takes up the politics behind race and periodical form in "Criteria for Negro Art," published in *The Crisis* in 1926. The essay, which appeared one year before *The Crisis* instituted the Charles Waddell Chesnutt Honorarium for outstanding writing, is most famous for its argument that "Beauty" and "Truth and Goodness" are "here and now and in the world in which I work . . . unseparated and inseparable," a point that leads him to the conclusion that "all Art is propaganda and ever must be, despite the wailing of the purists."[29] I have more to say about this statement—particularly about its oscillation between the "here and now" of Du Bois's working world and the gesture toward eternity that links Art with propaganda—but for now I want to note how Du Bois illustrates his point. "You all know the current magazine story," he writes. "A young white man goes down to Central America and the most beautiful colored woman there falls in love with him. She crawls across the whole Isthmus to get to him. The white man says nobly, 'No.' He goes back to his white sweetheart in New York."[30] For the lifelong magazine editor, of course the most obvious place to see a political aesthetic in action would be in another magazine. Unlike the intrinsically local representations of race and racial politics we find in Chesnutt's antilynching newspaper article, the above "magazine story" is something "you all know." The specific content varies, but the narrative is archetypal: it gets retold with different names and places and in different literary and journalistic forms, but Du Bois frames the "current magazine story" as the foundation for a popular understanding of racial difference.

In doing so, Du Bois highlights the ideological undercarriage of seemingly objective, neutral news coverage. His point here is that the nationalized popular press practices an Art that is propaganda, one that looks a lot like the racist doggerel that Carteret puts in his paper. Not surprisingly, he adopts the sociologists' perspective on such an arrangement: rather than insist on what artistic and journalistic work *should* be, he describes them as they are. "It is not the positive propaganda of people who believe white blood divine, infallible and holy to which I object," he claims. "It is the denial of a similar right of propaganda to those who believe black blood human, lovable and inspired with new ideals for the world."[31] The only way for African Americans to make headway, he insists, requires attuning themselves to the medium at hand. First, by acknowledging that everything they produce will be read in overdetermined, racialized ways, and second by producing work that takes advantage of this.

The Mechanics of a Race Magazine

Martha Jane Nadell summarizes the opinion of African American intellectuals such as Du Bois, William Stanley Braithwaite, and others regarding how
mainstream outlets represented African Americans as "object[ing] to the
mechanism by which these representations operated. Specifically, the critics objected to the way in which literary and visual images, ranging from
'caricature' to 'sentiment,' made the Negro into a 'genre stereotype.'"[32]
Though "stereotype," like the closely associated "cliché," now refers primarily to a widely held belief about the shared characteristics of a group, it
originally referred to a new printing technology: the eponymous method
for making exact papier-mâché copies of a metal printing plate that could
be cheaply distributed among many different printing plants. Thus, the
term "genre stereotype" (taken from Alain Locke's introduction to *The New
Negro Anthology* [1925]) perfectly encapsulates the way that new tactics
for African American self-presentation are at once reliant on print technology, narrative convention, and formal innovation. Put another way, African
American writers' and intellectuals' shifting position in American culture at
large offered an ideal vantage point from which to see how uneven access to
institutions of cultural production placed limits on the openness of this new
print market as well as on the pages on which its ideas circulated.

When we unpack the many ways that Du Bois and others at *The Crisis*
contested these "genre stereotype[s]," we see what Brent Hayes Edwards
calls the "compulsively documentary" side of the New Negro movement,
the "flood of energy in modern print culture" that took collectively produced print forms (for Edwards, especially the anthology) as a place to
"fram[e] race . . . [and] articulate[e] an epistemology of blackness."[33]
From the beginning of his career in periodicals, Du Bois realized the integral role of that new print technologies could play in creating "a proper
Journal" and circulating "certain ideals, racial and cultural, [that] must be
brought home to the rank and file."[34] In a fundraising letter for *The Moon*,
he emphasized that he and a partner had purchased a printing plant and
itemized its holdings:

new type,
one (1 horse power)
electric motor,

1 Whillock cylinder press,

1 Job Press (7 × 11) in exchange,

1 perforating machine[35]

Alongside this list he estimated the cash value of each piece of equipment and the expected income from serving as the go-to print house for the black community in Memphis. By playing up his technical knowledge of the mechanics of printing, he contrasts his potential magazine with the "small weekly sheets" and "thousands of small papers" that "have sprung up and died" in the last fifty years. He also differentiates his own magazine from other relatively successful African American monthlies like *Colored American* and *Voice of the Negro* by listing their formal and managerial deficiencies. He describes them as "fairly good periodicals of the ordinary sort" even though "they lack (a) careful editing on broad lines, (b) timely, readable articles, (c) an efficient news service, (d) good illustrations, [and] (e) modern aggressive business management." Or, to summarize his list of grievances, the other periodicals lack every positive characteristic of a "high class journal" and therefore have no hope of expanding their circulation and revenue beyond the black middle class.[36] In *The Horizon*, Du Bois went so far as to equate ideological autonomy with his ownership and production of the magazine. It was right on the masthead, which in large type assured readers that the magazine was "owned by" its editors, who "write it, type it, and print it."

Owning the means of production and sharing those means with other racially progressive print endeavors will help establish a culture of black readers and provide the material for them to buy. As we saw in chapter 1, S. S. McClure built his magazine subscription on the back of his profitable news service, and here Du Bois is just as interested in piecing together the institutional arrangements that will produce a national African American print culture. Just how big he thought this could get, though, depended on whom Du Bois was talking to. In 1905 he cites as a potential readership the "million Negro families who can read & write"; when later addressing a potential investor, he envisioned his magazine for "the nine million American Negros and eventually for the whole colored world."[37] He usually was more tempered in his estimates, though. In 1903 he claimed that an efficiently managed and aesthetically pleasing weekly could reach fifty to one hundred thousand readers. The upper end of that range is the most frequent number he cites for the highest possible circulation of *The Crisis* in the mid-1910s. The goal of one hundred thousand readers in the United States roughly corresponds with his ideas about the "Talented Tenth." As he would write in a report to the NAACP Board of Directors in 1912, "With proper agents and methods, there seems no reason why of the one million Negro families in the United States who can read and write well, 1/10 or 100,000 could not in time be induced to read the CRISIS."[38] The pathway to complete saturation of the periodical market, he conjectured, would be "by combining a knowledge of modern publishing methods with a knowledge of the Negro people."[39] Du Bois's emphasis on the mutual necessity of technoprofessional and cultural acumen ("modern publishing methods" and "a knowledge of the Negro people") is representative of the way he'll theorize the mechanics of a race magazine throughout his career. Of course, *The Moon* never reached those nine million African Americans, let alone the more modest goal of one-tenth of African American households—it topped out around 250—but Du Bois's ambition to do so marks his periodical endeavors as related to the popularity of *McClure's* and the Time Inc. titles I'll discuss in the following chapters. Du Bois would even name-check the former when he explained his ideas about *The Crisis*. "Our covers and our publishers talk may sometimes savour the 'penny-dreadful,'" he wrote, but "the methods that have built up McCLURE'S and the LADIES HOME JOURNAL cannot be altogether ignored by The CRISIS." The "methods" refer to the new editorial processes at *McClure's*, but here he seems to be talking about the look of big magazines: "[It] must be attractively gotten up for a people who love color and who have been starved in their cries," he wrote.[40] This aesthetic dimension is what hamstrung previous black periodicals, in his opinion, and Du Bois believed that they would need to invest in new printing equipment if they were going to sell more copies to a wider range of readers.

Hence, despite operating at a deficit and owing money to both their printer and the NAACP, he oversaw the purchase of their own multigraph for typesetting and page design. Though the multigraph is more or less a forgotten office technology today, when Du Bois bought one for *The Crisis* it was touted as a flexible and frugal way to design and make copies of any kind of print material that a business would need. Multigraph printers combined the capabilities of multiple typewriters and a small printing press; at a single machine a member of the editorial staff could mock up a page design and run copies. Because it allowed

design work as well as the printing and copying of high-quality advertising circulars to be done in house, Du Bois felt that it would save the
magazine money. Advertisements from the time he bought the multigraph claimed that it could save a company over 50 percent on printing
costs and improve the quality of the finished product as well. "It was
good printing, in real ink," one exclaims. It made production cheaper,
but it also allowed for extraordinary personalization in the page design
and visual style; users could feed office letterhead into the machine, cus-
tomize the ink they used, and, as the advertising claims, create "the most
intimate, personal, convincing and economical" advertising and editorial
materials. In a letter to Joel Spingarn, the new president of the board at
the NAACP—and a perennial hard sell on the usefulness of *The Crisis* in
achieving the organization's goals—Du Bois mentions the multigraph
as a primary example of his own editorial and economic ingenuity. His
decision to purchase it proves, in Du Bois's reasoning, that *The Crisis* can
be financially independent: as he made clear in *The Horizon*, ownership

FIGURE 2.1 W. E. B. Du Bois and staff in *The Crisis* office, featuring Du Bois's multigraph
(bottom left).
Source: Courtesy of the Schomburg Center for Research in Black Culture, Photographs and Prints
Division, New York Public Library.

meant fiscal as well as ethical accountability. Du Bois claims that the machine will save *The Crisis* around fifty dollars per month in printing and copying costs: in his annual balance sheet that he submitted to the NAACP in 1913, he lists the machine under "revenue," and he claims that it produces $175 per month.[41]

FIGURE 2.2 American Multigraph Sales Company advertisement.
Source: *System* (August 1910).

The multigraph registers Du Bois's investment in the mechanics of producing his magazine and the representational possibilities of printing machines, but it also ties into a wider concern with amassing an archive of racial work. That's because the multigraph allows Du Bois to document and track the increasing independence of the magazine. In Du Bois's narrative, it becomes a symbol of his break from Springarn and Villard in achieving that goal. First, it gives him a partial excuse for leaving their former editorial office on Vesey Street in Manhattan, which was subsidized by Oswald Villard Garrison, an NAACP board member and editor of the New York *Evening Post*. Garrison repeatedly tried to wrestle control of *The Crisis* away from Du Bois, and Du Bois justifies leaving Garrison's office space because of the multigraph's need for "space, light, and electric motor."[42] More broadly, Du Bois's investment in the well-being of this printing machine allegorizes the black intellectual work taking place at *The Crisis*. That is, the multigraph simultaneously creates and archives the magazine's expanding autonomy and influence. It lets him and his staff design *The Crisis* and its advertisements in-house. But it also makes it much easier to make multiple copies of every letter, memorandum, and internal communication received by, circulated within, or sent out from the *Crisis* office, a job that would grow increasingly important as Villard and others attempted to get Du Bois removed from his position as editor and from the leadership of the NAACP.

This internal documentation and archiving of work at *The Crisis* became a corollary to the magazine's documentation of uplift. The multigraph assists in Du Bois's bid for editorial independence while also helping him create the most professional and commercially viable magazine that explicitly racializes its periodical work. These two jobs come together in Du Bois's mind when he articulates his ideal affiliation with the NAACP. "If we can make the magazine one that is read increasingly for its own sake—its news, its stories, its opinion, its facts, then this large, strong and far going vehicle can be made to carry the message of this organization and its ideals not only to its friends but to the great public and even to our enemy," he wrote in a memo to the board.[43] And when the mechanical and aesthetic production of *The Crisis* is perfected, he surmises in a letter to Spingarn, "the real machinery of the N.A.A.C.P. can be perfected."[44] The multigraph makes "the machinery" of the NAACP and *The Crisis* both literal and metaphoric: it brings together the magazine's focus on the technologies of aesthetic representation with the organization's goal of equal political representation. Both, for Du Bois, depend on amassing an archive of black intellectual work.

This concern about the archival possibilities of print technologies also inflects how *The Crisis* imagines competition between media. A 1923 article about the dearth of black photographers finds Du Bois asking, "Why do not more young colored men and women take up photography as a career? The average white photographer does not know how to deal with colored skins and having neither sense of the delicate beauty of tone nor will to learn, he makes a horrible botch of portraying them."[45] Here, Du Bois characterizes the visual reproduction of race as a matter of professionalism and, particularly, a lack of black professionals. White photographers are not inclined to learn how to capture best the "tone" of "colored skins," and there are not enough black photographers to help overcome the deficit. Yet, as a 1922 article on "Moving Pictures" makes clear, Du Bois's and *The Crisis*'s interest in the circulation of other media always comes back to its relationship to the periodical. The article congratulates the NAACP for its long fight against public exhibition of that "slanderous moving picture," D. W. Griffith's *Birth of a Nation* (1915). The organization successfully stopped the film from being shown in California and

MOVING PICTURES   THE Association continues to fight slanderous moving pictures. We picketed "The Birth of a Nation" when it recently appeared in New York and distributed printed matter. Our pickets were arrested bu⁺ .e secured an opinion of the court which pronounced the distribution of printed matter under such circumstances legal. Our branches stopped this film in the State of California and helped induce the Board of Censors to refuse permission to exhibit it in Boston.

ANNUAL CONFERENCE   THE twelfth annual conference of the Association was held in Detroit, Mich., June 26 to July 1. The conference was opened with an enormous protest parade on Sunday afternoon. There were 4,000 persons in line, representing every organization among colored people in Detroit. In this parade banners were borne protesting against injustices perpetrated upon the

THE CRISIS   THE CRISIS during the years of its publication, since November, 1910, has distributed 5,259,899 copies. The figures showing its income, average net paid monthly circulation and total circulation follow:

	Circulation per month	Total Circulation	Income
1910	1,750 copies	3,500 copies	$375
1911	9,000 "	} 108,000 "	6,572
1912	22,000 "	} 264,000 "	13,217
1913	27,000 "	336,000 "	19,739
1914	31,450 "	377,400 "	22,124
1915	32,156 "	385,872 "	23,865
1916	37,625 "	451,500 "	28,193
1917	41,289 "	495,477 "	32,836
1918	75,187 "	902,250 "	57,367
1919	94,908 "	1,138,900 "	70,502
1920	62,417 "	749,000 "	77,706
1921	49,750 "	-597,000 "	62,582

The total income of THE CRISIS since its inception, November, 1910, has been $414,979.75.

FIGURE 2.3 "Moving Pictures," *The Crisis* (March 1922): 214.
Source: Courtesy of the Charles E. Young Research Library, University of California, Los Angeles.

Boston, and the way it did so, according to the article, is "through the distribution of printed matter" that brought on its own court case (214). The article on the national conference directly below "Moving Pictures" highlights the "enormous protest parade" and the "4,000 persons in line" in the streets of Detroit. The best way to "stop films," to take them out of circulation, is to clog the system with bodies and print, an argument reinforced in the page's layout: "Moving Pictures" sits next to the circulation numbers and income of *The Crisis*, which gives proof of the nation's rising investment in material supporting racial equality. The juxtaposition of the magazine's circulation numbers with this article about inhibiting films places the two media, as well as attitudes toward race, in direct competition. We'll see how the racial component of this felt competition between media forms comes up in Jessie Fauset's treatment of African American characters; however, here *The Crisis* in its layout and content stages a jointly political and aesthetic conflict. Columns of numbers arranged chronologically, building to the present, attest to the contemporary consolidation of a black print culture, one that can simultaneously distribute positive images of African Americans and take out negative ones.

The explicit inclusion of the magazine's total paid monthly circulation as a news item is a fairly typical example of an almost obsessive self-accounting in *The Crisis*. The first issue of every new volume included an auditor's report of its finances; every year the magazine listed the number of applicants for its numerous awards, such as the Spingarn Medal and the Charles W. Chesnutt Memoriam; it annually counted up the exact number of high-school and college graduates in the education issue; and "The Horizon" column kept track of the articles about race in other American magazines, tallying which other magazines covered race that month. Perhaps the strangest version of this hypernumeracy in *The Crisis* is the "Debit and Credit" feature, which ran for the first twenty years. It had little to do with finances and instead compared the progress and setbacks regarding race relations since the last edition. It ended with a statement of "Balance on Hand," which simplified the wide array of events into a single, seemingly objective statement about whether it had been a good or bad month for African Americans. Read alongside Du Bois's financial investment in multigraphs and printing presses, this psychic investment in the numerical proof of African American participation in American life suggests that *The Crisis* is, among other things, producing a counterhistory of race.

Du Bois's Problem with "Plain Ink"

Du Bois's comments on photography link the professional and mechanical skills necessary for expanding a race magazine as well as the representations of race that such a magazine will include. Especially as *The Crisis* began to reach wider audiences in the middle to late 1910s, it confronted an increasingly diverse readership that had ambivalently responded to the magazine's representations of African American life. Du Bois makes explicit the special difficulty of appealing to such a diverse audience, explaining the special combination of desire and fear that accompanies reading as a person of color. In the 1920 *Crisis* article "In Black," he writes, "Colored folk, like all folk, love to see themselves in pictures, but they are afraid to see the types which the white world has caricatured." There is an added irony here, because Du Bois in the article discusses a slew of negative responses by black readers to a *Crisis* cover portraying a middle-aged Caribbean woman. Du Bois thought of the reproduced photograph, "Woman of Santa Lucia," as a positive image of black femininity, but it was interpreted by a vocal set of readers as sensationalist. Like every photograph reproduced in *The Crisis*, the image was intended as a correction to racist caricatures of " 'grinning' Negroes, 'happy' Negroes, 'gold dust twins,' 'Aunt Jemimas,' [and] 'solid' headed tacks."[46] Though the magazine is mostly remembered now for its focus on the black bourgeoisie, "Woman of Santa Lucia" instances the broad range of individuals that Du Bois chose for his cover images. More than this, his spirited defense of the image emphasizes the incompleteness of such claims about the magazine's limited purview. Rather, it is his coworkers and readers that are flustered by considering the woman as a positive racial depiction. He summarizes the complexity of their complaints:

> Our photograph of a woman of Santa Lucia, with its strength and humor and fine swing of head, was laughed at by many.
> Why?
> "O—er—it was not because they were black," stammer some of my office companions, "but they are *too* black. No people were ever so——"
> Nonsense! Do white people complain because their pictures are too white? They ought to, but they do not. Neither do we complain if we are photographed a shade "light."[47]

The negative reaction to this photograph, according to Du Bois, taps into certain readers' and even *Crisis* workers' intraracial color prejudices. However, as Du Bois recounts the conversation here the description of race becomes simultaneously a conversation about print technologies. The move from "It was not because they were black" to "they were *too* black" subtly shifts the site of discomfort from racial identification to the mechanics of printing. That is, Du Bois's line of reasoning shifts from the issue of light-skinned African Americans identifying with darker-skinned African Americans to the well-documented practice in racist journals of darkening reproductions of African Americans to make them look more sinister. It is a move from blackness as group identity to blackness as an aberration in textual reproduction and hence an inaccurate transmission of visual information about a single body's physical appearance.[48] When the unnamed office companions complain about the image being "*too* black," they question the magazine's ability to reproduce skin tone accurately on the periodical page. And when Du Bois distinguishes between these two versions of black, he shifts the crux of the article from a racial to a typographical problem. That is, Du Bois articulates how the readers' discomfort is not necessarily about the content of representation; instead, it is about the uneven valuation of reproductive inaccuracies. Elsewhere he states this more directly: "The Negro race was a little afraid to see itself in plain ink."[49] Like Chesnutt did in *Marrow*, Du Bois literalizes the link between racial types and printed type so as to make sense of the way that representing African Americans is always read as a charged and uneven activity—notice the article's title, "In Black," as opposed to the colloquial "in black and white"—even when done with the best intentions.[50]

Du Bois's article fits in the broadly modernist tradition that questions the assumed transparency and objectivity of representation, particularly in regards to the photographic image, but it goes further than that.[51] He not only reminds the reader that the photographic image is not coextensive with the world but also surmises that even the most sympathetic and adept representations of racialized bodies will be undermined simultaneously by a history of racist caricature and the material limitations of reproducing skin color with cheap ink on cheap paper: the material that he saw constituting African American print culture. Thus, Du Bois points out the simultaneously technical and psychological impediments he faces when trying to "document the 'fact' of blackness" as an "object of knowledge production."[52] In fact, *The Crisis* repeatedly calls into question the neutrality of this representational process. Its interest in the impact of an ostensibly value-neutral media and a value-laden typology of racial characteristics can be read into Du Bois's self-presentation in the magazine, which often thematizes the racial overtones of white paper and black ink. For example, *The Crisis* began titling Du Bois's bylined contribution "Opinion of W. E. B. Du Bois" in 1919, at the very height of the magazine's popularity. In the capitalized "O," a lit candle sits on top of an open book, which visualizes the metaphoric abilities of a book to enlighten its reader. The representation, both of the flame and the beams of light that the candle emits, consist of black lines on a white page, so that illumination, and the knowledge that a candle metaphorically represents, are literally created with the imprint of blackness. Du Bois's "Opinion," then, is double coded as black: first, because of his status as an African American who writes the text and, second, typographically, as black ink on a white page. And in this way, the visual iconography of *The Crisis* insists that the two valences of blackness that were at odds above in "In Black"—that of group identity and accurate reproduction in print—can be brought into a more mutually beneficial alignment. And, importantly, it insists on a similar alignment of *The Crisis*'s reputation and Du Bois's, whose "Opinion" here might be seen as competing with the more official party line of the NAACP. In a small way, the conflict is resolved as the image figures *The Crisis* as inherently keyed to "the color line" because of its double-coded blackness.

   This rather specific example opens up a way to see Du Bois's investment in the multigraph, his representation of black magazines clogging the distribution networks of racist films, his concern over the lack of black

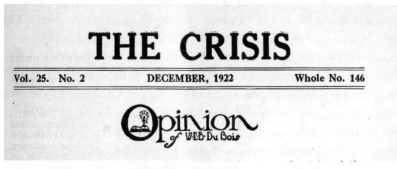

FIGURE 2.4 Masthead for *The Crisis*: "The Opinions of W. E. B. Du Bois."
Source: Courtesy of the Charles E. Young Research Library, University of California, Los Angeles.

photographers, and his ire at intraracial color prejudice as a densely lay-ered preoccupation with the media specificity of African American artistic practice. From this perspective, for example, the transcription of "Sorrow Songs" into the seven-tone occidental music system in *Souls of Black Folk* (1903) takes on added meaning. The Sorrow Songs are originally com-posed for oral production and aural consumption, and when Du Bois transforms them into a written form he points out the reorganization of signal and noise that occurs during that re-mediation. As Jonathan Flatley has argued, Du Bois's attention to the medium specificity of the Sorrow Songs' cultural circulation also puts pressure on the viability of a racially authentic art form, as the first "race records" were almost exclusively per-formed by white singers and musicians.[53] Thus, we see Du Bois not only commenting on the circulation of the Sorrow Songs but also showing how circulation in the aural or textual register, respectively, inflects the interpretation of a cultural artifact. Reading the score of a Sorrow Song, or any song, on the page is inherently different than listening to it (either performed in person or mechanically reproduced) and requires both a unique set of hermeneutic skills and a separate method of evaluation.

It's important, too, to point out how dissatisfying it is to read Du Bois's transcriptions of the Sorrow Songs in *Souls*. Purposefully dissatisfying, I think, because with all of his attention to the connected mechanics and thematics of print, it is only fair to assume that Du Bois figures the songs' change in content that accompanies their change in media as a loss. One can glimpse this attitude in his 1925 review of James Weldon Johnson's anthology *The African American Spirituals*. It begins by using Johnson's collection as an opportunity to muse over the self-reflexivity of black artis-tic production: "It is one thing for a race to produce artistic material; it is quite another thing for it to produce the ability to interpret and criticize this material."[54] Initially, it seems like Du Bois finds Johnson's collection as an example of the latter, evidencing the interpretation and criticism that mark it off as sufficiently self-knowing. "Never before have the 'Spirituals' had just this sort of original and yet true musical accompaniment," Du Bois writes, and "one must hear [it] to appreciate the peculiarly high and unique quality of the work."[55] However, it is a rather strange compli-ment for a book to say one must hear its content to appreciate its quality. Instead of unqualified praise, it seems Du Bois highlights the incongruity of a textual project that can only be appreciated when it is heard. More than this, he figures the translation of aural to textual form as a type of enslavement: the review concludes, "It is as though something unknown and wild and yet sensed in the song of black folk had been caught and caged forever."[56] Framing this endeavor as one that "caught and caged forever" the songs of "black folk," songs that are indelibly marked by slavery, is at best a backhanded compliment. It isn't that Johnson's collection is done poorly or incompletely but that, for Du Bois, the project of bringing oral forms into textual circulation brings with it a number of conceptual problems that cannot be solved by greater fidelity.

In this way, the notational translation of the Sorrow Songs offers a cautionary example of making a "record of the darker races," as it circulates a version of artistic production that is not keyed to the specific possibilities of print. When "In Black" protests against the feeling that any representation of race is excessive—it's always "too black"—he calls for an artistry that prioritizes the compositional techniques of print. Or, put another way, representing race in print, and especially in periodicals, requires a different set of attentions than writing or listening to a song, so a racialized print form dependent on "voice" will inevitably be drowned out by texts that conceive of themselves primarily as printed artifacts— those caricatures that have so influenced public perception. *The Crisis* sought to sponsor such self-consciously printed artistry and, in the process, as Henry Louis Gates puts it in a different context, to "re-present [African Americans'] public selves in order to reconstruct their public, reproducible images."[57] *The Crisis* imagines the possibility of new political representation as bounded by the technologies of print, an attention to medium specificity that pushes back against notions of racial "voice" while also firmly placing it within a modernist tradition.

Frank Walts's Flat Pictures

Neither Du Bois nor *The Crisis* is often characterized as particularly interested in the contingencies of mimetic practice or the materiality of the signifier, two aesthetic practices broadly aligned with literary modernism. Rather, Du Bois's fiction and magazine work are known for a realism that, if anything, verges on the archetypalism and abstraction of romance.[58] Critics often highlight *The Crisis*'s portrayal of contemplative light-skinned women, successful black businessmen, and well-proportioned babies as representative of Du Bois's investment in the politics of a black bourgeoisie.

THE CRISIS

A RECORD THE DARKER RACES

Volume One   APRIL, 1911   Number Six

Edited by W. E. BURGHARDT DU BOIS, with the co-operation of Oswald Garrison Villard, J. Max Barber, Charles Edward Russell, Kelly Miller, W. S. Braithwaite and M. D. Maclean.

EASTER NUMBER

Photo by Scurlock, Washington, D. C.

PUBLISHED MONTHLY BY THE

National Association for the Advancement of Colored People

AT TWENTY VESEY STREET   NEW YORK CITY

ONE DOLLAR A YEAR   TEN CENTS A COPY

FIGURE 2.5 Cover illustration, *The Crisis* (April 1911).
Source: Courtesy of the Modernist Journals Project, Brown University and University of Tulsa.

The magazine does often contain such images, but they are in constant tension with other versions of African American identity, as the "In Black" article exposes. The pictures of the bourgeoisie-as-uplift are often taken as evidence of Du Bois's aesthetic conservatism or, more sinisterly, his unconscious internalization of the period's eugenic discourse.[59] Features like "Men of the Month," full-page spreads of cherubic children, and class photos of well-heeled black teenagers—along with negative reviews of novels and poetry that represent lower-class Harlem life—signal the magazine's limited perspective on what counts as authentic African American identity. However, even these uplift images can present complex questions about the relationship between mimesis and identification. This section will look at how two visual strategies for representing African American identity exemplify the way *The Crisis* counteracts the prevalent caricatures of black bodies.

Take, for example, the cover from April 1911, which depicts a young, light-skinned woman reading *The Crisis* who appears so absorbed in the magazine that she does not notice being photographed. It's an image we might read as the magazine visualizing its own imagined readership. Rhonda L. Reymond has shown how *Crisis* covers use the painterly convention of *repoussoir* to dramatize themselves as both aesthetic and pedagogic objects.[60] *Repoussoir* brackets the content of the painting within another setting—placing one scene "deep" in the representational space of the canvas so that a character on the "surface" is looking at the image alongside the viewer. *Crisis* covers borrow this technique to access the cultural prestige of painting, according to Reymond, but the illusion of three-dimensional space also offers a way to embed a historical and political interpretation: on one cover a shackled black body looks in on a crumbling classical building, on another a young artist watches as busts of Dumas and Dunbar float into a cloudy sky. The covers teach history, but they also teach the *Crisis* reader how to look at visual information.

The above image seems to be after something different: rather than repurposing didactic painting it replicates its own medium, with the subject reading a magazine. And instead of teaching a specific lesson it withholds whatever the depicted reader might be learning. Garret Stuart calls this type of iconography "seen reading," claiming that it short circuits the narrative pleasure a viewer receives from images of people in action. Action, Stuart says, leads a viewer to parse the intentions, motives, or actions of a painted subject—all of which imply that the painting and viewer share psychological depth. "Seen reading," on the other hand, outlines "the composition of an inner event" and provides "the story of reading rather than the reading of a story."[61] Put another way, these images do not dramatize psychological movement or depth; instead they dramatize the flatness of the canvas or page. Understood in this manner, the "seen reading" on this *Crisis* issue's cover undoes any pedagogical message that one might read into it. Unlike a political cartoon or historical drawing that makes its message clear (and both of which *The Crisis* often included), the viewer does not have access to whatever this woman might be learning. Instead we find what Michael Fried refers to as the motif of absorption, in which the painted subject appears unaware that it is an aesthetic object created to be looked at. For Fried, and in the *Crisis* cover, absorption offers a way to close off the implicit structural similarity between the artist's fixation on the act of painting and the viewer's rapt attention on the aesthetic object. The painting does not return the viewer's attention, and thus it is a way to "screen that audience out, to deny its existence, or at least to refuse to allow the fact of its existence to impinge upon the absorbed consciousnesses of [the painted] figures."[62] Solitary, silent, absorbed, with eyes averted, this woman is in every way the opposite of the woman from Santa Lucia who looked directly into the camera eye and smiled; it is also the opposite of the historically themed covers that Reymond reads. The aestheticization of reading presented above, as opposed to the woman from Santa Lucia or images of other arts, points to a medium-specific version of black intellectual work. In the visual logic of the image, the audience does not identify with the woman reading but with the reading material itself. Though she is oblivious to the eyes of the viewer, the magazine and its title are on full display. *The Crisis* faces its reader from the flat pane of the page, theatrically (in Fried's sense) reciprocating the viewer's gaze. It is not the reader's eyes that are doubled in the image but the face of the reading material, which prominently displays "*The Crisis*" in black ink. Thus, the woman's absorption is contrasted with the magazine's theatrical self-presentation, its flattening of itself into the visual space of its cover.

A slightly different version of this paired emphasis of the flat page and its racialized content can be seen in a series of covers by Frank Walts, whom Du Bois explicitly named in the "In Black" article. "In the last few years," writes Du Bois, "a thoughtful, clear-eyed artist, Frank Walts, has

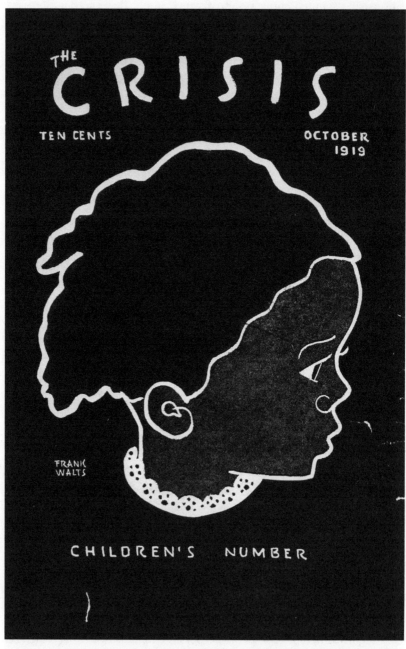

FIGURE 2.6 Frank Walts, cover portrait of Hasel Hensley, *The Crisis* (October 1919).
Source: Courtesy of the Modernist Journals Project, Brown University and University of Tulsa.

done a number of striking portraits for *The Crisis*. Mainly he has treated black faces; and regularly protests have come to us from various colored sources."[63] Walts composed cover images for a wide range of magazines in the 1910s and 1920s; he provided over a dozen covers for *The Crisis* between 1917 and 1922 as well as over half the covers for *The Masses* from 1915 to 1917.[64] However, Walts has received almost no critical attention from scholars of little magazines or African American periodicals.

Walts supplied three covers in 1920, the year of "In Black," and each was a portrait or bust of an African American woman or child—like many *Crisis* covers. And, like the above image of the woman reading, they thematically play with the spatial flatness of the page. Though Walts often worked in pastels or with charcoal on a white page for *The Masses* and *The Liberator*, his work for *The Crisis*, such as his October 1919 cover for the "Children's number," inverts this arrangement so that the black body represented is the same color as the background it stands out against. Like the image of the middle-class female reader, the child portrayed on the cover of the October 1919 issue averts her eyes from those of the reader. But unlike the previous image, it would be hard to characterize Walts's portrait as realist—by which I mean that one cannot argue that it strives for a mimetic identification of the viewer with a realistic representation of a projected, idealized reader. Instead, this image presents a flattened representational space so that everything depicted seems to reside on the same two-dimensional plane as opposed to providing the illusion of three-dimensionality.[65] Here and elsewhere in Walts's work for *The Crisis*, the pictorial style emphasizes its physical surface: a flat piece of paper that circulates in a magazine.

This flatness is even more apparent in the Walts work that appears on the November 1920 cover of *The Crisis*, which immediately follows the issue in which "In Black" appears. He depicts another female figure, but here she is even more abstractly drawn than the child. Once again, the figure refuses to make eye contact with the reader, this time appearing to look over her own left shoulder and off to the right-hand side of the page. There is even less detail than the previous image, with the entire outline of her hair, neck, and face comprising only three lines, which is characteristic of Walts's spontaneous, almost off-handed style for *The Crisis*. Along with his emphasis on the flatness of the page, this cover reiterates the trope in Walts's *Crisis* covers of inverted color schemes. These two covers are literally "in black": the content of the image is placed in a black context, and the figural representation is set off from the background with white lines. The background and foreground are a uniform shade of black and both coequal in their representational flatness, occupying the same two dimensions as the page on which they are drawn. And in this way Walts's covers parallel the same visual rhetoric as Du Bois's "Opinion": they metaphorically transform racial content into a racialized form, and they literalize the black artistic work required to create the magazine as a visually black page. In effect, he turns the magazine page into a "colored" material so that the racial and periodical forms correspond.

Certainly Walts's work for *The Crisis* is not the only place one finds this literalization of textual blackness in periodicals associated with the New Negro movement. Aaron Douglas's silhouettes and Winold Reiss's line drawings use the stark contrast between black and white on the page to "negotiate the boundaries between type and individual identity."[66] Douglas also produced a number of covers for *The Crisis*, and in a letter to Langston Hughes, he charged himself with the task of establishing an essentially black aesthetic: "Not white art painted black. . . . Let's create something transcendentally material, mystically objective."[67] Caroline Goesser argues that Douglas turned to silhouettes in his art because of their easy "typification": the silhouette "clarified the contours of the form while refusing to specify particular internal information. For example, the silhouette would not allow the reader to discern the specific hue of the figure's skin."[68] Douglas's cover for the lone issue of *Fire!!* (1926) echoes Walts's emphasis on representational flatness, but the differences make evident the competing goals of each artist and each periodical. The *Fire!!* cover, composed in black and red, deploys a perspectival trick so that the image of a Sphinx initially appears to be part of a repeating figurative pattern, and only after closer attention does one notice that it is a piece of jewelry hanging from the ear of a heavily stylized silhouette. With its geometric shapes, refusal of spatial depth, and binary color scheme, the *Fire!!* cover pushes the boundary between racial and representational abstraction. The black space on the page initially appears as a background against which the earring stands out, which forces the viewer to toggle between competing interpretations of the image's object and ground. Like in Walts, the stylistic flatness draws attention to the spatial plane of the print media. And, as Goesser points out about Douglas's silhouettes, the flatness here refuses interiority or depth of consciousness in favor of highlighting the medium specificity of the periodical.

FIGURE 2.7 Frank Walts, cover drawing, *The Crisis* (November 1920).
Source: Courtesy of the Modernist Journals Project, Brown University and University of Tulsa.

FIGURE 2.8 Aaron Douglas, cover of *Fire!!*, 1926.
Source: Art © Heirs of Aaron Douglas / Licensed by VAGA, New York, NY.

Yet unlike Walts's clearly hand-drawn covers, Douglas's image is highly composed, even monumental, like the Sphinx it depicts. Indeed, according to one critic it "looks more like a work of art than a mere medium for conveying information about price and publication, for in no way does it call attention to itself as a commercial enterprise," an interpretation bolstered by the magazine's miniscule circulation and failure to get beyond one issue.[69] Walts, on the other hand, made dozens of covers for the most popular black magazine of its time, and in his work there is no illusion of a self-contained and singular object that exists outside of publishing economies. Rather than read Walts's covers as an example of art failing to announce its autonomy in the face of commerce, it seems more interesting to read their repetitions, sprezzatura, spatial flatness, and transposition of color as an allegory of the materiality of the popular black periodical. Walts's covers are the ensign of the reflexively black big magazine: they aestheticize the specific type of black intellectual work needed to create a formally and politically daring periodical. Or, more precisely, they capture Du Bois's goal for hundreds of thousands of copies of such a periodical, produced once a month for decades, bought by just as many black readers whose existence as a collective readership would embody a sustainable, nationalized, routinely refreshed black print culture. *Fire!!* is a powerful aesthetic object, but its very singularity is exactly what Du Bois wants to overcome with *The Crisis*. Walts's covers double down on the ephemerality, iterativeness, and reproducibility of the big magazine, and in the process they discover an aesthetic form perfectly suited to that medium.

It is no coincidence that each example from *The Crisis* so far has been culled from the late 1910s and early 1920s. This rather narrow window of selection emphasizes that when the magazine peaked in terms of circulation and finances, it was also daring and innovative in its visual and editorial style. On the one hand, this simply reiterates its status as a big magazine, but more importantly it pushes back against the notion that commercially successful periodicals maintain their popularity by sanding down their difficulty or stroking the egos of a self-satisfied readership. On the contrary, *The Crisis* was purposefully jarring in both its imagery and rhetoric, and Walts's covers are only the most public examples of how the magazine's editors and artists developed a house style that allegorized print-based African American artistic production. This attention to the materiality of cultural transmission is not limited to Walts's entries in *The Crisis*; as the next section will show, Jessie Fauset's short stories, especially "The Sleeper Wakes," also thematize the political implications of racial flatness. As will become more evident in my discussion of Fauset, *The Crisis*'s repeated invocation of the link between race and print media can also be read in terms of the seriality of its periodical circulation. Unlike a standalone book, *The Crisis* reiterates its message about race and media on the first day of every month, when its cover image hits the news racks and subscribers' mailboxes.

Jessie Fauset's Serial Stories

Jessie Fauset served as literary editor between 1919 and 1926, the same period that the other visual and typographical tropes of blackness discussed in this chapter take place. During that time she was an integral part of the magazine's staff and did much to secure its cultural standing, especially among the younger generation of writers, such as Claude McKay and Langston Hughes, whom Du Bois never fully embraced.[70] Because of her engagement with the new literary experiments taking place in Harlem and her investment in the production of *The Crisis*, it's not surprising that her fiction engages with the various institutions that mediate black cultural life, not least of which is the magazine itself. In particular, her three-part novelette "The Sleeper Wakes" sets up shop in this generational struggle as it narrates the life of a young woman who is already fantastically efficient at internalizing the things she reads and sees. The story appeared in *The Crisis* from August to October 1920, ending in the same issue that contained Du Bois's "In Black" article; as such, its reads as a further elaboration of the particular problems the magazine faced regarding the possibility of representing race in a periodical form.

Fauset's quasi-passing narrative follows the racially ambiguous Amy, a foster child raised by African American parents, as she runs away to bohemian New York and passes as white; marries an aristocratic Southerner and moves to his Georgia home; outs her own past life as a black child to save the life of an African American servant; returns to New York and becomes a working professional in the fashion industry; and, finally, rejects her estranged husband's attempt at reconciliation. At one level, Fauset's treatment of the "tragic mulatto" motif is thoroughly generic: the sentimentalism and heavy-handed moralism, the culture clash of Old South and Modern North, the treatment of the female body as the site of political conflict.[71] However, she spins the story's premise in a number of ways. Unlike other contemporary versions of this plot, such as Mary Ovington's *The Shadow* (1920), Charles Chesnutt's *Paul Marchand, F.M.C.* (1919–1920), or Nella Larsen's *Passing* (1929), and especially unlike the epic panhistorical Pan-African image that ends Du Bois's *The Dark Princess* (1928), Fauset never discloses Amy's biological race.[72] Amy does not know whether her biological parents were African American, and the story is completely uninterested in that information. Instead, Fauset treats Amy's racial identification—black then white then black again—as constituting something like a personal style that can be changed, "some phase such as cubism or syncopation," without recourse to an originary or authentic form.[73] I will come back to the connection between "phases" and Fauset's invocation of artistic movements, but first I want to unpack how the iterations of Amy's racial identification expound upon the flatness I have discussed in Du Bois and Walts. The story's first paragraph links the iterative quality of Amy's racial identification with her simultaneous experience of media and "color" as such:

> Amy recognized the incident as the beginning of one of her phases. Always from a child she had been able to tell when "something was going to happen." She had been standing in Marshall's store, her young, eager gaze intent on the lovely little sample dress which was not from Paris, but quite as dainty as anything that Paris could produce. It was not the lines or even the texture that fascinated Amy so much, it was the grouping of colors—of shades. She knew the combination was just right for her. . . .
>
> The saleswoman slipped the dress over the girl's pink blouse, and tucked the linen collar under so as to bring the edge of the dress next to her pretty neck. The dress was apricot-colored shading into shell pink and the shell pink shaded off again into the pearl and pink whiteness of Amy's skin. The saleswoman beamed as Amy, entranced, surveyed herself naively in the tall looking glass.
>
> ("Sleeper," August 1920, 168)

The first sentence emphasizes the seriality of Amy's life without disclosing what "the incident" or "phases" allude to. Instead, the story turns to Amy's "young, eager gaze intently on the lovely little sample dress" in a shop window. The fabric and female body "shad[e] off" into each other, blurring both their visual appearance and their materiality. And, as Fauset makes clear, the encounter hinges on the dress as an imitation: it is *like* Parisian fashion, but it is not actually from Paris. This is a distinction that Amy does not notice but one that the narrator clearly does, which allows for perspectival distance between Amy as a flat character and the possibly ironic intrusions of the narrator. What's more important in the scene for Amy than the authenticity of the fabric is its ability to blend into her own skin, a visual blurring over which the narrator relishes. The gradation of apricot-colored cloth into the "pearl and pink whiteness" of Amy's skin transforms the politics of her racial identity into something both aesthetic (the beauty of the "grouping of colors") and media-like: the "whiteness of Amy's skin," like both the colored cloth she wants to buy and the white page on which the reader encounters Amy's story, becomes a material on which information is housed and circulated but without making any claims to originality—like the imitation Parisian dress. Yet it also shows her medium-like whiteness to be anything but self-evident: Amy's skin tone obscures her racial ambiguity. Her race is indecipherable from her skin, and Fauset never clears the air, suggesting that her concerns are elsewhere.

The "incident" that initiates the story, it turns out, hinges on a film that Amy recently saw, or, more accurately, on Amy thinking about how a specific kind of "looking" extends from inside the world of the film to her encounters outside, in the real world. As she shops for dresses, she watches in a mirror as two men stop to look at her:

> Two men walking idly though the dress-salon stopped and looked— she made an unbelievably pretty picture. . . .
>
> "Jove, how I'd like to paint her!" But it was the look on the other man's face that caught her and thrilled her. "My God! Can't a girl be beautiful!" he said half to himself. The pair passed on.
>
> ("Sleeper," August 1920, 168)

One admirer articulates his desire to turn her into an aesthetic object, and the other simply looks; Amy prefers being looked at to being remade as art. The whole experience feels like déjà vu to her: "She had seen it before in men's eyes, it had been in the eyes of the men in the moving-picture which she had seen that afternoon" (August 1920, 168). There is a complicated refraction of gazes—from Amy to the men through a mirror, from the men to Amy through a shop window (and metaphorically through a painting), from the men to other men through Amy's memory of the film. Each is associated with a lens or medium, sometimes competing but often combinatorial, through which the visual information passes: the mirror, the window, the picture, the movie screen, and ultimately the periodical page on which the story takes place. Fauset, then, places Amy's racial meaning, or possible lack thereof, in a dense network of mediated gazes that redundantly repeat each other.

By including references to the European visual arts and American music (cubism and syncopation, respectively), Fauset situates her discussion of race and serialized fiction within contemporary discourses of aesthetic form and nationhood that attempted to delineate between national and cosmopolitan modernisms and to establish an authentic African American literature. Fauset was deeply involved in these discussions on multiple fronts throughout her life, but here the characterization of these artistic movements as mere "phases" analogous to the phases of a young woman's maturation and growing self-awareness minimizes both the newness and singularity of these ostensibly modern styles. Instead, Fauset emphasizes how modern painting and music are easily folded into Amy's experience of the contemporary media landscape. Cubism and jazz happen alongside the melodramatic films she sees and romance novels she reads, each occupying a similar cultural register to the faux-Parisian dress. She then goes further: because both the appearance and obscuration of Amy's racial information operate analogously to the "phases" of art movements, Fauset positions race as an aesthetic experience dependent, as is this story, on the presupposition of past knowledge built into the serial form.

Rather than arguing that new styles of artistic expression either respond to or influence the way Amy organizes her life, Fauset suggests that Amy's experiences are fundamentally made of the narrative fragments that she's absorbed. Within her own conscious experience, they subtly blur into one another—just as the materials of her dress and skin do—and make up her ostensibly unmediated life outside of the theater. Early on the narrator explains, "The only reading that had ever made any impression on her had been fairy tales . . . and descriptions in novels or histories of beautiful, stately palaces tenanted by beautiful stately women" (August 1920, 169). This is the same type of woman who is gazed upon by the men within the diegetic world of movies as well as by girls like Amy from the audience. In fact, the film she sees before going to the shop seems to be about her, about "a girl—such a pretty one—and she was poor, awfully. And somehow she met the most wonderful people and they were so kind to her. And she married a man who was just tremendously rich and he gave her everything" (August 1920, 169). Even her own teenage ennui is overrun with the language and tone of the stories she reads and watches. " 'Trenton is stifling me,' she would have told you, in her unconsciously crescendo. Amy rose and went downstairs. Down in the comfortable, but rather shabby dining-room which the Boldins used after meals to sit in, Mr. Boldin, a tall black man, with aristocratic features, sat reading; little Cornelius Boldin sat practicing on a cornet, and Mrs. Boldin sat rocking. In all of their eyes was the manifestation of the light that Amy loved, but how truly she loved it, she was not to guess till years later.

"Amy," Mrs. Boldin paused in her rocking, "did you get the braid?" Of course she had not, though that was the thing she had gone to Marshall's for. Amy always forgot essentials. If she went on an errand, and she always went willingly, it was for the pure joy of going. Who knew what angels might meet one unawares? Not that Amy thought in biblical or in literary phrases. She was in the High School, it is true, but she was simply passing through, "getting by" she would have said carelessly The only reading that had ever made any impression on her had been fairy tales read to her in those long remote days when she had lived with the tall, proud woman; and descriptions in novels or histories of beautiful, stately palaces tenanted by beautiful, stately women. She could pore over such pages for hours, her face flushed, her eyes eager.

At present she cast about for an excuse. She had so meant to get the braid. "There was a dress—" she began lamely, she was never deliberately dishonest.

Mr. Boldin cleared his throat and nervously fingered his paper. Cornelius ceased his awful playing and blinked at her shortsightedly through his thick glasses. Both of these, the man and the little boy, loved the beautiful, inconsequent creature with

her airy, irresponsible ways. But Mrs. Boldin loved her too, and because she loved her she could not scold.

"Of course you forgot," she began chidingly. Then she smiled. "There was a dress that you looked at perhaps. But confess, didn't you go to the movies first?"

Yes, Amy confessed she had done just that. "And oh, Mrs. Boldin, it was the most wonderful picture—a girl—such a pretty one—and she was poor, awfully. And somehow she met the most wonderful people and they were so kind to her. And she

"Huh! I don't want to look at no pretty girl!"

married a man who was just tremendously rich and he gave her everything. I did so want Cornelius to see it."

"Huh!" said Cornelius who had been listening not because he was interested, but because he wanted to call Amy's attention to his playing as soon as possible. "Huh! I don't want to look at no pretty girl. Did they have anybody looping the loop in an airship?"

"You'd better stop seeing pretty girl pictures, Amy," said Mr. Boldin kindly. "They're not always true to life. Besides,

---

FIGURE 2.9 Illustration accompanying Jessie Fauset's "The Sleeper Wakes," *The Crisis* (October 1920): 169.

Source: Courtesy of the Modernist Journals Project, Brown University and University of Tulsa.

adopted movie-diction" (August 1920, 170), which suggests not so much a chosen affective posture as an "unconscious" internalization of the narratives around her.

Rather than depict Amy as psychologically complex and self-consciously unique, Fauset fills Amy's interiority with the surfaces of stories culled from other media: movies, paintings, music, and novels. This also happens in the drawings that accompany Fauset's story in the magazine, such as one that shows Amy, having returned from her trip to the movie theater and dress shop, talking with her adoptive family. Her father reads a newspaper, her mother reads a magazine, and her younger brother plays the coronet while Amy stands in the middle, the only figure whose skin is not composed of black ink and the only person who is not engaging with some kind of media device. This image visually reinforces the story's attention to the coupling of race and media, and it doubles back on Amy's own interiority as self-mediation; when she prepares for sleep at night, "in the mirror she apostrophize[s] the beautiful, glowing vision of herself. 'I'm like the girl in the picture,'" she exclaims, which can refer both to the female actor in the "pretty girl picture" she saw and to the picture of Amy that shares page space with her pronouncement (August 1920, 170). Her foster father warns, "You'd better stop seeing pretty girl pictures, Amy . . . They're not always true to life" (August 1920, 169). But for Amy, who "grow[s] up as the average colored American girl does grow up, surrounded by types of every hue" (September 1920, 227), "pretty girl pictures" are the average material of an average life. In fact, life is exactly like "pretty girl pictures" because Amy narrates her experiences as one of many iterations of that genre.

Amy, in this regard, offers a narrative equivalent to Walts's pictorial flatness. The lines between her interior motivations and the world outside—between the figure of her body and the ground of its context—are sketchy at best. She becomes nearly coterminous with the media environment in which she exists, both within the "deep" world of the story and in the textual space of the magazine page. In Fauset's telling, there is nothing overly tragic in this tragic mulatto story; Amy is all surface, her racist husband loves her for her "shallowness," and Fauset repeatedly insists that she does not have the psychological depth to sustain such a personal or even historical tragedy (August 1920, 172). The political liabilities of such a statement are treacherous, to say the least. But Amy's superficiality, or her existence as a pure surface that alternately houses and hides racial information, takes on its own positive evaluation by the end of the novelette.

Broken into three serialized sections, the middle installment of "Sleeper" focuses on Amy's decision to pass so that she can marry a rich and power-ful Southerner, Stuart James Wynne. She leaves New York and moves to Wynne's ancestral home, where like Clare in Nella Larsen's *Passing,* she must swallow any residual race pride to maintain her newfound economic and social status. When Wynne goes to strike a black servant, though, Amy steps in front of the blow and declares herself "colored," a scene that finds her "phasing" from black to white, then from white to black. Wynne, outraged, throws her out, and she moves back to New York, where she gets a job designing dresses with a "modiste," sometimes living as white and sometimes as black.

In the last installment, which appeared in the same issue as Du Bois's "In Black," she finally returns to her family. Just before deciding to write the family she abandoned years before, her ex-husband visits to ask her to become his mistress. When she goes downstairs to let him in the door, "Some leaves—brown, skeleton shapes—rose and swirled unnoticed about her head":

> She took him into the drawing room—a wonderful study in browns—and looked at him and looked at him. . . . As she sat there in the big brown chair she was, in her yellow dress, like some mysterious emanation, some wraith-like aura developed from the tone of her surroundings. . . . She sat down heavily in the brown chair, all glowing ivory and yellow against its somber depths.
>
> (October 1920, 269–270)

The "brown, skeleton shape[d]" leaves, the room as a "wonderful study in browns," the two references to a brown couch—each of these serves to contrast the "glowing ivory and yellow" of Amy's skin and figuratively reenacts the color palette of Walts's line drawings. It also inverts the way that the reader has been encountering Amy—that is, as black ink on a white text—by describing her as white set out against a dark background. Yet Fauset suggests that Amy, a character composed of typed letters on the page, at once depends upon the media that has made up her life and transcends it. She is "some mysterious emanation, some wraith-like aura developed from the tone of her surroundings." Amy's flatness is an ema-nation of her environment, but it is also still extremely intriguing and intellectually appealing, as all the other characters in the story make clear.

Even though Amy is flat, she still elicits the narrator's attention. And with this, Fauset exposes the narrative limits of taking media literally; she shows how even a story about a character who is all surface can, "wraith-like" and auratic, expand outside of the ink on the page into a collective body of periodical readers. Though entirely flat, the multiple perspectives that repeatedly look at Amy (and that she returns—"she looked at him and looked at him") provide the illusion of perspectival depth that goes beyond the flat representational field of the periodical page. More than this, it temporally extends Amy's narrative out from a single issue of the magazine. In the story she travels geographically across the country while the story spreads out serially over three months. Amy, because she is not deep, individual, and singular, can be anyone.

It is at this moment, sitting on a brown couch, that Amy gains some perspective on her own situation. She asks herself if she has turned out "like the women in those awful novels? . . . Not like those women!" (October 1920, 272). Alone, she strikes herself in the face: " 'You *thing*! She said to the image in the glass, 'if you hadn't been so vain, so shallow!' " (October 1920, 272). This self-objectification makes explicit the literal shallowness of Amy's characterization, though it makes available to her, however late, a self-awareness of the story's connection between race and typographic form. It also makes the mental image Amy conjures even more loaded when, in the story's final paragraphs, she returns to her adoptive family. The decision is prompted by a memory of her younger brother, Cornelius, "spelling out colored letters on his blocks, pointing to them stickily with a brown, perfect finger" (October 1920, 273). The "brown, perfect finger" that spells out "colored letters" once again brings together racial identification and typographic form while doubling back on Fauset's own magazine composition. More than this, though, it shows how Du Bois's concern about the contagiousness of magazine stories and those "magazine mad" readers can find a literary counterpart in his own journal as it transforms the flat black and white of the page into a vehicle for imagining the possibilities and limits of representing racialized intellectual work in print.

* * *

The contingencies and limitations of such representations would have been felt on a much more practical level at *The Crisis* in the early 1920s, as well as at most periodicals in the United States. A nationwide paper shortage was so serious that a special hearing was held in the House of Representatives to discuss possible federal action. Just two months prior to the first installment of "The Sleeper Wakes," Du Bois warned that "the stringency in the paper market is so acute that THE CRISIS has been reluctantly compelled to take radical precautions." Not only did the magazine reduce its circulation in response to a lack of material on which to print, but it was forced to shrink the magazine to forty-eight pages "in order to avoid any contingency of finding ourselves in mid summer absolutely without paper."[74] An article in the *New York Times* summarizes the conversations about the shortage, both in periodicals and in Congress, as revolving around two issues: first, the cause of the depleted paper stock and how to find new sources of pulp, and, second, what it would mean to the freedom of the press if the government stepped in to ration the size of newspapers.[75] When the House did in fact put forth the possibility of rationing, many believed it would provide the federal government with justification for shutting down journals that it did not approve of. Thus there was quite literally a crisis of representation in print culture. The war over images, in this case, takes on an added urgency; it is not just that certain images will take over the public imagination but that competing depictions of race may never even make it to the printing press.

David Levering Lewis reasons that the combined effect of the paper shortage—which caused *The Crisis* to raise its cover price from $1 to $1.50—and an economic recession in 1920 can explain the drastic reduction in subscriptions to *The Crisis* that begins that year.[76] Within two years, the circulation dropped to fifty thousand. Others attribute the fall in popularity to fundamental changes in the field of black periodicals.[77] New magazines, most famously the Urban League's *Opportunity*, edited by Charles S. Johnson, brought competition for potential subscribers, big-name authors that would help newsstand sales, and prestige as the standard bearer of black political and artistic positions. However, a more fundamental shift had occurred in African American periodical culture: Claude Barnett founded the Associated Negro Press in Chicago in 1919, providing a weekly packet of news stories about African American interests to subscribing newspapers and magazines. Barnett's institutionalization of a national black clipping service made it much easier for local papers to carry national coverage, and it helped consolidate and standardize the production, distribution, and consumption of news about African American life. *The Crisis* admits that this innovation forces a change in their own mission, especially in their section "The Horizon," which, like its namesake magazine that Du Bois edited in the early 1900s, compiled a "monthly history of the Negro race." This task, the magazine claimed, "was increasingly difficult to do and increasingly unnecessary as the weekly Negro press progressed in efficient news gathering."[78] Thus, we find causes for *The Crisis*'s contraction related to changes in the organization of news gathering, its relationship to a stable body of readers, its place among competing journals, and to the material concerns about paper sources. Most of these developments in the black press are, generally speaking, a good thing for the mission statement of *The Crisis*. The field has expanded, become more complex, founded institutions that codify the production and dissemination of African American news, and developed the "self-criticism" that Du Bois says must exist for an intellectually mature black public body. Yet, as Mary Ovington tells Du Bois in a letter, these advances put *The Crisis* in a tough spot: "As time has gone on . . . the *Crisis* [is] less important. . . . It is not unique as it once was."[79]

As we'll see in the next chapter, other magazines born in the 1920s found innovative ways to take advantage of the increasing consolidation of news services and sought out new periodical genres to accommodate those changes. The decade gives rise to the newsmagazine, most famously *Time* in 1923 and *Newsweek* in 1933, a format that conveniently repackages and stylishly rewrites the reportorial work of other institutions. For a long list of reasons both internal to its relationship with the NAACP and external to the changing market, *The Crisis* never rebounds to its 1919 and 1920 numbers. But, as a result of the magazine's newfound smallness relative to the wider world of black print culture, we find Du Bois making the case for the organizational advantages of being unpopular. "*The Crisis* must be an *Unpopular* magazine," he declared in a draft report to the NAACP board. "If the cause which we espouse and the means by which we defend it were popular, then there would be no call for this periodical."[80] In 1925, after several years of stagnating circulation numbers, Du Bois anticipates the magazine's possible end, arguing that the journal's titular problem foresaw its own obsolescence. "How long may a *Crisis* last?, one might ask, sensing between our name and age some contradiction." The crossed message of the name and longevity of the magazine, he argues, has finally come to a head because of the changing print landscape: "There is no longer need of a monthly newspaper for colored folk. Colored weeklies have arisen with an efficiency and scope in newsgathering that was not dreamed of in 1910. Our news has transformed itself into a sort of permanent record of a few matters of widespread and historic importance."[81] The problem is not that the political crisis is over—that somehow racial inequality was abolished in the first fifteen years of the magazine's life—but that the crisis of black print culture has evolved. By the mid-1920s, *The Crisis* finds itself as merely one of a whole field of black periodicals, a situation Du Bois foretold in his 1907 article about the "magazine mad" nation. His former privileging of the book for its archival capabilities, by this point, has been subsumed by the "permanent record" of the periodicals, especially his own, even if by the mid-1920s it is indistinguishable from many others.

CHAPTER 3

On the Clock

Rewriting Literary Work at Time Inc.

The author is, in the last analysis, merely a working-man, and is under the rule that governs a working-man's life.
—WILLIAM DEAN HOWELLS, *Literature and Life*

I wish I knew how to work.
—JAMES AGEE, IN MIA AGEE, "Faint Lines in a Drawing of Jim"

Finding Work

James Agee might be the first American writer to stake his literary career on making fun of his employer, and the particular form of his joke says much about the way his generation understood how literary writing related to market-dependent definitions of writing as work. During his undergraduate years at Harvard, Agee studied T. S. Eliot and James Joyce, took classes with I. A. Richards, and fashioned himself as a Southern romantic poet. He was relatively well known among the campus literati; his first and only volume of verse, *Permit Me Voyage* (1934), was published in the Yale Younger Poets series and consisted mostly of work composed during college. In 1931, however, he was a senior looking to land a job, and corporate journalist promised a far more secure route than professional poet. As the president of the *Harvard Advocate*, he dedicated six months to compiling a parody issue of, in the words of his biographer, the "newest, flashiest, and most successful magazine around, *Time*." His premise was simple: he imagined *Time* unhinging itself from contemporary coverage and reporting on major historical events of the Western world: for instance, he wrote about "J. G. Caesar," who "scribbles a good deal;

not for publication, just for the pure fun of the thing," and reviewed the first performance of Aeschylus's *Electra*, his "latest nerve-shatterer," a play "well worth a trip to the new State Theater."[1]

Unfortunately the young Agee could claim neither the lucrative occupation that allowed Caesar to write for personal amusement nor the literary prestige (and state subsidies) of Aeschylus. However, he did possess a growing number of literary-minded acquaintances who worked in the growing Time Inc. media empire: Dwight MacDonald and Robert Fitzgerald, both hired after college, were school friends of Agee (MacDonald from Phillips Exeter Academy, Fitzgerald from Harvard), and both encouraged him to apply. Thus, he sent multiple publicity notices to *Time*'s offices before the *Advocate*'s publication as a means of self-promotion. In one particularly forward letter he begged Roy Larsen, a manager at *Time* who also had cut his journalistic teeth at the *Advocate*, to

> imagine your staff set down in Ancient Greece, Rome, Egypt, and Palestine, with an uncommonly long nose for news, several amphoras of rye, vivid but confused recollections of the 20th century, a somewhat cockeyed sense of TIME, and no sense whatever of chronology; and take note. *The Harvard Advocate* has already imagined you there; has used this as a device whereby to parody TIME.[2]

To parody *Time*—a news magazine by definition attached to and dependent upon contemporaneity—Agee deploys the "device" of temporal dilation: Aeschylus rubs shoulders with Caesar; Rome, Egypt, and Greece sit side by side in a version of history that ignores the pesky problems of anteriority. This temporal dilation takes the form of spatial compression as he neatly fits all the major talking points of Western history between the covers of a single, slim volume. Which is to say, Agee takes what he learned from *The Waste Land*—immense historical perspective combined with radical spatial compression—and applies it to parodying *Time*'s idiosyncratic approach to news coverage. What initially looks like Agee's apt pun on a "cockeyed sense of TIME" ends up not being a pun at all but instead a substitution of the common noun for a trademark. As chronological specificity falls away, the tonal uniformity of *Time* style steps in to take its place. In Agee's formulation, "TIME" has little to say about lowercase "time"; any notion of either the writer's or the subject's historical context is "vivid but confused," with the writing itself providing the only correlation between one instance and the next. In this trade of title for temporality, the linear timeline on which *Time* operates stretches so thin that it disappears, and narrative style replaces historicity as "TIME's" operative logic. As long as one writes like *Time*, any subject is up for grabs.

Agee was not the only artist to court Time Inc. for a job; in fact, for a period in the 1930s it can begin to feel like everyone worked there, even if their reasons for applying and responses to being accepted vary considerably. This chapter surveys the field of novelists and poets who found a home and steady paycheck in the offices of Time Inc. and considers how this institutional affiliation can be read into their literary form and ideas about authorial work. In the first two chapters, we saw how Willa Cather's theory of the autonomous text and W. E. B. Du Bois's attention to the materiality of representation—two aesthetic concerns at the heart of modernist practice—grew out of the specific editorial work they undertook at big magazines. In the cases of *McClure's* and *The Crisis*, the goal of increasing readership (for *McClure's* along class lines, for *The Crisis* along racial lines) produced a series of formal innovations that bled out of the periodicals and into the individual literary style of the authors who worked there. In what follows, I'll track the paired development of modernist form and magazine work into the offices of Time Inc. from the company's inception in 1923 until the early 1940s. This historical and organizational context expands the scope of the story I've been telling in a number of ways, not least of which is an explosion in the number of writers involved. This is not incidental, as Time Inc.'s ability to standardize and scale its idiosyncratic style is the company's signal contribution to magazine history and to the history of media companies in the United States.

From the beginning, Time Inc.'s cofounders Henry Luce and Britton Hadden planned to add "an appreciable something to American prose," and as Agee saw in 1932, that "appreciable something" entailed redefining newsgathering and -writing.[3] Time Inc.'s expansion into business news with *Fortune* in 1930, then photojournalism with *Life* in 1936, as well as its many other print-based and multimedia endeavors (for example, the "Time Marches On!" newsreels), created what was at the time the largest media corporation of the twentieth century. More recently, Time Inc. became Time Warner in 1990 when it merged with Warner Communications, and then in 2001 it became AOL Time Warner (reverting to TimeWarner in 2003) in what is usually described as "the worst merger of all time"—even by its own publications.[4] And while the shifting face of the company is more recognizable today for its market share, at the beginning of its existence as the publisher of a single magazine, it distinguished itself by its style. The linguist Joseph Firebaugh writes of *Time*, "Here for the first time is a popular medium of information whose editors are using the language so freely and boldly as to suggest conscious experiment."[5] Luce and Hadden wanted to enliven the drab tone of newspaper journalism, the content-over-form approach alluded to when one refers to the *New York Times* as "the gray lady."[6] *Time* borrowed the newspaper's staff system, a move we also saw twenty years earlier at *McClure's*, but countered the in-depth reporting and organizational protocols of news writing with an inventive editorial voice: inverted sentence structures, a chatty tone, and the aggressive compression of content and words. The result, referred to as *Time* style, consists not only of highly compressed stories (at the beginning, no more than four hundred words apiece) but also the compression of words together: *Time* made a point of employing portmanteaus such as "cinemactor," "socialite," "filmen," "Hindenburglary," and "detectifiction."[7] One might claim the transition in 1927 from self-identifying as "News-Magazine" to "Newsmagazine" marks the full internalization of this tendency. The magazine distinguished itself by its uniformly idiosyncratic style, so it is both ironic and telling that the most famous single instance of *Time* style comes from outside of the magazine's own pages: Walcott Gibbs's acerbic 1936 *New Yorker* profile of Henry Luce, in which he lambasts how, in *Time*, "backwards ran sentences until reeled the mind!"[8]

Agee came of age at the perfect moment to take advantage of Time Inc.'s expansion. He was born in 1909, graduated college in 1932, and arrived on the doorstep of adulthood during the Great Depression, a period that largely did away with the bohemian dream of moving to Paris and either finding a patron or eking out a living by writing for the little magazines. As the patronage systems of the modernist little magazines dried up, working at a mass-market periodical sat alongside finding a job in one of the New Deal arts programs or moving to Hollywood as the obvious career options for those trying to write for a living.[9] Depression-era literature, and especially photography, is more familiarly associated with the public sector, such as the New Deal's Works Projects Administration and Federal Writers Project. However, the more lasting institutions of artistic patronage from the period, the ones that have only grown in influence and financial reach over the second half of the century, are those of the culture industry: massive media corporations like Time Inc. and its flagship magazine.[10]

Time's utter squareness today could not be further from its reputation in the first half of the century, and unlike those federal arts programs—which have been nearly completely dismantled—media corporations like Time Inc. remain integrally connected to the vast majority of cultural production in the United States. As Michael Szalay has pointed out, to "quite a staggering extent . . . contemporary culture is underwritten—financially and otherwise—not by government agencies but by a small cartel of media conglomerates."[11] Thus, this chapter measures the increasing amplitude of the big magazines' effect on literary production as media corporations increasingly standardize editorial practice. Time Inc. and the development of the newsmagazine expands the history I've been tracing of modernism's relationship to big magazines by looking at the emergence of a corporate voice (rather than a single magazine's) by a rather large group of artists (rather than a single person) who grew up internalizing the insights of modernism. As we'll see, the anonymity of that voice can look like modernist impersonality held up to a dark mirror: at *Time* the author is decoupled from the textual artifact he or she creates but, in accomplishing this feat, does not accumulate the cultural prestige associated with artistry. And looking forward in time, modernist writers' ambivalent participation in the success of Time Inc. foreshadows what will happen in the late 1940s, when big magazines will reimagine the iconoclastic posturing of certain modernists as a description of postwar American life. Chapters 4 and 5 will elaborate on the unexpected frequency with which modernist texts are used to describe life in the "American Century," a term that first appears in *Life*, another Time Inc. publication, to describe the increasingly international influence of the United States. At the same time that the New Criticism was transforming modernist novels and poems into autotelic objects—ones that only referred to themselves and could only be understood on their own terms—big magazines popularized a thematic reading of texts from the 1920s, with T. S. Eliot and Ernest Hemingway as the mastheads, which positioned modernist ennui as the collective, affective condition of American life.[12]

During the Great Depression, though, Time Inc. was known for its support of struggling artists. Alfred Kazin claimed that the company invented a new kind of a writer, the "poet-reporter," and provided those writers with a legitimate path to literary prestige: "Never as in the Thirties, when history proclaimed itself every day in the significances of daily struggle, could a story in *Time* have seemed so significant to a writer." He describes how, for those at *Time*, writing a story became "a literary feat because of the harsh stylistic frame to which a story had to be fitted," one for which "you got paid well, praised as only great writers are ever praised, and felt like you were an artist, of sorts."[13] Archibald MacLeish, who spent time on the Left Bank with Hemingway in the mid-1920s, began at *Time* in 1929, and would later write the preface to Agee's *Permit Me Voyage*, refers to the juxtaposition of poetry and journalism, or creative and corporate writing, as the "two ends of the typewriter keyboard," suggesting that because the activities share so much *materially*—they require the same tools, so to speak—it is difficult to cordon off one from the other cleanly.[14] The sticking point, of course, is buried in the implications of that "of sorts" tacked on to Kazin's assessment: the economic, aesthetic, and, in the end, epistemological baggage that accompanies a creative writer's corporate affiliations.

The first two chapters have been extending that sociological investigation into an analysis of literary form by tracking the historically and institutionally specific ways that writers have squared the demands of their editorial day jobs and their desires for psychological and economic space to produce the art of their choosing. This chapter examines how the context of corporate news writing impinges on the literary output of several writers. First, it describes the characteristics of *Time* style, what aspects of magazine culture it responded to, and how it transformed from a specific approach to writing into the primary "mental discipline" of working at Time Inc. From here, we'll see how *Time* style and its implicit definition of writerly work reemerges in two literary texts written by Time Inc. employees. The indignities of corporate journalism provide the plot and theme in Kenneth Fearing's crime novel *The Big Clock* (1946), which takes place inside a fictionalized version of Time Inc. and ends by killing both the boss and the company. Then I'll turn to James Agee and Walker Evans's breathless tirade against corporate work and mass culture, *Let Us Now Praise Famous Men* (1941), which began as a three-part *Fortune* article. *Famous Men* is probably the most well-known collaboration between Time Inc. and one of its employees, and reading it alongside other Time Inc. works highlights the text's indebtedness to Agee's editorial job, even though he tries to write himself out of that history. The sociologist Robert

Vanderlan and the literary critic Jeff Allred have begun this work by changing the focus to the way that artists such as Agee and Evans, in Allred's
words, enact a "modernist dissent against the 'continuity style' of mainstream journalism." Allred especially seeks to describe a more nuanced
"explanation of the interplay of attraction and repulsion that linked artists
with mass cultural institutions," though he, perhaps justifiably, maintains
a "pessimistic outlook" on the tenability of coupling corporate work and
experimental aesthetic practice.[15] I depart from that pessimism and, if
only temporarily, withhold judgment so as instead to offer historical interpretation of an employment arrangement that produced dozens of truly
astounding literary and visual texts: *The Big Clock* and *Let Us Now Praise
Famous Men*, to be sure, but also much of Archibald MacLeish's poetry
and Margaret Bourke-White's photography, several of Robert Cantwell's
novels, most of James Gould Cozzen's stories, and John Hersey's *A Bell
for Adano* and *Hiroshima*.

The possibility that *Time* style is fungible—that it can move off the
magazine page and into the prose and poetry of its employees—is apparent from Agee's first interaction with Time Inc. It is not his literary
prowess that provides the opportunity for a remunerative position; it is
the ability to replicate *Time*'s voice. By writing like *Time* before writing for it, Agee demonstrates how its style can be transported and par-
roted by any writer bright enough to pay *Time*'s editors the flattery of
imitation. However short his parody might fall of actually being funny,
Agee accomplishes his larger goal. The stunt changes him from a student writing like *Time* for free into an employee now paid to do the
same task for *Fortune*. When Agee substitutes "TIME" for its uncapi-
talized homonym and then economically capitalizes on his work done
in the magazine's image, he shows how *Time, Fortune*, and *Life*—he
wrote for all three—might provide an ideal setting for the simultaneous
production of literary professionalism and professionally subsidized literature. In the same way, the periodical prehistory of *Let Us Now Praise
Famous Men* and Agee's highly publicized problems with finishing the
text provide a model for how the feedback between big magazines and
literary modernism changes in the 1920s and 1930s. Agee and Fearing
came of age in the wake of literary modernism, and at Time Inc. they
became coworkers with a number of its biggest proponents: MacLeish,
Fitzgerald, and Dwight MacDonald, among others. By pairing these corporate and aesthetic interests, I hope to shed light on the institutional

situation of American writers who attempted to suture modernism's aesthetic claims onto the economic reality of writing for a paycheck.

Administrative Poets

In a letter to Dwight MacDonald, Agee recalls his elation from receiving the news of a job offer: "Words fail me . . . Besides the fairly fundamental fact that I don't want to starve, there are dozens of other reasons why I want *uh* job and many more why I am delighted to get this one."[16] The reasons go unstated, but many other writers share the sentiment of delight at getting the invitation to work at Time Inc. MacLeish recalls that receiving a job offer from Luce was "one of the luckiest things that happened to me in a fairly lucky life":

> In 1929, when the offer was made, jobs were not easily available, particularly jobs for writers of verse with wives and children, and, more particularly still, jobs such as Luce was willing to provide. . . . I had begun by saying that I needed a job desperately, so desperately that there was only one thing I needed more—time enough to finish a long poem I had started in Paris two years before.[17]

That poem was *Conquistador* (1932), the Pulitzer Prize–winning modernist epic that MacLeish finished in his off-time over the next two years. Alfred Kazin, who alternately wrote for *Time* and *Fortune*, recounts with awe the stable of writers he encountered on his first visit to the offices at *Time*: "Part of the fascination of going up to see Harriet [his friend] in the new *Time* offices in Rockefeller Center was running into James Agee, Walker Evans, Robert Fitzgerald, John Hersey." When Kazin's colleague John Chamberlain became an editor at *Fortune* in 1936—the same year of Walcott Gibbs's *New Yorker* parody—Kazin met and befriended Dwight MacDonald, MacLeish, Robert Cantwell, Ralph Ingersoll, Louis Kronenberger, and James Gould Cozzens.[18] Not only does Kazin depict Time Inc. as a focal point for the circulation of literary talent, but for him and presumably for those employed there, it represents a desirable line of work at a respectable print organ.

A big part of its reputation comes from an active interest in the aesthetic form of news language. *Time*'s intervention into news writing had everything to do with form and little to do with content. Or, to be more accurate, it had to do with developing a form that made the news stay new. Take, for example, the opening paragraph of *Time*'s coverage of the Scopes trial, from 1925:

> Scene. In the fastnesses of Tennessee, the quiet of dawn is split asunder by wailing screams from a steam siren. It is the Dayton sawmill, waking up villagers and farmers for miles around. From 5 until 6:30 the blasts continue. The hamlet and the fantastic cross between a circus and a holy war that is in progress there come slowly to life.[19]

In *Time*'s rendering the Scopes trial becomes a logical extension of a broader shift toward the scientific rationalism of modernity and also how those very proclamations of social progress might belie elaborate confidence games. The passage depicts Dayton as "split asunder" like a plank in the mill by, on the one hand, the businessmen who orchestrated the legal battle as a means of publicizing the city and, on the other, the fundamentalists who use that publicity as a religious soapbox. The "wailing screams" of the steam siren replace the bucolic calls of the rooster, forcefully waking the town to a new day of industrial technology. The narrative voice becomes analogous to the siren; it comes into being with the aural representation of industrial progress. Even more, it situates the technologies of communication as fundamental for bringing this scene "slowly to life" and shapes the terms in which one can discuss it. Instead of journalistic objectivity, the story takes an explicitly literary stance: the extradiegetic stage directions of "Scene" and later "Jury" and "Trial" transform news coverage into something like a closet drama with a complicated narrative point of view; the wailing siren brings about something like free indirect discourse. This use of dramatic structure abounds in *Time* stories as a way to organize information while supplying a narrative arc to news events. The novelty of reading *Time*, as opposed to the *New York Times*, is the novelization of news information.

Agee grew up eighty miles from Dayton in Knoxville, Tennessee, and in several *Fortune* articles on the Tennessee Valley Authority he describes the rise of the New South in remarkably similar terms. He refers to the "Dayton of blessed memory" as one of many "down-at-heel" villages on the verge of a delayed industrial revolution. New Deal projects such as Norris Dam, rural factories, and, yes, sawmills make farmers "come to" after generations of existing in the ahistorical utopia that Agee mocks *Time* for describing in his parody. These farmers'

> forefathers settled this country in the 1700's when the effete civilization east of the Alleghenies stuck in their craws. They whipped the British- ers and Loyalists at King's Mountain. They kept much to themselves and their great-grandsons do likewise and live in much the same way, while slowly the sawmills and the mines and the railways and the highways and now TVA burn seclusion from about them.[20]

In a letter, Agee claims Luce said that a TVA piece he wrote "was one of the best pieces of writing he'd seen in *Fortune*," which forces one to question the notorious mutual antipathy felt between Agee and "The Founder," as Agee was known to call Luce.[21] Perhaps more importantly, though, Agee's nativist romance of a Southern existence outside of time, where folks speak "pidgin-Elizabethan and some of their songs are still of the sea and of England," sits awkwardly next to his critique of *Time*'s form as the end of historical difference.[22] Robert Fitzgerald argued that Agee's style "was so conspicuous that it might as well have been signed"; Alfred Kazin wrote that Agee was "the only writer whose individual voice could be distinguished from the anonymous smoothness" of its surroundings.[23] Above, the Scopes Trial coverage is more interested in allegorizing the machine in the garden than the specifics of the case at hand, and, despite Kazin's and Fitzgerald's claims, after only a year of working on Time Inc.'s clock Agee adopts the same tone, without the arched eyebrows that marked his collegiate parody.

It would be easy to chalk up this allegorical model of *Time* style to bad history, but it might be more productive to read it as another local manifestation of the inextricable tie between aesthetic and bureaucratic tendencies in editorial work that we saw in *McClure's* and *The Crisis*. In important ways, the innovations at *Time* cannot happen until after these previous iterations of the big magazine, which help diversify the offer- ings of and expand the readership for periodicals, because *Time* reacts to and capitalizes on the superabundance of print culture. That is, *Time*'s desire to aestheticize the historical moment can be seen as a response to what Luce and Hadden described as an overproduction of information in the newspapers and an inattention to the wants and needs of the aver- age reader. "As it is now," wrote Luce in the early 1920s, "people have to think too hard as they read."[24] Though one might assume that modernism is to blame, Luce's most immediate referent is not "the difficulties of modernism," to use Richard Poirer's phrase for the "proposition that the act of reading should entail difficulties analogous to those registered in the act of writing."[25] Certainly, these difficulties are plentiful; one might convincingly, if vaguely, define modernist style as that which requires people to "think too hard." And *Time* repeatedly disparaged modernism: it dedicated its first book review to a takedown of T. S. Eliot and James Joyce as representative of a massive "hoax." "There is a new kind of literature abroad in the land," the magazine claimed, "whose only obvious fault is that no one can understand it."[26] However, here Luce is responding to the difficulties of an oversaturated print landscape, one that offers no method of evaluating the relative worth of publications before actually reading them. Not only had what scholars now call the "print revolution" drastically increased the number of titles available, but the size of individual magazines and newspapers had also exploded. For example, a typical issue of the *Saturday Evening Post* in 1926 —one of the most popular magazines in the United States—exceeded two hundred pages, and it was not uncommon for *Cosmopolitan* or *McClure's* to close in on 150 pages; a 1926 *Ladies Home Journal* was 270 pages.[27] Counterintuitively, Luce points out the difficulty of mass culture, which is difficult precisely because there is so much of it. A *Time* advertising circular from 1925 dramatizes this: two distraught characters, "Busy Man" and "Busy Woman," sit sadly in a living room surrounded by newspapers. The man laments, "I bought this mass of printed matter to find out what is going on in the world, but it's no use! I am not abreast of the news in anything outside of my business." Lo and behold, "TIME" knocks on the door and saves the day, representing "a new idea of journalism. In my twenty-six pages is every fact of significance in all those newspapers and periodicals on your floor."[28] For *Time*, modernism and mass culture both fall short of the reader's needs, though they do so in different ways: the former by a dearth of readily available meanings, the latter by supplying too many.

Time's narrative mode, then, responds to a seemingly paradoxical anxiety about the loss of knowledge at the hands of unfettered and disaggregated information. And, as Niklas Luhmann argues, when communication becomes faster and more complex, it also makes knowledge more quickly obsolete.[29] In other words, what we might call the "information economies of scale" tip toward strategic ignorance: there is a decreasing payoff for staying current as the timespan of "current" shrinks and the amount of information in that interval expands. Agee's depiction of *Time* as unhinged from historical specificity, in this light, looks like a response to the feeling that contemporaneity is awash in unprocessed data. Stretching back to at least to Matthew Arnold and forward at least to Allan Bloom, the fear of intellectual dissipation at the hands of mass media is a familiar story. We saw it occur in the responses to the first iteration of big magazines in the 1900s, though it more commonly surfaces as an impetus for the development of modernism.[30] The epistemological and material foundations of Time Inc. force a reconsideration of this trajectory: they suggest that a crisis of mass culture's informational overproduction was also felt *within* mass culture. Though *Time* positions itself against modernist literature from the beginning, it shares what F. R. Leavis describes in *New Bearings in English Poetry* (1932) as the central modernist literary technique: "a compression approaching simultaneity—the co-presence in the mind of a number of different orientations, fundamental attitudes, orders of experience."[31] Despite this shared technique, the answer that the magazine offers is not what Aaron Jaffe compellingly theorizes as modernism's "aversion to oversupply"; instead, it takes the approach that defines the big magazines.[32] That is, it massifies aesthetic taste and expands the reader's linguistic and cultural skills, employing creative artists to presort the paralyzing crush of news into a manageable quantity. In its "Prospectus," *Time* decides that a news organ matters "not in how much it includes between its covers—but in HOW MUCH IT GETS OFF ITS PAGES INTO THE MINDS OF ITS READERS."[33] What distinguishes it among big magazines, though, is that *Time* compresses so as to make reading easier and more rational; it becomes an interface between the raw data of history and the upwardly mobile reader. Rather than make reading as difficult as writing, *pace* Poirier, the magazine reduces the effort that goes into reading while expanding the benefits of that activity.

To remodel the work of news gathering, Time Inc. did not employ typical reporters; instead it hired editors who would read the dailies and, like a Dadaist collage, remake the content of newspapers into an aesthetic object. Justifying his approach Henry Luce said, "It is easier to turn poets into business journalists than to turn bookkeepers into writers." The *Time* editor's work is not investigation but collation; Luce writes, "It takes *brains and work* to master all the facts dug up by the world's 10,000 journalists and to put them together in a little magazine."[34] The magazine does not found itself on informational originality but on the way that it translates other people's research into its own voice. And because of this emphasis on a uniform voice, all of the Time Inc. publications excise bylines in favor of a staff list in the frontmatter of each issue. The end products of different writers, after passing through the hands of the editor, Britton Hadden, were supposed to be indistinguishable, so attaching names to the stories became counterproductive for establishing a single periodical persona.

As the magazine's editorial methodology gets up and running, the combined goals of aesthetic singularity and managerial organization become a compositional method in their own right. Though *Time* style originates with Hadden, the style slowly matriculates from his personal affect to a work ethic distributed across the corporation. T. S. Matthews, a longtime Time Inc. employee and an early biographer of T. S. Eliot, remembers, "All neophytes were expected to memorize Hadden's invented words and phrases and to use them at every opportunity." The task had lasting effects, according to Matthews; when he and his colleagues tried to stop writing in *Time* style, "the iron had so far entered our souls that the attempt at reform was never successful."[35] William Gottfried, another Time Inc. lifer, also describes how the magazine's doctrine of compression and its stylistic tics quickly moved from Hadden's and Luce's insistence on short, snappy blurbs to self-censure: "The original Prospectus said that no story would occupy more than about seven inches of type. We tried to write this way, but gradually we found our medium changing under our hands. . . . *Time*-style became not a formula of words, but a kind of mental discipline."[36] Gottfried describes the mutation of formal or spatial constraints into an approach to thinking about writing and then into an automatic way of writing that no longer requires thinking—a reflex, in the non-self-reflexive sense. Thus, we can see how a formal experiment in the content of the magazine shapes the way that workers approach the task of writing. The corporate identity is thoroughly particularized by its aesthetic form, but it cannot be attached to a person.

In this respect, a *Time* editor begins to take on the definition of individual talent that T. S. Eliot discusses in *The Frontiers of Criticism* (1952): "poetic originality is largely an original way of assembling the most disparate and unlikely material to make a new whole."[37] Both imagine their project as organizing the sum total of one's reading into a new form. Just as the shared technique of compression brings Time Inc.'s style into conversation with literary modernism, the sublimation of individual writ-ers into a corporate voice can look like a bowdlerized version of modern-ist "impersonality," especially the one laid out in Eliot's "Tradition and the Individual Talent." Here, Eliot claims that an artist does not have a "personality" to express but rather "a particular medium which is only a medium and not a personality." "The poet cannot reach this impersonal-ity without surrendering himself wholly to the work to be done," Eliot claims.[38] Ironically, this theory of impersonal authorship, in which "the work to be done" overrides the writer doing the work, also guides the editorial model at Time Inc. The difference is that no one questions who wrote either *The Waste Land* or *Ulysses*. Eliot's ideal author still gets to sign the finished product—and, in the case of Joyce, to stamp the date and location of composition. There literally is a name attached to the poem or novel as well as the figurative signature of an individual style—what Jaffe calls the modernist imprimatur.[39] At Time Inc., the lofty hand that guides Eliot's individual poet, what he calls "the historical sense," materializes in the suspect form of a corporate "house style," a purely textual identity that supersedes the agents that work in its name. The Time Inc. model begins to raise questions about how one might pinpoint the creative act in an anonymous and collective text, a problem hinted at by the combination of plural and singular in Luce's assertion of "*brains and work.*"

Punching the Clock

The "mental discipline" of *Time* style carries over into the "corporation story" of *Fortune*, the "photomagazine" format of *Life*, and the ethos of "group journalism" that guides Time Inc.'s overarching editorial system. Though each magazine develops its own style, the organizational model that makes editorial work transferable between writers also makes the administration of that work transferable between titles. Perhaps the best evidence of this is the promiscuous reappropriation of writers between periodicals within the organization. Archibald MacLeish, something like the Platonic ideal of an administrative artist, started as an education writer for *Time*, went on to be a manager at *Fortune*, and also wrote for *Life*. James Agee spent four years at *Fortune*, began writing book and later film reviews for *Time* in 1939, and after 1945 served as a "rover," writing in any capacity and for any magazine that Luce required of him.

In 1949 Agee published "Comedy's Greatest Era" in *Life*, a long piece on silent comedies, which one might read as his self-reflexive comment on the pervasiveness of Time Inc.'s mental discipline. The argument that "the only thing wrong with screen comedy today is that it takes place on a screen which talks" fits quite well into the photograph-before-writing emphasis of *Life*. In chapter 5 we'll see how the magazine's nonlinguistic aesthetic helps make sense of its long engagement with Ernest Hemingway and his famously terse prose. For now, it's enough to say that verbalization in either the aural or written form becomes antithetical to *Life*'s aesthetic mission, and Agee repurposes the silent comedians as evidence of language's fundamental inadequacy. He refers to the "figure[s] of speech, or rather of vision" that the comedians develop not as creative acts but as "a ruthless discipline." The "business of being as funny as possible" becomes a strictly organized type of work developed to suit best the media form in which it will be distributed. The problem, though, is that learning the grammar of silent film's performative work makes the comedians unfit for the talkies: "The only comedians who ever mastered the screen cannot work, for they cannot combine their comic style with talk. Because there is a screen, talking comedians are trapped into a continual exhibition of their inadequacy."[40] And, for Agee, the sad consequence of their overspecialization provides an allegory for the plight of the poet-reporter. After only a few months at *Fortune*, he wrote to his longtime friend Father James Flye about the troubles of writing outside of the corporate style: "For the past two weeks, particularly, writing has been very much on my mind. I've been steadily trying to do it, and haven't written a single good thing. The only writing I do which approaches decency is on this job—and on other stuff I seem to be pretty well congealed."[41]

Time style shuts down Agee's ability to write "other stuff," but other authors would use the working conditions at Time Inc. as inspiration for their extracurricular, fictional writing. Kenneth Fearing's novel *The Big Clock* (1946), for example, reimagines the "*brains and work*" that produce *Time* style as an "empire of intelligence" dedicated to overseeing the minutia of daily life, which seems to be entirely made up of thoughts about the corporation.[42] For this reason the novel offers a valuable entry point into the thematic resonances between Time Inc.'s "mental discipline" and the artistic work of even its most stridently anticorporate employees. Unlike MacLeish's and Agee's shared delight at receiving jobs at Time Inc., Fearing took pains to keep his worlds separate. Throughout

the 1920s and 1930s, Fearing was a fairly well-known leftist poet; he associated with the Dynamo school, and with the support of two Guggenheim
fellowships he published several books of poetry that received high marks
from reviewers.[43] All of this cultural capital, however, did not quite translate into the kind that consistently pays the rent. To make ends meet he
worked as "a professional freelancer" at large media companies to support
his literary writing. He wrote for *Time, Newsweek,* and several other news
publications while also contributing pornographic crime stories to the
pulps.[44] This for-hire writing was strictly "hack work" in Fearing's eyes,
though with a deep skepticism of the second word. "I always begin to get
suspicious," he told his son, "when I hear a poet talking about his *work,*"
implying that even using the same word for art and occupation is to allow
the logic of labor into one's vocation.[45]

   This suspicion of work and the uncomfortable places it might lead a
writer who takes it too seriously colors every aspect of *The Big Clock.* The
novel revolves around a murder witnessed by George Stroud, an editor
at *Crimeways* newsmagazine, one title in a vast media company called
Janoth Enterprises that is clearly modeled on Time Inc. Though Fearing
firmly inserts the novel into the detective genre, the narrative spends
much more time detailing the daily work of a magazine editor than it
does in introducing clues or setting up a murder mystery. Echoing Kazin's
bewildered litany of literary types that fill *Time*'s office, Stroud describes
the strange scene of an office building filled with "frustrated ex-artists,
scientists, farmers, writers, explorers, poets, lawyers, doctors, [and] musicians" (107). The aggregate knowledge of this employee pool means that,
though ostensibly a crime blotter, the magazine can handle any topic:
"Whatever the subject, it scarcely mattered," says Stroud. "What did matter was our private and collective virtuosity," which turns the raw material of news into a Janoth story (23). "What we decided in this room,"
he thinks, "more than a million of our fellow-citizens would read three
months from now, and what they read they would accept as final . . . they
would follow the reasoning we presented, remember the phrases, the tone
of authority, and in the end their crystallized judgments would be ours"
(24). What Luce and Hadden intimated, Fearing makes explicit: it is the
memorable phrases and "tone of authority" that are the wellspring of his
magazine's appeal.

   The problem for Stroud, as for Fearing, resides in the collective pronoun repeated above: the "we" of a depersonalized corporate voice that erases the author. In his 1956 essay "Reading, Writing, and the Rackets," Fearing reflects on how this collective composition model presents a "curious reversal of custom that once prevailed in print." "The writer is paid (and very well paid) by the sponsoring corporation, while he himself has become a corporate writer, one member of a large team," he explains. "The writer has a private name, probably, and he probably has a distinct personality. But his divorce from the transmitted material is complete."[46] Fearing laments how corporate media entities, or what he calls the "theaters of communication," transform from the intermediary between writer and public into the primary agent. For Fearing this dissolves the "distinct personality" of a writer into the editorial protocols of his office work. He was not alone in his concern, as Dwight Macdonald, another longtime Time Inc. employee, attests. For Macdonald, this all-encompassing vision of the "sponsoring corporation" extends into every aspect of writing. While working for *Fortune*, he also contributed to a little magazine, the *Miscellany*, in his "spare time." When he sent an issue of *Miscellany* to Luce, he received an irate letter in return, arguing that by writing for another publication Macdonald had "betrayed Time, Inc." Writing for *Fortune* was not just a job; it was a vocation worthy of a man's whole effort, and pay and time schedules weren't the point at all:

> Why, the very name Fortune was thought up by so-and-so [one of my fellow editors] late one night on the West Side subway between the Seventy-second and the Seventy-ninth street stations [Luce was a Time man always]. This is a twenty-four-hour profession, you never know when you may get an idea for us, and if you're all the time thinking about some damn little magazine

then Macdonald is not fulfilling his writerly obligations to Luce.[47] *Time* style, then, becomes a methodology that forecloses the possibility in its practitioners of other types of writing. As the company style becomes both a disciplined competence and a method of work that can be applied equally to all subjects, then to write for someone else, even if that person is oneself, becomes theft.

Luce's claim that a writing job at Time Inc. gives him full control of his employees' "thinking" points out the difficulty of compartmentalizing the intellectual work of writing. The sociologist Andrew Ross refers to this as "the mental labor problem" and finds it especially troubling for artists employed by large institutions, who assume that their employee's love of their craft means that they do not need to be paid very much.[48] Along with fair compensation, Fearing turns his attention in *The Big Clock* to where and when one's ideas come from and whether they belong to the company. When George Stroud asks himself what, exactly, provides him and his fellow writers with the words they disseminate to the millions of readers, he can't quite explain: "The moving impulse simply arrived, as we, on the face that the giant clock turned to the public, merely registered the correct hour of the standard time" (24). Uncovering the source of that "moving impulse," and how one connects to it, generates the fairly standard murder plot of the novel. Earl Janoth's girlfriend, Pauline Delos, is found dead in her apartment, and George Stroud is handpicked to lead the investigation into who killed the woman. The novel builds its dramatic irony on the fact that Stroud's higher-ups do not know that he was having an affair with Pauline Delos and that they thus have put him in charge of finding himself. To take the informational imbalance between the employee and the employer one step further, Stroud also knows that Earl Janoth is the real killer. The plot that actually provides the novel's thrust, then, is not a whodunit—the reader and main character know that from the beginning—but instead a kind of shadow story in which we see Stroud redirecting the path of the investigation away from clues that lead to him and toward clues that lead to Janoth.

To cover up his affair and expose his boss's guilt requires Stroud to see "the face of the giant clock" everywhere, which results in paranoid visions such as this:

> The big clock was running as usual. . . . Sometimes the hands of the clock actually raced, and at other times they hardly moved at all. But that made no difference to the big clock. The hands could move backward, and the time it told would be right just the same. It would still be running as usual, because all the other watches have to be set by the big one, which is even more powerful than the calendar, and to which one automatically adjusts his entire life.
>
> (3–4)

Though the novel clearly has no love for the automatic adjustments that one makes inside the clock, it does make a case that the impulses that it imparts are not necessarily malevolent. Stroud describes the organization's

perfect bureaucratic movement as "big and smooth and infinitely pow-
ered" (91), running on the energy of "five hundred sightless eyes" (138),
"all of whom spent their lives conforming . . . to a sort of overgrown, aim-
less, haphazard stenciling apparatus" (107). This sentiment has been read
as a "reaffirm[ation] of humanism and individualism through the often
frightening image of their opposites" and as a "warning" to Fearing's
readers "against the dangers of modern American corporate life: the sac-
rifices of individualism and creative, satisfying work."[49] Yet to Stroud's
surprise, the clock's machinery is extremely easy to manipulate. Part of
the system's efficiency comes from being "blind, clumsy, [and] unreasoning"—that is, automatic (91). When Stroud describes his goal to turn
this unreasoning clock against itself, he says, "If I picked the right kind
of staff, twisted the investigation where I could, jammed it where I had
to, pushed it hard where it was safe, it might be a very, very long time
before they find George Stroud." All of this pushing, jamming, and twist-
ing of the investigative machine is just, as Stroud repeatedly says, "the big
clock running as usual." And rather than getting squashed, or crushed, or
defiantly stripping the gears, he discovers the pliancy of its systematized
work—really, its total indifference to the content that the machinery produces. From the outside, the clock looks monolithic, cold, and inhuman.
But Stroud, with his jamming and pushing, discovers the opposite: how
easily, even if unintentionally, someone aware of the way that the administration functions can take advantage of it. As an outsider on the inside, so
to speak, Stroud can make the system work for him.

So "the big clock" describes the media corporation, Janoth Enterprises,
and its role as a "haphazard stenciling apparatus" that standardizes the
lives of its workers and readers by way of highly organized editorial work
and the "tone of authority" housed in the periodical's content. However,
when Stroud describes it as "haphazard," "blind," "sightless," and
"clumsy," it is hard not to direct a little bit of Fearing's suspicion about
the indignities of work back at the author. The ease with which Stroud
uses the clocklike media corporation for his own purposes makes it hard
to read Janoth Enterprises as the embodiment of machinelike conformity
or, in turn, to read the novel as an outright excoriation of Fearing's corporate work. Part of the allegorical ambiguity of the clock comes from the
difficulty of pinning down exactly where the technological center of that
clock resides or how it functions. Unlike the 1948 film adaptation, which
places a clock tower in the center of the corporate offices and features a

fight scene inside of it, there aren't any actual clocks in the novel. In fact, Stroud uses the metaphor of a clock to describe the cocktail parties, dingy bars, secondhand stores, and motels that he frequents during his daily work, so that everything in the novel looks like "the big clock." Early on, Stroud philosophizes, "For of course the clock that measures out the seasons, all gain and loss, the air Georgia [his wife] breathes, Georgette's [his daughter] strength, the figures shivering on the dials of my own inner instrument board, this gigantic watch that fixes order and establishes the pattern for chaos itself, it has never changed, it will never change, or be changed" (13). The clock is now so big that one can only glimpse its movements in the changing of the seasons, and at the same time it is so particularized one can breathe it in, an invocation of scalar extremes that will also turn up in Agee's attempt to imagine a space outside corporate work. With the almost identical names in Stroud's nuclear family (George, Georgia, Georgette), Fearing weds a critique of the anonymous suburbs to the flattened individuality of corporate life. Yet the references to the perennial jangling of Stroud's "own inner instrument board" flattens time, and particularly historical change, so that in this instant at least Fearing cannot imagine a pre- or postclock mode of being. Stroud, after all, is clocklike, too, so that company, employee, family, and environment are seamlessly integrated. "The big clock," then, transforms from agent to background, from evil mover of things to a more banal medium through which things move. Put another way, Fearing's work evidences the way that *Time* style turns everything into company work, but it does so without Macdonald's outrage. The representations of Stroud's work as an editor in *The Big Clock* look increasingly like what one usually does outside of work: he eats with his family, goes to restaurants and bars, buys antiques and paintings, talks with friends. For Stroud, each of these actions now constitutes work, as his "work" at Janoth Enterprises is to investigate himself. Or, as Mark Seltzer might phrase it, when the media system that is the novel turns its attention to the daily work of media systems, in this case Janoth Enterprises, then the narrative has no choice but to see everything as itself: an endless regress of clocks. And, ultimately, this reflexivity is how the novel imagines modernity—it is simply "the big clock running as usual," with no judgment attached.

This view of the clock as an inevitability, a type of background noise, forces a reconsideration of how we look at Stroud's seemingly heroic stance against the injustices of working on the salaried time of corporations, a type of temporal organization in which everything one does belongs to someone or something else. Even when he works in self-interest against the clock, defending his name and hiding his identity from the investigation, Stroud works from within it: figuratively, as an employee in the clocklike corporation, and literally in the material object of the novel that, to borrow Stroud's phrase, "fixes order and establishes the pattern for chaos" (13). As much as Stroud looks for the space that should be outside of his work, it never shows itself. Neither Stroud nor Fearing take the most obvious way out: quitting. Instead, the greatest revenge against Luce that Fearing can muster at the novel's end is to manufacture a hostile takeover of Janoth Enterprises and have Stroud work for the new company. When Janoth, wallowing in shame after being removed from office, commits suicide in the final lines of the novel, Stroud reads the news in a *Crimeways* headline: "EARL JANOTH, OUSTED PUBLISHER, PLUMMETS TO DEATH" (166). As it turns out, Stroud isn't the only one who can't escape: even after his death, Janoth is reanimated as editorial content.

If one can read reception history back into the novel, then *The Big Clock*'s grand statement about the effect of writing on company time is at best a tortured one. Despite the disapproval of Fearing's former avant-garde literary circle, who interpreted his trade of poetry for the detective novel as giving in to economic demands, *The Big Clock* became a runaway bestseller. A laudatory review in none other than *Time* was followed by brisk sales and popular approval. All told, he made over $60,000 from royalties, republications, and film rights, which included a condensation for *The American Magazine*. Fearing always supported himself through the "work" side of writing. And ironically it's only when his novels—which he emphatically declared not to be work—begin to incorporate the details of his day job—which he most surely did consider to be work—that he makes enough money to quit.

Unwriting *Famous Men*

The Big Clock starts as a riposte to Luce's and Time Inc.'s notion of all-encompassing work but ends up reproducing that very logic in its transformation of all of Stroud's rebellions against Janoth into extensions of his office work. The novel goes even further, though, showing how the corporation subsumes even unrelated artists and art objects under its masthead.

Stroud collects the abstract paintings of an unfashionable artist, Louise Patterson, and in a nod to Henry James's *The Golden Bowl*, one particular painting he buys at an antique store on the night that he spent with Pauline will later provide the material proof of his infidelity. The location of this painting, rather than that of the killer, becomes the subject of a media frenzy: articles are written about its importance to the case, the magazine sends a team of investigators in search of it and the person who painted it, and, as one *Crimeways* reporter puts it, "we'd automatically find the picture when we found the man," a phrase that both semantically and syntactically prioritizes the radically singular artwork over the nondescript identity of a common criminal (153). In the course of all this publicity for the painting, its price tag skyrockets, as does the reputation of its artist. By the end of the novel, Patterson paintings are the new trend in art, and Stroud's painting is the most valuable piece. As information about the painting circulates among artists, dealers, collectors, and popular magazines—each with an opinion about the artistic merit and financial worth of the object—Patterson's painting begins to look like the novel recursively accounting for its own reputation. In another book, one produced under different organizational circumstances, this might be characterized as a degradation of artistic value by bringing it into contact with a financially motivated media company. But Fearing has something else in mind. The painting depicts two hands exchanging a gold coin, for which different characters decide to name it *The Temptation of St. Judas* and *Toil*. But Patterson, the artist who produced it, corrects them, calling it *Study in Fundamentals*.

Patterson's paintings begin to transform Fearing's thematic treatment of corporate life into a formal one, but the prepublication history and narrative structure of James Agee and Walker Evans's *Let Us Now Praise Famous Men* provides a far more robust example of how *Time* style reappears in the style of extracurricular work. The text, which began as a three-part story on Southern white tenant farmers for the "Life and Circumstances" section of *Fortune*, followed a rather circuitous route to its final—if still incomplete in Agee's mind—form. In June 1936, shortly after returning to New York from a six-month vacation, Agee's editor at *Fortune* offered him the story. Unlike his usual "commercial-poetic prose" that "wasted enough time not to be by any means worth the forty dollars that was the best it could bring in," this assignment offered a return to the rural Southerners he had covered in his articles on the Tennessee

Valley Authority. He describes the three parts coming together with "the first on the family, the second a generalized piece, a big fatassed analysis of the situation of cotton economics and of all Governmental efforts to Do Something about It, which latter I was quite sure could beautifully hang themselves in their own rope; and a straight union piece."[50] In true "group journalism" fashion, he imagined Archibald MacLeish writing the middle section. Despite Agee's lofty vision, the three-part submission to *Fortune* was quickly rejected by his editors, though they did not give up the rights to the manuscript he produced. The legal status of the document became increasingly important as Agee continued to write throughout 1937 under the encouragement of Edward Answell, a literary agent at Harpers & Bros. who showed interest in printing the manuscript in book form. Because Luce refused to publish the manuscript in *Fortune* but also refused to give up his right to do so, there was a year-long period when Agee had no legal claim to the work that he considered his great artistic statement, "the best assignment I have ever had, and the only one I have a hundred per cent worked to do."[51] After a year Luce relinquished the manuscript, but Harpers eventually rejected the project because Agee refused to make suggested revisions. It was not until 1940 when Eunice Jessup—an editor at Houghton Mifflin and the wife of John Jessup, a colleague of Agee's at *Fortune* and the unnamed author of *Time*'s tepid initial review of *Famous Men*—showed interest in the manuscript that it finally found a permanent home.[52]

It is difficult to characterize Agee's activities after *Fortune* kills the story, at least from the position of a writer-employee. Is revision considered office work—after all, Time Inc. still owns the words that he has written, and he is still their company man—or has Agee become like his imagined Caesar, writing without hope of eventual publication? In his Guggenheim fellowship application from October 1937 (an award that Fearing, and not Agee, would be awarded) he states that any approach falls short of an assignment that technically now resides in the limbo between work and not work. The text about three tenant families aims "to tell everything possible as accurately as possible: and to invent nothing. It involves therefore as total a suspicion of 'creative' and 'artistic' as of 'reportorial' attitudes and methods."[53] Authorial autonomy and the bureaucratic strictures of corporate employment are now untenable, creating a vacuum where neither writing on the clock nor writing for oneself adequately represents what Agee sees himself doing.

All of this anxiety over the substance of writing becomes a primary motif in *Famous Men*. In a text that could reasonably be described as one long, breathless tirade against the indignity of bureaucratic abstraction, Agee early on attempts to lay out what nonexploitative aesthetic work might look like: "If I could do it, I'd do no writing at all here. It would be photographs; the rest would be fragments of cloth, bits of cotton, lumps of earth, records of speech, pieces of wood and iron, phials of odors, plates of food and excrement."[54] Along with his petition to have the work printed on cheap newsprint that will disintegrate before the next generation has a chance to read it, this might be the most famous example of Agee's Pyrrhic desire for textual self-immolation. Michael Szalay finds the above passage characteristic of Agee's attempt to "disavow the means of production that sustain him," namely, corporate writing (27). Of course, the irony lies in the fact that Agee does "do" writing, and lots of it. The conditional form of "If I could do it, I'd do no writing at all here" attests to the impossibility for Agee to abstain from the activity. He is compelled to write because his livelihood depends on it, just as his coworker Walker Evans must take photographs, and just as all other staffers must write news stories that will not be attributed to them. Yet because of his institutional context, Agee equates writing with betrayal:

> These I will write of are human beings, living in this world, innocent of such twistings as these which are taking place over their heads; and that they were dwelt among, investigated, spied on, revered, and loved, by other quite monstrously alien human beings, in the employment of still others still more alien; and that they are not being looked into by still others, who have picked up their living as casually as if it were a book.
>
> (12–13)

The greatest offense that Agee can envision would be to treat his subjects as a textual artifact, which is exactly what they become as soon as he leaves Alabama and begins to document his experience. To encounter the plight of the tenant farmers "as casually as if it were a book" would be to flatten the gestural register, the one that silent-film comedians perfected before it was ruined by words.

Agee faces the competing methodological problems of either creating a form that can directly communicate his subjects or reducing his experience into words that are owned by a corporation. The problem with the first method is that sending a plate of food and a bag of excrement to *Fortune* as his report on the plight of tenant farmers does not exactly fulfill his contractual obligations. Agee finds work because of his ability to write like *Time*, and to refuse to write eliminates his most marketable skill. While "If I could do it, I'd do no writing here" may refer to a deep skepticism of mediation, in context it looks to be about something far more banal: work. More specifically, it finds him chafing at the way that writing has become a particularly depersonalized type of work in which he can be classified as a Northern spy, a New Deal do-gooder, or a corporate lackey. By organizational affiliation his work is part of the "twistings" taking "place over their heads," yet the corporate machinations also take place over his head. Not writing—that is, not working— would allow him to square the circle, to erase any trace of his own labor from the document he is supposed to be compiling on his subjects. In other words, or in Agee's words, to remove the work of writing from the equation resembles displaying "plates of food and excrement" side by side. Pragmatically, this would have unappealing consequences: it would mean giving up his income and the prestigious writing position that sends him on paid trips to Alabama, an area he claims to be familiar with only through the rather textual examples of "Tobacco Road, some passages in Faulkner, and a few meetings of the Committee for the Defense of Southern Workers."[55]

If one way to work through the logic of *Time* style that situates all writing as work is to extract the writing from the finished product, then another avenue, and the one that ultimately guides *Let Us Now Praise Famous Men*, is to insert text frantically so that the finished product never reaches completion. In the preface, Agee writes, "Ultimately, it is intended that this record and analysis be exhaustive, with no detail, however trivial it may seem, left untouched, no relevancy avoided, which lies within the power of remembrance to maintain, of the intelligence to perceive, and of the spirit to persist in" (x). "The present volume is merely portent and fragment" (xi), the first installment of what he still imagines as a three-volume opus. Ideally, it will not even end there; it will incorporate letters from readers, alternate accounts of tenant life, other journalistic attempts to describe the situation, and anything else that will keep the text from ending. In practice, this encyclopedic aesthetic results in the laboriously intricate descriptions of clothing, furniture (or lack thereof), and worn accouterments in the farmers' houses; these passages bore down to uncover how "each texture in the wood, like those of a bone, is distinct in the eye as a razor: each nail-head is distinct: each seam and split" (142). Rita Barnard characterizes Agee's aesthetic as "the 'anorexic' response to consumer culture" because of its "fascination with the authenticity of scarcity."[56] But *Famous Men*'s form is anything but anorexic; Agee is fascinated by the fact that, when he looks closely, these people are surrounded by an indescribably complex array of things that he simply must describe so as to do them justice. If we stay with Barnard's metaphor of pathologized consumption, then Agee exhibits something much closer to compulsive eating. His method of giving each minute part of every object its due does not erase what Agee calls the "digestion into art" (11), nor does it simply refuse to take part in the consumption-production loop (which would be Barnard's formulation). Instead, Agee takes Time Inc.'s work model to its epistemological limit. If all of his time belongs to his employer and if his job is to write, then everything he experiences must be documented. He transforms productive "workman-ship" into pathological graphomania.

With this methodology, it is conceivable that *Famous Men* could spread out forever by inserting more and more text into the middle, thus remov-ing itself from the market relations of corporate writing by drowning them out with textual noise. The result of this approach is something like an inversion of fractal geometry, in which scalar levels that superficially look the same are actually infinitely inassimilable. He writes, "How am I to speak of you as 'tenant' 'farmers,' as 'representatives' of your 'class,' as social integers in a criminal economy, or as individuals, fathers, wives, sons, daughters, and as my friends and as I 'know' you?" (100). First the common nouns, then knowledge as such become impossibly general. Agee expresses a desire for the historical, personal, and contextual specific-ity that is erased in Time Inc.'s disciplinary and aesthetic model. Yet just as soon as he arrives at this particularity, the sheer existential weight of infinitely regressive singularity falls apart:

> I might suggest, [the text's] structure should be globular: or should be
> eighteen or twenty intersected spheres, the interlockings of bubbles on
> the face of a stream; one of these globes is each of you. . . . We should
> first meditate and establish its ancient, then more recent, its spreaded
> and more local, history and situation: how it is a child of the substance
> and bowels of the stars and of all space: how it is created forth of an

aberration special to one speck and germ and pollen fleck this planet,
this young planet, on that broadblown field.

(101)

Here we see him toggling between the very far and very near in time,
space, and situation. Telling the tale of three families quickly becomes the
mind-numbingly vast project of cataloging the particularity of every atom
in the universe. And even if he could complete this universal encyclope-
dia, the structure is absolutely arbitrary, a jumble of spheres bumping up
against one another that are interlocking *but interchangeable*. Eighteen,
twenty, twenty thousand globules: when forced to organize, we are back
in the realm of representativeness and classification. Even more, Agee
must think analogically to conceive of this particularity: the structure is
arrived at by comparing his subjects to "bubbles on the face of a stream."
He atavistically reimagines the unique humanness of each of the tenant
farmers as surface phenomena of the natural order, undermining any singularity that might be achieved through his endlessly specific descriptions. While he can take pleasure in the solipsistic isolation of nails and
boards, his methodology evaporates any trace of the human; the bubbles
that float on the stream are empty of all but air. What constitutes "the
human," in this context, looks like nothing more than the unacknowl-
edged middle register that exists between Agee's microscopic particularity and cosmic abstraction.

Incorporating the Porch

With this in mind, Agee's attempt to write outside of the Time Inc. model
strangely dovetails with the editorial style he hopes to evade. This happens
in the most basic organization of the text, which repurposes the original
tripartite structure of the magazine in the recurring "On the Porch" sections that provide the nominal beginning, middle, and end of the work.
And while those sections are not exactly "globular," they do exemplify
the book's repetitive attempt to hollow out the limited subjectivity of its
own narrative voice. The "On the Porch" portion serially describes two
people, ostensibly Agee and Evans, laying on the Gudgers' porch and
preparing for sleep. As the house goes silent, the men hear a call and
response between two animals they take to be foxes, whose noises become

a stand-in for the ideal form of Agee's text, "never repeating a pattern, and always with what seemed infallible art . . . the frightening joy of hearing the world talk to itself, and the grief of incommunicability" (468–469). With the appearance of the foxes, Agee's desire for radical, nonrepeating singularity comes together with his desire for a now undisciplined, because "incommunicabl[e]," transmission outside of language. As the foxes take over, they push Agee and Evans so far out of the narrative that they become senseless and inanimate, "left like dim sacks at one side of a stage," as the animals have "what at length turned out to have been the most significant, but most unfathomable, number in the show" (470). Like the unnamed *Time* writer whose point of view is supplanted by the wailing siren and who uses stage directions to organize the Scopes Trial, Agee ends *Famous Men* in an unconscious sack-state. His and Evans's subjectivities are erased from the action; the final line finds them melting into the senselessness of the house as talk "drained rather quickly off into silence . . . until at length we too fell asleep" (470–471).

   Each of the three sections of "On the Porch" expands from the last, reusing the closing words of the previous installment to begin the next, replicating the serial format in which Agee's original report would have been published. The first opens with a description of the Gudgers' house, as it and "all that was in it had now descended deep beneath the gradual spiral it had sunk through; it lay formal under the order of silence" (19). The passage ends with a parenthetical, italicized restatement of the section's title, " *(We lay on the front porch:*" (21), which is picked up and promoted to the diegetical level for the opening of "On the Porch: 2." Then in the second paragraph, it expands: "We lay on the front porch to the left of the hall as you enter" (225). Paralleling the sentence's expansion, the section itself dilates into a long diatribe against journalism, art, science, abstraction, naturalism, realism, and description as such before returning to the porch and foreshadowing the entrance of the foxes: "From these woods a good way out along the hill there now came a sound that was new to us" (253). Just as the second "On the Porch" begins with the last words of the first, "On the Porch: 3" begins with a restatement of the new sound Agee hears. It then redescribes the silence of the opening section before ending at what appears to be the beginning of the first "On the Porch," with everyone asleep and the house standing alone without the intrusion of human consciousness. These sections make the text an endlessly repeating loop, narratively closing off the possibility of reaching completion.

The entirety of "On the Porch" in the published version pushes seventy pages, but it began as a five-line poem in the journal Agee kept after returning to *Fortune* from a vacation with his wife in 1936:

On the porch.

We got back to town late in May.
The winter before.
The shape of the mind.
Home.   Friends.   Back to work.[57]

"The porch" he describes here does not seem to be the Alabama porch he shared with Evans, because the "we" alluded to above is not he and Evans but he and his wife. In fact the biographical content of the last line—"Home.   Friends.   Back to work."—predates the *Fortune* story completely, suggesting that this aesthetic reverie must always return to the ambiguous definition of "work." Though Agee attempts to extricate himself from *Famous Men*'s narrative loop by playing dead and letting the foxes take over, the lesson of "On the Porch" is the translation of his personal writing into the work of *Time* style. The poetry he writes about his vacation comes back to his day job, and the seedling of this poem provides the organizational structure for his prose *Fortune* assignment. But the affiliative pull of Time Inc. goes even deeper: as these five lines expand into the skeleton of *Let Us Now Praise Famous Men*, they also find Agee depersonalizing his own work and giving over authorial control to the "incommunicabl[e]" noise of the world talking to itself. The text's last gesture is to erase its narrator so that, rhetorically, "On the Porch" stands on its own, absent of an individual consciousness, like Eliot's ideally impersonal literature. Authorial impersonality offers an escape hatch from bureaucratic complicity, but it is a strange consolation considering that the very problem of *Time* style begins with the refusal of writerly autonomy. From a certain angle, Agee's formal evacuation of personal voice from the finished product looks surprisingly like what Luce and Hadden expected of their writers all along.

The central contradiction of *Let Us Now Praise Famous Men*, then, is that Agee's version of a liberated modernity—one in which he takes the paycheck of Time Inc. but writes himself out of what that paycheck symbolizes—ends up reenacting the formal, editorial, and political problems he has with his employer. The structure of *Famous Men* creates a closed circuit, removing Agee's complicity with corporate work, but in the process it gives up on the possibility of a nonexploitative mode of representation that might actually do something for the rural sharecroppers. Paula Rabinowitz is correct that at the end of the final "On the Porch," "the movement from the documentary image of the tenants to the narrative of his own subjectivity is complete, and with it, the movement from visual to descriptive, from the people to the self."[58] But if that "subjectivity" and "self" are given over to the incommunicable forces of nature, as they appear to be, then Agee's impersonality is a rather unimaginative answer, really a restatement, of Time Inc.'s desire to write about, then write off, "the people" and the policy issues they present. For Agee, it is better to cordon off the economic question of his own corporate work—and by extension the tenant farmers' lack of access to that system—and approach it as an aesthetic problem, as a crisis of textual rather than political representation. In this way, the fact that Agee's narrative ends up mimicking a depersonalized *Time* style should not be all that surprising. Both are designed to leave things exactly as they are because when faced with the choice between rural poverty and urban, corporate modernity, Agee cannot imagine that the sharecroppers' hell can be any worse than his own. "I could not wish any of any one of them that they should have had the 'advantages' I have had: a Harvard education is by no means an unqualified advantage," he writes late in the text (311). It may not be an unqualified advantage, but it places him in an ideal position to equivocate between two very different types of disenfranchisement.

If *Let Us Now Praise Famous Men*'s periodical prehistory shines light on some formal traces of Agee's anxiety over midcentury corporate work, then its afterlife says something about how that anxiety has become an enormously productive topic in postwar culture. After flopping in 1941 and going out of print for nearly twenty years, *Famous Men* was republished in 1960 on the heels of his Pulitzer Prize–winning *A Death in the Family* (1957) to quite a different response. In the book's postwar resuscitation, we see that Agee's desire for an endlessly proliferating project comes to fruition in a number of ways that will forecast the situation of the next chapter. First, the book actually expands: in the 1960 reprint, Walker Evans doubles the number of photographs from thirty-one to sixty-two, some of which predate his trip with Agee or do not portray Alabama at all; he also writes a memoir about his time with Agee that has been included in every subsequent edition. In Bruce Jackson's formulation, these inclusions "cracked the structure of the book," but they also show "the book really wasn't about that very specific place but rather was about a larger slice of human experience and therefore the expansion was legitimate."[59] The particularity of "the people," it turns out, was never all that important. Along with this literal expansion of *Famous Men*, a recently unearthed copy of the manuscript that *Fortune* rejected was published in book form as *Cotton Tenants: Three Families* (2013), which adds an ur-text to the Agee and Evans canon. It contains neither the recursive self-analysis nor the circular structure of *Famous Men*, and in its relatively stable, ostensibly objective narrative voice it looks far more like a typical piece of journalism than the lore around Time Inc.'s rejection would lead one to expect.

But the text also expands in a more ironic, if only metaphoric, way. As the range of biographies and critical studies of his work attest to, everyone can now claim a piece of what Alan Speigel calls "the legend" of Agee: Catholics and atheists, communists and Jeffersonian democrats, journalists and artists, naturalists and modernists and postmodernists.[60] Also, like a real-life version of George Stroud's boss in *The Big Clock*, Agee is endlessly reintegrated as the content of popular long-form journalistic articles. These treatments of Agee cyclically return to Alabama to keep his report up to date and are always surprised to find that nothing has changed except the residents' attitudes toward journalists. The most elaborate of these re-creations, Dale Maharidge and Michael Williams's Pulitzer Prize–winning *And Their Children After Them* (2008), revisits the same families that Agee and Evans documented and finds them in a remarkably similar economic situation as in 1936. The economic collapse of 2008 has inspired a number of similar excursions, such as Christina Davidson's April 2010 *Atlantic Monthly* essay "Let Us Now Trash Famous Authors." It discusses her "Recession Roadtrip" to Alabama, where she finds herself one of many "like-minded tourists" who want to talk to a real-life "Gudger" about Agee's "timeless and powerful . . . principal theme that material poverty holds no inherent shame." Davis is astonished that the descendants of the three families in *Famous Men* "had tired of journalists, researchers, and filmmakers turning up in Moundville looking for 'Gudgers.'" Finally, even Agee's former employer reassesses its discarded text. In its review of the 1960 edition of *Let Us Now Praise Famous Men*, none other than *Time* claims that the work provided a "sort of readers' underground" outside of mass cultural consumption. As the still-unnamed reviewer concludes his fawning tribute to Agee's individualism, he writes, "Agee steadily retains the artist's supreme gift: he can bring even a reluctant reader into the heart of his own experience."[61] The lesson that these writers learn from Agee's corporate work, then, is to find a form capable of writing oneself out of political responsibility without writing oneself out of a job.

In fact, after hibernating through the Eisenhower administration, Agee's showy antibureaucratic stance and fetishization of particularity fit right in when baby boomers and the New Left make radical individuality the new normal. By the time of *Famous Men*'s republication, when it is reclaimed as a forerunner of the New Journalism, the lessons of David Reisman's *The Lonely Crowd* (1950) and William Whyte's *The Organization Man* (1956) had time to blossom. These works of popular sociology seemed to verify the white-collar worker's growing unease with the conformity of corporate life, and, alongside Sloan Wilson's *The Man in the Grey Flannel Suit* (1955), they offered the nonfictional half of a diptych on the death of the artistic spirit. However, read with an eye toward the changes in corporate culture that were already underway when Wilson's novel and Whyte's study were published, these texts also signal how 1920s artistic individualism will be reinvigorated in the mid-1950s and 1960s in the form of the entrepreneurial spirit. This is the situation Thomas Frank describes in *The Conquest of Cool* (1997), when postwar businesses grew quite adept at combining managerial organization with creative personality, a mixture Agee learned and then replicated in the offices of Time Inc. Employees, not to mention writers, are not tacitly allowed the artist's ennui; their displeasure with institutional order is *expected*, so that "thinking outside the box" can become market "disruption," the most prized term in twenty-first-century business. Whyte's critique of an employee's willingness to sacrifice personal benefit for economic security is especially relevant here both because of its popularity in the early 1950s and because, like *Famous Men*, his study of the "organization man" started as a series of articles in *Fortune*—by now, it should be clear the magazine was quite skilled at packaging critiques of corporate standardization. In fact, Whyte was a managing editor at the magazine when he formulated his hypotheses about the bureaucratization of creativity; that is, he was one of the staffers whose entrepreneurial spirit was supposedly being hampered by institutions like Time Inc. Though his study does not directly mention the working conditions that he faced everyday, it is not hard to imagine him looking out over his desk, seeing a swath of poet-reporters such as MacLeish and Agee, and thinking that something interesting had happened to the patronage of creative work.

The big takeaway of Whyte's study is that individuals' reliance on massive corporations has created an uncritical championing of "the social" over one's own needs, robbing the worker of the "intellectual armor" required to participate fully in society.[62] It might come as a surprise, then, that his great investigation into the dulling of American ingenuity by faith in hierarchy was assigned to him by a manager. As he recounts in "How to Back Into a *Fortune* Story," "Managing Editor Del Paine called" and asked him "to do a story on the current college seniors" at Yale; supposedly "they were the best crop in years—wonderful for business."[63] Whyte, in his interviews, discovered exactly that: they were wonderful for business because they had no real desire to strike out on their own. Instead, "they wanted a storm cellar for the great depression ahead. And so, on the verge of the greatest peacetime boom in history, the class of 1949 girded for the future, looking to big business for security." Whyte contrasts the point of view of these risk-adverse graduates with his own hesitance to embrace the role of company man. Sure, he says, he and all his friends "went with the big organizations but at least we talked individualism in our bull sessions."[64] Like Agee before him, in Whyte we find a staff worker who makes a career out of decrying the indignities of corporate affiliation, and, like Fearing, Whyte's most lasting piece of writing implicitly analyzes the bureaucratic situation that produced it.[65]

The Organization Man, born in the newsroom as a "corporation story," works both inside of and against the influence of Time Inc. While Whyte might not have been conscious of the effect his own institutional surroundings were having on the methodology of his work, he certainly paid attention to the way it influenced how that methodology influenced his writing style. If *Time* style expressed the speed, attention, and sociability of the modern manager, then Whyte's florid prose did not quite fit with the program. He writes that his boss "Herb Solow, who detested ornamentation and the elaborate metaphors and analogies I delighted in, thought my leads were models of bad writing." He confesses, "I was so bad that I was not fired, but kept on as a kind of exhibit," evidencing a different type of writerly discipline than William Gottfried found to be the case.[66] Thus, in the example of Whyte we see an extension of how Agee's attempt to be radically inassimilable into corporate and artistic life becomes a model for bureaucratic individualism both in form and content. *Let Us Now Praise Famous Men* is championed retroactively as the most accomplished version of its genre because of Agee's refusal to kowtow to institutional pressures. Its reclamation ends up describing the postwar moment perfectly because it sidesteps the fact that those very institutions are what initiate his ability to play rebellious.

CHAPTER 4

Our Eliot

Mass Modernism and the American Century

My business is with words; yet the words were beyond my command.
—T. S. ELIOT, 1948 Nobel Prize for Literature Banquet Speech

The Uses of T. S. Eliot

"Has the Reader Any Rights Before the Bar of Literature?" asked the inaugural issue of *Time News-Magazine* in March 1923. It raised the question in response to the recent news that the American literary magazine *The Dial* had awarded T. S. Eliot its second annual prize for outstanding service to letters—and the hefty sum of $2,000 that accompanied it—partially because of *The Waste Land*, which *The Dial* published for the first time in the United States. Instead of directly answering his own rhetorical question about readerly rights, the *Time* reviewer laid out what he sees as the contemporary field of letters: "There is a new kind of literature abroad in the land, whose only obvious fault is that no one can understand it." The broken signal between poet and reader is not an accident, according to *Time*: "It is rumored that The Waste Land was written as a hoax" and that its poet thinks that "lucidity is not part of the auctorial task."[1] What's worse, though, is that the hoaxers are not limited to poets and novelists; they also publish, review, and publicize this new literature. Burton Rascoe at the *New York Tribune*, Edmund Wilson at *Vanity Fair*, and John Middleton Murry at *The Athenaeum* (referred to only as "a British critic") all positively review Eliot's experiment. They legitimize it, they rain down American literary awards on it—they make it circulate.[2]

At the onset of the modern news magazine, then, we find modernism as news. More than this, we find the positive evaluations of modernism from other periodicals reframed as news about the unhealthy state of literary culture. The reviewer, John C. Farrar, was a Yale friend of Henry Luce and Britton Hadden, and he had a personal stake in the success or failure of Eliot's formal innovations. Though he is now remembered more for his outsized influence on American literary production as a publisher, in 1923 Farrar was an up-and-coming poet in his own right. Yale published his first two books of verse, *Forgotten Shrines* (1919) and *Songs for My Parents* (1921), and *Forgotten Shrines* won the second annual Yale Younger Poets Prize. Placing Farrar's Yale prize alongside Eliot's *Dial* prize can help explain the animus behind Farrar's *Time* review, as both poets and their prizes fight for space in "the economy of prestige"[3] as representatives in the struggle between the academic poetry of university presses and the more aggressively experimental work taking place in little magazines. *Forgotten Shrines* displays a formal regularity and pastoral vision of poetry that provides a perfect antipode to Eliot's poem. The book is broken into three sections—"Portraits," "Miscellaneous," and "Stanzas"—and is full of tightly crafted, rhyming stanzaic portraits of rural simplicity such as "A Hill-Side Farmer," "A Hill-Woman," "A Coal-Miner," and "A Barge-Wife," among others. Farrar's poetry, then, devotes itself in subject and theme to folk life, despite its origins and almost exclusive circulation in the highest echelons of the Ivy Tower. He is just as well read and schooled as Eliot, but Farrar's poetry takes the pastoral as its primary touchstone, along with a strict adherence to regular meter and rhyme. *Forgotten Shrines* slightly loosens the formal and thematic reins in the "Miscellaneous" section, though the closing lines of "To an Intellectualist" make it clear that the poet's (relative) stylistic laxity here should not be taken as an endorsement of modern techniques such as *vers libre*, let alone the citational style that Eliot will employ in *The Waste Land*:

go back to your dull books,
And tired, dusty thoughts,
Until, perhaps, some day
A sudden mist will dim your eyes

And there,
Between you and your intellect—
God!⁴

For Farrar, at least, the stakes of what a poet discovers when he gives himself over to feeling rather than intellect is abundantly clear, and dead serious, even if the pathway to this direct communion with God is not.

Despite Farrar's paeans to poor folks, "To an Intellectualist" seems to be splitting hairs between two strands of roundly *un*popular poetry, the academic and avant-garde, both of which circulated in relatively small if overlapping circles in 1923.⁵ In the poem, the clear vision and "dusty thoughts" of the stodgy intellectual stand against the mist-dimmed eyes of the romantic poet, who sees God by shutting down his mind and simply experiencing the world. It's safe to say that, for Farrar, the undertones of the Grail myth in *The Waste Land* did not make up for all the footnotes that Eliot later added into his own version of poetic structure. With this context in mind, we might frame Farrar's denouncement of intellectualist, rather than intuitive, poetry as registering a fear that purposefully difficult poets like Eliot might become, if not accepted, then at least trendy.

As it turns out, he had good reason: Eliot's sense of the poetic had an outsize influence on those that came after him, and Farrar is remembered now almost exclusively for his second career, hinted at in his affiliation with *Time*, as an administrator rather than as an example of in-the-flesh talent. In the 1920s he wrote for and edited the New York–based literary magazine *The Bookman*, contributed film reviews to *Ladies Home Journal*, and edited the "Books" page of *Time* until 1927. After working several years as an editor at the publishing firm Doubleday, he founded his own in 1929, Farrar and Rinehart. Several permutations later it would become Farrar, Straus and Giroux, which in the 1950s, lo and behold, published several of Eliot's books of criticism. Farrar also founded the Breadloaf Writers' Conference in 1926, the self-proclaimed oldest writers' conference in the United States, where he employed Robert Frost, Willa Cather, and Louis Untermeyer, along with FSG authors such as Stephen Vincent Benet and Hervey Allen, to lead summer workshops for a budding generation of novelists and poets. These fledgling authors and poets undoubtedly benefitted from Farrar's deft career as a literary patron, but it is fair to assume they knew *The Waste Land* much better than *Forgotten Shrines*.

Eliot, of course, worked his own day jobs during this period. First in the foreign transactions department of Lloyd's Bank, where according to Aldous Huxley he was "the most bank-clerky of all bank clerks,"[6] and where he stayed—at his desk in a sub-basement, clocking in from 9:15 to 5:30, with two weeks of vacation every year—even after writing *The Waste Land*. Like Farrar, Eliot then went into publishing, working his way up to a director at Faber and Gwyer / Faber and Faber. Despite their similar career arcs, Farrar's devotion to and promotion of traditional poetic and cultural forms looks rather different from Eliot's appeal to "tradition" as found in his early essays. This difference justifies Farrar's dismissal of *The Waste Land*, but it is harder to square with the style of the magazine from which he began his ascent as a teacher and tastemaker.

Farrar's review in *Time*'s very first "Books" section mocks Eliot's experiments in compression as well as those periodicals that have bought into his reworking of poetic voice and form. Yet the parallels between Eliot's approach to poetic compression and *Time*'s own stylistic innovations suggest that there might be institutional, as well as personal, stakes for the magazine when it frames modernist experimentation as being antireader. That's because *Time* was pieced together out of other reading material and, like *The Waste Land*, marked a new experiment in approaching an old form. *Time* quite consciously upended the style of news writing and the organization of editorial work, developing a narrative voice commonly referred to as *Time* style, which attempted to counteract the pressing overabundance of printed information available in the early decades of the twentieth century. Perhaps most obviously, Farrar's review positions *Time* as both an aggregator and arbiter of literary taste. This fits neatly into its self-appointed task of reading and evaluating all the printed material available, then compressing it each week into stylishly worded, easily digestible recaps for "the busy reader." In this way *Time* flattens literary culture into another kind of news: Eliot and his "new kind of literature" are one of many pieces of information that *Time* reads and summarizes so that the magazine's readers need not waste their time.

But *Time*'s appraisal of literary modernism as the new thing implicitly suggests that *Time* stands behind, and hence becomes, the old thing, the thing that the reader already knows and enjoys. This despite the fact that it was the magazine's first issue and despite the possibility that in 1923 this "new kind of literature" was not all that new anymore. If we are to believe Ezra Pound (admittedly a big if), what we now call modernism

had peaked in 1914; Eliot only "added certain complexities."[7] On the fac-
ing page of Farrar's review of *The Waste Land*, *Time* makes this very claim
about visual art. It quotes Clive Bell, "English critic and pontiff of modernism," who argues that cubism "has served its purpose . . . and is in danger
of becoming itself a mere convention."[8] In its early days, *Time* repeatedly used "modernism" and "modernist" in reference to modern visual
art—here, modernism is synonymous with cubism—but rarely to fiction
or poetry. A 1930 article, "Sterile Modernism," assumes the "multitudes
of laymen" are familiar "at least by name with Matisse, Picasso, Zuloaga,
Augustus John, Rockwell Kent," but makes no mention of Joyce, Pound,
Eliot, Ernest Hemingway, or Gertrude Stein, all authors who, by the end
of the 1920s, had come to represent Anglophone literary modernism
in both academic and publishing circles. In fact, for *Time* "modernism"
most frequently designated religious unorthodoxy. In 1923 the magazine
contrasted religious fundamentalists with "Liberals or Modernists, who
believe they are more fundamental than the Fundamentalists." In fact,
its only use of modernism to describe literature before 1937 occurs in a
one-paragraph review of a translation of Guillaume Apollinaire's *The Poet
Assassinated*, which refers to Apollinaire as an "idol of the professional
modernists in literature."[9]

It is only after the fact, in the 1940s, that *Time* finds a stable vocabulary for describing the "new kind of literature," but it is not alone in this.
This is the same period in which American literary critics and poet-scholars
such as Cleanth Brooks and Robert Penn Warren helped consolidate and
define a subset of 1920s art as "modernism" rather than as an array of
loosely connected avant-gardes.[10] Though Eliot's poetry in the 1910s
and 1920s occupies a separate sphere from academic poetry, from the
late 1930s on modernism becomes inextricably linked with the college
English classroom. New Critics like Brooks and Warren would perfect the
methodology of close reading by emphasizing the irony, ambiguity, and
autotelic coherence of poems like *The Waste Land*, rather than its frag-
mentation. In fact, according to some critics from the period, modernism
is synonymous with higher education. "If . . . we are on the hunt for *the*
modern element in modern literature," wrote Lionel Trilling, "we might
want to find it in the susceptibility of modern literature to being made
into an academic subject." Though he believed strongly that modern literature should be taught precisely because of its ability to say something
about the student's contemporary moment, he also found it necessary to

present it in "as *literary* a way as possible": as "a structure of words, in a formal way, with due attention paid to the literal difficulty which marked so many of the works."[11] When Eliot, Joyce, and Proust made their way onto Trilling's literature syllabus at Columbia, even he became something of a formalist.

Modernism's firm canonization in the midcentury university is only half the story, though, as it also gained increasing prominence as an issue of national identity in mass media. Serge Guilbaut has approached modernism's salience during the Cold War in terms of visual art, arguing that the postwar realignment of European political power brought with it a chance for American art dealers and critics to assert themselves. Guilbaut traces, through American journals such as the *Partisan Review* as well as popular magazines, how the political and aesthetic "rebellion of the artists . . . gradually changed its significance until ultimately it came to represent the values of the majority," drifting from the "ideology of the avant-garde" to the "dominant ideology" of "the vital center." In the face of McCarthyism, the hermeneutic difficulty of abstract expressionism and color-field painting (in contrast to Soviet realism) could be watered down to signify "individualism and the willingness to take risks" and "freedom of expression," so that "expressionism stood for the difference between a free society and a totalitarian state." Guilbaut shows just how easily this slide from cutting edge to comfortable middle can be when artistic intentionality is severed from interpretation.[12]

The entrance of modernism into the university signals the end of competition between "academicism and avant-gardism." At roughly the same moment, though, cultural critics attempting to explain the difference between serious art like *The Waste Land* and its commercial opposite establish a different binary: that of avant-garde and kitsch, to paraphrase Clement Greenberg's influential 1939 essay. Though kitsch as of late has experienced a second life in scholarship on twentieth- and twenty-first-century poetry,[13] Dwight Macdonald's correlate term "masscult" has proven the more durable category for American critics contrasting the serious artistic achievements of the twentieth century with the vast amount of dreck that "is imposed from above," "fabricated by technicians hired by businessmen," whose audience consists of "passive consumers, their participation limited to the choice between buying and not buying."[14] However bad masscult may be, though, the more insidious problem for Macdonald is "midcult"; unlike masscult, which makes no pretension of High Culture—"It is not just unsuccessful art. It is non-art. It is even anti-art," writes Macdonald—midcult cannibalizes the look and feel of 1920s artistic experimentation but hollows out the interpretive difficulty. By way of example, Macdonald contrasts the "disciplined, businesslike understatement" in Ernest Hemingway's early story, "The Undefeated," with "the drone of the pastiche parable" in *The Old Man and the Sea*, first published in *Life* in 1952. The latter reeks of the midcult for Macdonald because of its "constant editorializing"; that is, it includes an interpretation of the story and its characters within the story itself, thereby removing any readerly participation. The concluding line of *Old Man*'s opening paragraph—"The sail was patched with flour sacks and, furled, it looked like the flag of permanent defeat"—with its predigested interpretation of the sail's faded glory, epitomizes the tendency. Turning to Thornton Wilder's *Our Town*, Macdonald asserts that the narrator's editorializing about the Old Man and Editor Webb's invocations to the audience are methods of "constructing a social myth, a picture of a golden age that is a paradigm for today," where "the past is veiled by the nostalgic feelings of the present, while the present is softened by being conveyed in terms of a safely remote past."[15]

Macdonald's assessment of the midcult, or middlebrow, toggles between considering it as a structure of social relations and prestige—it confers High Culture on the middle class—and an aesthetic category. That duality continues to guide scholarship on the middlebrow even as critics, seeking to understand how different texts and authors settle into the sediment of literary culture, have been more accepting of the genre than Macdonald.[16] Macdonald's disdain for all commercially minded art has aged rather poorly, but his discussion of the midcult is worth parsing further here for several reasons. First, the essay in which he develops the term was commissioned (but eventually rejected) by the *Saturday Evening Post* as part of its "Adventures of the Mind" series, which also published essays by Clement Greenberg and Randall Jarrell, among other prominent intellectuals. The essay's origin registers how popular magazines and other mass-media outlets were just as interested in "brow theory" as those ostensible outsiders who criticized it. In addition, Macdonald's concept of the middlebrow depends on some pure modernism unsullied by mass culture or its print media. "The special threat of Midcult," he writes, "is that it exploits the discoveries of the avant-garde," and his heroes from the 1920s who used to be above the commercial fray are the ones sponging off their former achievements. The high-water marks of the middlebrow are "the products of lapsed avant-gardists who know how to use the modern idiom in the service of the banal." The late-career novels and poems produced by Hemingway or Archibald MacLeish (another example, for Macdonald, of modernism gone to seed) come with built-in cachet because, no matter how insufferably preinterpreted they are now, "their authors were all expatriates in the 'twenties.'" Yet it is important for Macdonald that this is not a story of selling out for these authors; they seem to lack any knowledge or control over their downward slide into middlebrow cultural consumption. In fact, the category depends on it: "That they are not conscious of any shifting of gears, that they still think of themselves as avant-gardists is just what makes their later works so attractive in a Midcult sense."[17] Macdonald's retroactive separation of modernism from mass culture, his own long career in commercial magazines, and the origin of "Masscult and Midcult" in the same can make his delineation of the middlebrow look more like a new symptom of modernism's life inside mass culture rather than an analysis of it. Which, in some ways, makes Macdonald much like the authors he discusses: rather than decrying careerism or vulgar commercialism, he describes the unconscious seepage of modernist authors and their trademarked formal experimentations out of the coterie and into wider circulation. In short, midcult is what happens when modernism stops being able to control itself.

***

This chapter tracks that loss of control by way of T. S. Eliot's circulation in big magazines, particularly those published by Time Inc. It builds off the groundwork I laid on Time Inc. in chapter 3, particularly how the company imagined the corporate impersonality of its own narrative voice as an antidote to the glut of print media in the 1920s. In a number of ways, they contrast their own experiments during the 1920s to those of Eliot and other modernists as a version of market differentiation. But at the same time that *Time* becomes unprecedentedly popular in the late 1920s—as do *Fortune* and *Life* in the 1930s—modernism succeeds in a different cultural context, primarily the university, which affixes to it a unique readership and niche in periodical culture, one that Time Inc. does not see itself in competition with. This doesn't mean that modernist writers disappeared from the big magazines; to the contrary, the 1940s and 1950s witnessed an explosion of articles about Eliot, Hemingway, Faulkner, Stein, and other American writers from the 1920s. What does disappear, though, is the disapproval. Especially in *Time*, Eliot and modernism transform into ambassadors of American popular culture for Time Inc.'s increasingly international postwar audience. Eliot becomes a symbol of the political and epistemological uncertainties of postwar American cultural expansion as Time Inc. repatriates a version of Eliot's poetry, especially *The Waste Land* and "The Hollow Men," that is not formally opaque and sociopolitically cosmopolitan but instead transparent and realistic— even democratic.

When one is relatively unknown to the general public, as Eliot was in the run-up to the first three publications of *The Waste Land* in 1922 and 1923, controlling one's public image may be laborious, but it is a reasonably well-defined endeavor. However, after the initial spark of infamy inaugurated by the *Dial* prize, it becomes an increasingly attenuated project for Eliot to manage the narratives that circulate about his poetry. Instead of attempting to parse out Eliot's own feelings about mass culture or how magazines affected the production of his literary work, I want to give a genealogy of T. S. Eliot as a mass-cultural artifact; to see how and why the tenor of coverage changes over the interwar and immediate postwar periods; and, finally, to theorize how the popular reading of Eliot presents an alternative version of midcentury modernism, one in which the middlebrow has not diluted modernism so much as modernism has become more concentrated in popular American culture. This change in methodological perspective—from a tight historical focus on scenes of writing in the 1910s and 1920s to an overview of the massification of terms associated with Eliot, and by extension with literary modernism, in big magazines—allows a circulatory reading of Eliot rather than one attuned to literary production. From this perspective, I see a gradual reclamation of Eliot as an American writer and thinker as well as a recasting of the competition between modernist and journalistic practices of the 1920s as paired cultural endeavors in the 1950s. When the big magazines write about Eliot from the 1920s through the 1950s, they also implicitly write about themselves. Though big magazines, most notably *Time* and *Life*, first position their own cultural nationalism against a cosmopolitan Eliot, after World War II they repatriate him as a symbol of American internationalism. The modernist trope of exilic alienation morphs into Time Inc.'s Cold War image of America Everywhere.

In other words, this chapter provides a parallel story to modernism's institutionalization in the university and uncovers a different interpretation of modernist ambiguity, one that existed alongside the interpretation proposed by the New Critics. Tweaking Macdonald's idea of the middlebrow, what follows will theorize an emerging postwar *mass modernism*, where the tropes of modernist exile and alienation become part of U.S. postwar culture. Rather than emphasize how modernism becomes mainstream, then, we'll see how the mainstream becomes modernist. As Macdonald is fully aware, such a situation depends on a general openness to the shock of the avant-garde; unlike the academicism of the 1920s, "which was intransigently opposed to the avant-garde," a new class of cultural consumer "graduated to an appreciation" of it.[18] Especially in the United States, and especially with T. S. Eliot, this constituted modernism's "victory over reigning taste and at the same time an accommodation with the established literary order."[19]

Linking Eliot's poetry to midcentury nationalism rubs against a history of reading Anglo-American modernism in terms of cosmopolitanism, which goes back at least to Delmore Schwartz's "T. S. Eliot as the International Hero" (1945) and plays an integral role in the transatlantic turn in modernist studies. Rebecca Walkowitz's "critical cosmopolitanism" is exemplary here, as it builds bridges between high-modernist and contemporary writers—Conrad to Ishiguro, Woolf to Sebald, Joyce to Rushdie—by way of their engagement with the aesthetics and politics of cosmopolitanism, and in doing so it generates compelling reassessments of modernist aesthetic and political stances while also recalibrating the timeframes by which one defines modernism.[20] Yet it is hard not to see this otherwise powerful reassessment of contemporary writers in light of modernism as, in Jon Wiener's words, forgetting the Cold War, when cosmopolitanism was something of a dirty word among politicians and intellectuals alike.[21] More specifically, this critical stance toward cosmopolitanism makes it hard to see the strange ways that modernism surfaces in the discourse of midcentury American *nationalism*. For instance, Eliot appears on the cover of *Time* in 1950—then the most widely circulated newsmagazine in the world—with an accompanying article about Eliot's boundless popularity. When Eliot won the Nobel Prize for Literature in 1948, an award that is the height of international acclaim, *Time* wrote: "The Twentieth Century needed a poet (at least) to explain it to itself, and a good place for a Twentieth Century poet to be born was St. Louis, Missouri."[22] Even though Eliot had not lived in St. Louis for over forty years—or the United States for over thirty—his intractable "Americanness" remained essential to the interpretation of his contemporary relevance in *Time* and other outlets of mass print culture. The repatriation of Eliot-as-modernism and the exportation of America as world culture were in fact deeply intertwined. These magazines latched on to both Eliot's Midwestern origins and his transnational popularity to present him as a figure of American culture writ large.

The Outside of Modernism

In several publications Lawrence Rainey meticulously works out the facts behind what Farrar and *Time* suspected in 1923; as it turns out, the cards really might have been stacked in Eliot's favor concerning the *Dial* prize. In the process of parsing out the complicated backroom dealings of the poem's American publication, Rainey famously refuses to read the poem, citing his methodology as "the modernist principle of reading" and concluding, "the best reading of a work may, on some occasions, be one that does not read it at all."[23] There is no evidence that the *Dial*'s editors read *The Waste Land* before offering Eliot the prize, and a number of well-placed reviewers and poets presented the poem as a watershed without actually seeing it, let alone studying it. Instead of closely reading *The Waste Land*, Rainey's attentive history of the poem's publication is a close reading of, in his words, "how modernism negotiated its way among the 'contrived corridors' of its own production"—to financial stability and canonical status. The moral of Rainey's narrative is about the puff work associated with *The Waste Land*; long considered by scholars a well-wrought urn, it has now been recast as "the output of a specific marketing-publicity apparatus."

Rainey's investigative work into the "institutions of modernism" has produced an entire subgenre of literary history intent on getting to the bottom of the processes that enshrined modernism as a dominant literary movement.[24] Unlike the New Critics, particularly Cleanth Brooks, who assert that modernist poetry wins out over other contemporary modes because of its inherent aesthetic quality—its ambiguity, paradoxicality, autonomy, and structural integrity—scholars of modernism in the late 1980s began to insist that, in the words of Rainey, the afterlife of a

particular author or work in the critical tradition is subject to "historical contingencies as varied and intricate as those that also informed the
poem's composition."[25] However, from a somewhat bent angle, Rainey's
story about modernism can look like a slightly expanded version of the
New Critics' autonomous texts. In Rainey's account, the autonomous aesthetic object, the *inside* of the poem, is transferred to an insulated coterie
of culturemongers on the outside of it. Pound, Eliot, Gilbert Seldes, and
the other players in Rainey's story have free rein over defining and publicizing their literary endeavors, with little input from or care for the other
writers, magazines, or publishing houses, such as Farrar's, that might want
to define modern literature in a different way. In this way, the self-enclosed
poem of the New Critics transforms into the self-defining literary culture
of the New Modernists.

Contemporary reviews of Eliot's "new kind of literature" share Rainey's
belief that its formal difficulty might hide organizational underhanded-
ness. *Time* fills its "Books" section with questions about the openness of
the literary market and implies that the lack of transparency (in aesthetic
and organizational registers) signifies a threat to American nationality.
One month after its review of *The Waste Land*, the magazine echoed a
"charge" that "has been repeated" against American literature in towns
such as Boston and Chicago: "Is There a 'Literary Dictatorship' in New
York?" Writers in these cities fear being shut out of literary opportunity
by a "semisecret cabal of radical young critics":

> The youthful intelligentsia, occupying strategic positions in the publicity
> section of the literary world as editors and contributors to the "high-
> brow" weeklies, critics of books and drama, colyumnists [*sic*] and readers
> for publishing houses, have combined to form not alone a mutual admi-
> ration society; but also an exclusive literary coterie, admission to which
> is denied candidates who have not the personal friendship of the charter
> members. Only thoroughgoing social radicals are welcome. Clearness
> and cleanness, coupled with a sound belief in American institutions, is a
> fatal bar.[26]

This reaction against a coterie of literary elites certainly does not originate with *Time*, nor does it end in the 1920s. Similar charges are waged
in Harold Stearns's *America and the Young Intellectuals* (1921), Brander
Matthews's 1922 *New York Times Book Review* article about "juvenile

highbrows," and Joel Spingarn's manifesto from the same year, "The Younger Generation," which explains that the new class is a "somewhat narrow and unorganized but very articulate group."[27] A more recent version is Thomas Strychacz's account of the simultaneous professionalization of literature and criticism in the period: specifically, that difficult texts coupled with a new, jargon-filled literary criticism professionalized both literary production and interpretation by keeping out the amateurs. Unlike the article above, which conflates literary experimentation with radical politics, Strychacz exposes the nascent conservatism contained within the will to professionalize. Yet the two early articles in *Time* give us an alternative perspective: they portray modernism from the outside— a tentative and skeptical picture of the literary coterie from the position of those who can only access the modernist prestige system through the cloudy window of what they feel to be inscrutable texts. Thus, the terms of literary exclusion here are a little counterintuitive. *Time*, itself only two months old, does not say the older generation refuses to let them in. Instead, they paint a literary market quietly overrun by a minority of young "highbrow[s]" who are cutting out their forebears and "traditional" younger writers.[28] And when we think about this as the opinion of an organ that will, over the next two decades, become the face of American mass culture, the implications of the terms of the debate take on national significance. As the references to a "semisecret cabal" and a "literary dictatorship" make clear, this new social formation is profoundly undemocratic—and the denial of meritocratic access to the literary field quickly mutates into a charge of un-Americanism. As the article states, "a sound belief in American institutions" ensures one's exclusion from the new world order. "Clearness and cleanness" are "coupled" to American nationality, both in literary production and in the social fields that encompass individual works.

My point here is not to show that the free market of ideas has never actually been all that free, nor is it to mock archly the outrage of a new mass-market periodical that has stumbled upon this hypothesis. Instead, the preceding debate shows how the projection of a meritocratic literary market, and the recognition of the shortcomings of that projection, quickly transforms into a discussion of national character—an American "clearness and cleanness" positioned against its offshore opposite. In a move that may seem strange from our vantage point, which has inherited a vision of Eliot as the embodiment of royalism, classicism, and

Anglo-Catholicism, the article goes on to say that the "social radicals" that can be found walking the halls of *The Dial* and *Vanity Fair* are scheming "to 'put over' T. S. Eliot as the greatest modern American poet" on an innocent reading public.[29] The threat that the "social radicals" and their metonymic leader represent, then, is not only the rise of difficult texts or even that of a literary cosmopolitanism in competition with a nationalist tradition. Instead, the problem is the redefinition of which poetry counts as both legitimately modern and canonically American as well as of the periodical context in which it circulates.

Though Time Inc. magazines have come to be something like the background noise of American popular culture, in 1923 the company found itself in a rather similar situation to T. S. Eliot and other modern authors: attempting to differentiate itself among a field of more established and reputable competitors. Henry Luce and Britton Hadden, the magazine's founders, publishers, and editors-in-chief, represent in their pages a "faith in the things money cannot buy," "respect for old manners," and "interest in the new"—three tenets that could sit comfortably next to Eliot's version of the literary "Tradition," which reads true innovation as consciously speaking to and augmenting the past.[30] Time Inc.'s version of experimentation, then, could very well suffer the same critique that they level against Eliot—and in fact it does, again and again. The inverted sentence structures, chatty tone, and aggressive compression of content and words that define *Time* style were consistently mocked by other publications. Walcott Gibbs's 1936 *New Yorker* profile of Henry Luce, which contains his joke about *Time* style, is not alone in this regard. A longer list would include the 1931 *Harvard Advocate*, edited by James Agee; a similar issue of the University of Washington's magazine; a Naval Academy newspaper article; Hotchkiss's student magazine *Index*; a 1934 White Company (manufacturer of trucks and buses) promotional pamphlet that included the "Truck of the Year"; a Rochester, New York, newspaper; an Edmonton, Alberta, newspaper; and even Henry Luce's own mother, who mocked his magazine's style in a 1926 letter.

In this light, the authors of *Time* had to worry not just about how to interpret Eliot and his new literary movement but that they might be mistaken for a similar group of hoaxers. *Time*'s "organization" becomes a way to tie into the professional-managerial class's desire for specialized knowledge as well as mark itself as the torchbearer for a national American culture—"Curt, Clear, Complete," to quote another *Time* self-description that diametrically opposes the magazine's representation of the "secret cabal" of youthful literati. Just when the new magazine *Time* enters the print ecology hoping to contribute something to American prose, the new kind of literature represented by Eliot's *The Waste Land* starts winning American literary awards and making a name for its own type of experimentation. The magazine marks modernism as simultaneously foreign and meaningless so as to distinguish its own formal experimentation as the rightful descendent of American letters.

Time Inc. places itself as the true innovator of American letters at the same time that it invents a nationalized readership in its own image, on view in a 1924 advertisement, "The Spread of the News-Magazine Idea." It portrays a map of the United States with subscription numbers written over the outline of each state. Making allowances for differences in population between states, the advertisement numerically visualizes its own spread from New York to California, with every corner of the country represented as being full of *Time* readers. From here, one can see the implicit nationalizing project of *Time:* if everyone is reading the same news magazine, and that magazine makes sure that everyone has the time and inclination to read it cover to cover, then readers separated by geographic distance can still occupy and participate in the same informational and textual space. In the publishers' minds, the cover of *Time*'s famous red border becomes a national border as well as a recognizable corporate insignia.

As it becomes the self-styled voice of the nation, *Time* deports Eliot and modernism across the Atlantic. How the magazine does this becomes clearer with the section of Eliot's poem that *Time* reprints in its 1923 review and how it chooses to do so. It excerpts the last eight lines of *The Waste Land* with no attempt to contextualize how they relate to the rest of the poem. If one wants to make Eliot's poetry appear as unintelligible as possible, this final section certainly does the job. Five languages, only three lines in English (one a nursery rhyme, one typographically marked as antique); references to London Bridge and "Le Prince d'Aquitaine"; no discernible meter, rhythm, narrative, or any other organizational logic to provide an interpretive scaffolding. Unlike the poem's opening line "April is the cruelest month," or one of the scenes from "A Game of Chess," or even the typist's tryst with the young man carbuncular, this section is completely dependent on the preceding 425 lines for even the most basic of interpretations. The polylingual section is made even more difficult by the specific typographical appearance of this reproduction. The quoted lines are pushed tightly together, almost bleeding into one another. Also, the font size is noticeably smaller than the rest of the article, making it more difficult to read. The American and British periodical publications in *The Dial* and *Criterion* and the book publication by Boni & Liveright present the lines (mostly) intact, center the text with wide margins, and provide plenty of kerning space between lines, which gives the poem a visual integrity. As Jerome McGann has argued, small-press magazines and vanity book publishers treated the materiality of the page and presentation of the poem as artistic practices that were equal to the content of the words.[31] *Time*'s reprint of these lines, then, shows the darker side of how the space of the page can inflect interpretation. By refusing Eliot even the logic of his line breaks, *Time* takes away the excerpt's basic formal logic. When the magazine quotes and reproduces these lines as representative of Eliot and claims Eliot as representative of "a new kind of literature abroad in the land," it marks both the individual and the artistic movement as examples of a foreign decadence antithetical to a definition of American literature based on "clearness and cleanness." All of these non-English languages crashing against one another becomes indistinguishable from the string of syllables in James Joyce's *Ulysses*, which *Time* describes as composed of "some half million assorted words—many such as are not ordinarily heard in reputable circles—shaken . . . up in a colossal hat, [and] laid . . . end to end."[32] Only now it isn't benignly meaningless: cosmopolitan cross-cultural sampling becomes a politically suspect formal mode.

Though the terms change a little, one can trace this reading of an un-American Eliot in *Time* through the 1939 article "From Tom to T. S.," which takes great pains to mock both Eliot's collegiate affectations and his bourgeois banality. After establishing the bright field of Harvard graduates from which Eliot arose, the magazine writes that his contemporaries in college mockingly "say he was English in everything but accent and citizenship . . . and dressed with the studied carelessness of a future dandy."[33] They cast Eliot as an outlier at Harvard, but not for the usual reasons given in his biographies. His alienation often is attributed to his two-pronged identification with St. Louis and Boston, a simultaneous homesickness for the Mississippi River and northeastern pines—or, in other words, a feeling of permanent exile produced by his identification with two versions of American regionalism.[34] Instead, *Time* characterizes Eliot as an outlier at Harvard because of his European pretensions rather than his Midwestern upbringing. During a visit to Boston, he "seemed to enjoy flaunting his English ways: 'I tend,' said he, 'to fall asleep in club armchairs, but I believe my brain works as well as ever, whatever that is, after I have had my tea.'" Here we find a unique career arc: the dandy turned avant-garde poet turned stodgy bourgeoisie, a character Eliot ironized in his early poetry. On the cusp of World War II, Eliot appeared thoroughly decoupled from the current state or future of an American literature: he "winces at Americanisms" and "admit[s] he had little knowledge of U.S. Poetry or interest in it."[35]

How to Make *The Waste Land* American

So far this story lines up chronologically with how and when Eliot and modernism are usually positioned: 1922 as the *annus mirabilis* and the 1920s as the height of their cultural importance. However, when one looks quantitatively at Eliot's appearance in *Time*, the historical location of his dominance looks a little different.[36] From 1923 to 1960, Eliot is mentioned in 420 articles, but between its first issue in 1923 and 1929, *Time* only mentions him five times, all but ignoring (or forgetting) the colossal threat that Eliot and his ilk posed in the first issue. In fact, Eliot's peak does not occur until after World War II, when between 1950 and 1954 he is mentioned more than one hundred times. In 1950, he appeared in the magazine at least once every two weeks (see figure 4.1).

These numbers come from one magazine, and they could be the statistical idiosyncrasy of looking at a single title. However, in many ways *Time* is *the* magazine of midcentury American culture. During the 1920s and 1930s, Henry Luce had amassed the largest, most profitable print empire in the world while many of the little magazines that helped circulate modernist print culture folded under the financial pressures of the Great Depression.[37] By the 1940s, *Time* and the other Time Inc. publications, especially *Life*, unquestionably stood on top of the American print marketplace. Luce's photo-magazine *Life* was unprecedentedly popular: by the end of its first year in 1937, circulation reached 1.5 million per week—more than triple the first-year circulation of any magazine in American history. In 1942 it was over 4 million, and in 1952 over 5.5 million. A 1938 study concluded that the actual readership of *Life*

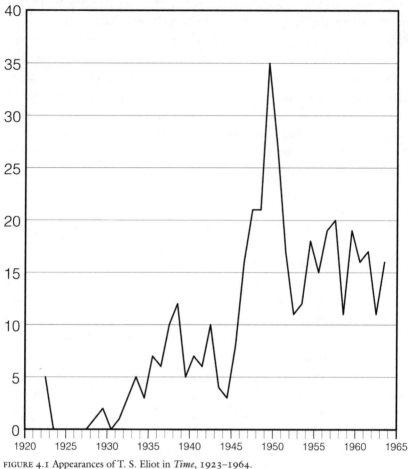

FIGURE 4.1 Appearances of T. S. Eliot in *Time*, 1923–1964.

exceeded 17 million if one counted the "pass-along" readers not represented in raw sales figures.[38]

Eliot's place in literary culture had changed just as drastically as that
of Time Inc. He founded his own English literary magazine, became
a British citizen in 1927, came out as an Anglo-Catholic cultural con-
servative, quit Lloyd's Bank and became an editor at Faber & Faber,
won the Nobel Prize, and wrote several popular and financially successful plays. That is, he migrated from the leading edge to the comfortable
middle of the world of letters, both on the literature syllabus and on the
pages of big magazines. While it shouldn't be a surprise that Eliot was

popular in the 1950s, the substance of that popularity is quite strange. That's because *Time* and *Life*, beginning with a 1948 article about Eliot winning the Nobel Prize, also frame this popularity as an American repatriation. In 1954, T. S. Matthews wrote in *Life* that "In England he seems synthetically American; in America he seems synthetically British." Matthews praises Eliot's postwar work for being "as smooth as a gumdrop," claiming that it "can be taken in with the same lack of effort." Though Eliot addresses serious topics and themes like "the mystery of reality, and loneliness, and love, and paying the piper . . . none of these themes intrudes itself in any painful or even provocative way."[39] However, *Time*'s coverage of the 1948 Nobel Prize makes similar claims about Eliot's prewar poetry, specifically *The Waste Land*, which has "the immediacy of a headline" and "the memorableness of a song that is easy to hum." That is, rather than the hallmark of difficulty, *The Waste Land* now might be mistaken by readers as too clear. However, *Time* saves the poem from oversimplicity: "the 20th Century had no difficulty in recognizing itself" in *The Waste Land*, but it insists that it is "not mere poetic journalism."[40]

The most compact and forceful reinterpretation occurs in March 1950, when Eliot appears on the cover of *Time*.[41] Over the caption "No middle way out of the waste land?" his face looks back at the reader, superimposed over a surrealist landscape of mountains, canyons, and flowing streams (see figure 4.2). Two disembodied arms, one on either side of him, raise a golden cross and a Manhattan glass—a reference to his play *The Cocktail Party* (1949), which had recently premiered on Broadway. Yet the imagery and headlines all allude to *The Waste Land*, linking his reputation in 1950 with the notoriety of his earlier poetry. The reddish-purple landscape seems to reference the nymphless dry stone and red rock of *The Waste Land*, but softened with undulating riverbanks and pastel hills. "What are the roots that clutch, what branches grow / Out of that stony rubbish?" the poem asks, which gets transformed into the hand-trees that stand to the side of Eliot's face.[42] All three (the head and two hands) grow directly out of an otherwise barren landscape; the hands sprout roots, and Eliot's shirt and tie blend seamlessly into the river in the foreground. Knowing Eliot's fondness for Grail myths, it's hard not also to see that cocktail glass and its golden elixir as a chalice, which provides an answer to the poem's question regarding which roots and branches can survive in such an unforgiving climate. The naturalized Christian

FIGURE 4.2 "T. S. Eliot: No middle way out of the waste land?" *Time* (March 6, 1950).
Source: © 1950 Time Inc. Used under license.

iconography suggests that Eliot's theological project is the middle way out the waste land and that *The Waste Land* is the way into Eliot's contemporary American appeal.

The accompanying article erases the cosmopolitan Eliot of the 1920s. It seeks to expand Eliot's influence beyond the "few Americans" who know him only as "an expatriate, an obscurely highbrow poet who wrote an unreadable poem called *The Waste Land*."[43] It recounts how "The American Master" taught his English students to play baseball; emphasizes the "human Mr. Eliot who loves Bourbon and the Bible, both of which he used to keep on his night table (in austerity England he settles for pink gin)"; and quotes Conrad Aiken reminiscing about "tall, dapper Tom Eliot" in his Harvard days, who takes up boxing and "proudly sports a shiner" (23). Baseball, bourbon, the Bible, bloodsport: the article attaches a list of homespun "American" characteristics to someone who voluntarily expatriated thirty years prior. And that, it would seem, is the point: Eliot, as an ambassador of national culture, exports America via his chosen exile and his cultural work, be it the poem or the classroom—or the poem in the classroom.

Time also reinterprets Eliot's poetry as an outgrowth of his native pragmatism. Instead of an avant-garde hoax, *The Waste Land* now evidences the clarity and representativeness of Eliot's social policy. It resembles a "kaleidoscopic mirror held up to the age—a patched mirror which at first seems to reflect only a heap of broken images, but which, to a longer view, blends them into a single bizarre picture, at once as strange and as familiar as one's own face (or one's own city)" (24).[44] The age itself was indecipherable until Eliot integrated it into a unified "tableau of aimlessess" (rather than aimlessness itself) full of "sharp, unsentimental lyricism" that "touched a hidden spring in the century's frightened, shut soul" (24). The article assumes the same permeability between literary and social form as *Time* did in 1923, but now the poem-as-mirror clearly sheds light on complexity rather than muddying a transparent literary market. The poem can now also be read as nationalist despite never actually mentioning the United States.[45] The contemporary barrenness in *The Waste Land*, according to the author, describes a specifically continental problem:

More & more clearly, Eliot saw and recorded the crumbling of European civilization; more & more sharply, his verse photographed the human ruins—an old man waiting for death in a rented house; a tuberculous courtesan calling for lights in decaying Venice; Apeneck Sweeney at an all-night party where, in a soaring descant above the all-erasing vulgarity, "The nightingales are singing near / The Convent of the Sacred Heart . . ."

(25)

European society is collapsing under the weight of its decadence and vulgarity. The problem is neither the mechanical automation of subjectivity (the typist's gramophonic arm) nor the vulgarization of high culture ("O O O O that Shakespeherean rag")—two decline narratives present in *The Waste Land* and often positioned as specifically American failings. Instead, continental culture becomes its own worst enemy, and, for *Time*, an American Eliot chronicles aristocratic demise. In 1923, a "semi-secret cabal" tried to "put over" Eliot as the greatest American poet, but here the literary society he represents looks like an Electoral College: "the lost generation . . . voted Eliot their most representative poet," his old expat coterie retroactively figured as literary democrats (24). Eliot sits at the center of an ascendant democratic impulse thoroughly associated with America and, now, with modernism, too. As T. S. Matthews writes in *Life*, Eliot's poetry works so well "because it put the modern situation into memorable words. Almost anybody who could read it could see and recognize that the waste land is the modern world. Almost anybody, whether he appreciated all the poem's ironies or not, could feel the force of [his] lines."[46]

Eliot's work not only holds a mirror up to his readers but to Time Inc.'s two most successful magazines as well. In this repatriated version of Eliot's poetry, the differences between modernist difficulty and the clarity of *Time* style disappear. The reviewer praises Eliot's "complex thoughts in catchy (if complex) rhythms" and claims that readers "like Eliot for being clever, and at the same time clear," all of which sounds remarkably like the characteristics to which *Time* aspires and diametrically opposed to the unclean and unclear social radicals that typified modernism in the 1920s. Eliot turns out to be engaged in the same project as *Time*: they both describe the contemporary scene in more accurate and efficient language. Modernist poetry no longer withholds meanings or forces the audience to read difficult texts; instead, it is exactly like *Time*, aggregating disparate types of knowledge into a uniform, accessible literary voice.

The Internationalism of American Magazines

Whereas in the 1920s Time Inc. asserted its Americanism by deporting Eliot and his "new kind of literature," its postwar reclamation of Americans abroad suggests a new mission statement: the expansion of American cultural products into other national markets. Henry Luce's "The American Century," published in *Life* in February 1941, lays out the plan. "We Americans are unhappy," it begins. "We are not happy about America. We are not happy about ourselves in relation to America. We are nervous—or gloomy—or apathetic. As we look out at the rest of the world we are confused; we don't know what to do."[47] Luce claims that Americans suffer something like national ennui because they haven't fully acknowledged "their nation became in the 20th Century the most powerful and the most vital nation in the world." Unlike the British, who "are calm in their spirit not because they have nothing to worry about but because they are fighting for their lives," Americans "do not have to face any attack tomorrow or the next day . . . so now all our failures and mistakes hover like birds of ill omen over the White House, over the Capitol dome and over this printed page" (61). The "ill omen" hanging over the page will only recede when the reader realizes that "we are in a war to defend and even to promote, encourage and incite so-called democratic principles throughout the world" (62).

While Luce's essay often, and rightly, is read as an argument against Roosevelt's perceived political and military isolationism (and an argument, paradoxically, for full-on militarization as an antidote to the fear of world war), it ends by stating that the binary between isolation and interventionism is a false one. Global exchange thoroughly colors all aspects of one's daily life, and a general ignorance of this fact, ultimately, underlies American dissatisfaction. Luce's real goal, as the essay closes, entails transforming the basic experience and scale of global connectedness into a specifically American enterprise. "We can make a truly *American* internationalism something as natural to us in our time as the airplane or the radio," writes Luce (64). For him to imagine the proliferation of American influence in terms "as natural to us" as transportation and communication technologies underscores the strangeness of such a statement. Airplanes and radios connect different people in different places, but Luce's vision of an American Century is the world as a singularity, something Marshall

McLuhan describes as the periodical press's presentation of the "the world as one city"—preferably New York.[48]

A cultural version of American internationalism already exists, Luce explains, and he advocates for the political sphere to take advantage of this foothold:

> We shall be amazed to discover that there is already an immense American internationalism. American jazz, Hollywood movies, American slang, American machines and patented products, are in fact the only things that every community in the world, from Zanzibar to Hamburg, recognizes in common. Blindly, unintentionally, accidentally and really in spite of ourselves, we are already a world power in all the trivial ways—in very human ways.
>
> (65)

The soft power of American culture "blindly" seeped over foreign borders, and, Luce surmises, American cultural hegemony is as inevitable as the nation's entry in the war. Exporting a unified American culture becomes the seedbed for what Luce describes as "so-called democratic principles" and the free-market capitalism that will allow his magazine to thrive elsewhere. All it needs is a powerful image and a unified message: "a vision of the 20th Century to which we can and will devote ourselves," one that encapsulates "from Maine to California the blood of purposes and enterprise and high resolve" (65). The best way forward, as he alludes above, is to target the "human" element. Elsewhere he writes, "No idea exists outside a human skull—and no human skull exists without hair and a face and a voice—in fact the flesh and blood attributes of a human personality."[49] And again: "People just aren't interesting in the mass. It's only individuals who are exciting."[50] The most effective way to affix ideas to skulls, as the cover of almost every issue of *Time* and the photographs of every issue in *Life* show, is to focus on a single person who can stand in for everyone else. This fixation on representative individuals leads him to refute internal difference within the United States. Regionalism and provincialism are things of the past: "America is already the intellectual, scientific, and artistic capital of the world. Americans—Midwestern Americans—are today the least provincial people in the world" (65). And for the majority of the 1940s and 1950s, Time Inc. will attach its American internationalism to the "hair and face and voice" of T. S. Eliot, whose literary path from Midwestern provincialism to international renown provides the ideal model for Luce's postwar enterprise.

Eliot's 1948 Nobel lecture provides a clue as to why, of all possible professions, a poet should serve as the figurehead of American internationalism. In it he extols the transnational and utopian possibilities of poetry; one need only look at the Nobel Prize itself, its "function" and "peculiar symbol," to witness the "supra-national value of poetry." It is "the most local of the arts" because it depends on a common language, but this limitation provides a useful filter. Different nations, cultures, and languages interact through the "small minority" who can "acquire an understanding of each other which, however partial, is still essential." When poets and their work circulate among other traditions, they become part of a much longer and geographically wider collaborative project. A poet writes in "the voices of all the poets of other languages who have influenced him . . . and at the same time he himself is speaking to younger poets in other languages, and these poets will convey something of his vision of life and something of the spirit of his people."[51] Pascale Casanova calls this global literary field the "world republic of letters," in which innovation moves from the periphery and semiperiphery to the cultural centers. Eliot's Nobel speech, equally attuned to uneven development, envisions cultural cross-pollination as the height of a positively positioned cosmopolitanism. However, it's only a small step for Luce to turn this statement about poetry's cross-cultural influence into another form of American internationalism. In a less utopian tenor, a poet's transmission of "something of the spirit of his people" into the minds of other types of people is another way of saying that the American Century will be won with hearts and minds.

Like Luce's American internationalism, Eliot's rise also gets framed as unintentional. Anders Osterling's presentation speech claims that Eliot differs from his predecessors in that he accumulates prestige against his will: "His career is remarkable in that, from an extremely exclusive and consciously isolated position, he has gradually come to exercise a very far-reaching influence. At the outset he appeared to address himself to but a small circle of initiates, but this circle slowly widened, without his appearing to will it himself." Osterling offers a somewhat different take on the intentionlessness of modernism, one attuned to the author's inability to restrict an expanding readership rather than to literary form. In fact, it resembles Luce's understanding of cultural circulation more than an account of literary style, and as such it is attuned to the way an author's reputation travels outside of his control. Much like how Luce will refashion Eliot in the 1950s, Osterling's speech emphasizes the interpretive value of reading the poet as straddling American and continental culture. He was "born an American," but "his years of study as a young man at the Sorbonne, at Marburg, and at Oxford, clearly revealed to him that at bottom he felt akin to the historical milieu of the Old World."[52] Like Henry James before him, Eliot is the modern American abroad, the perfect vessel through which to perceive the changing of the cultural guard from "Old" European to "New" American.[53]

Forgetting "Mr. Eliot"

In a *Time* piece from 1960, T. H. White contends Eliot has become one of the "poets unfashionable." "He is out—due for the chop. Eliot is no longer cool. He's square."[54] The rough exterior of Eliot's modernist aesthetic has been smoothed away so that he becomes predictable and approachable. And to be called "square" by an author of young-adult fiction in the pages of *Time* (the blurb that follows this Eliot article carefully dissects the impact of Bob Hope's rheumatoid arthritis on his comedic persona) must be a truly difficult pill to swallow for one of those formerly outrageous "Men of 1914." At this moment, Eliot becomes shorthand for a wide variety of experiences; for example, his poetry introduced *Time*'s coverage of the 1963 Bay of Pigs incident, which begins, "April is the cruelest month breeding / Lilacs out of the dead land" and concludes that Kennedy "could subscribe to the notion of April's cruelty."[55] Or Eliot's poetry can describe the American disposition in general, as it did in *Life*'s 1948 "Report of the Roundtable," in which a handful of prominent intellectuals—Erich Fromm, Stuart Chase, Sidney Hook, Beatrice Gould (the editor of *Ladies Home Journal*), and Henry Luce, among others—came together to discuss "the pursuit of happiness" and young Americans' self-image. As it turned out, young people imagined themselves as descendants of T. S. Eliot. The report cites the case of a Yale student "who described himself as one of T. S. Eliot's 'hollow men' because he did not believe in anything and consequently could find nothing to say."[56] Hugh Kenner begins his book on Eliot with a similar claim about the poet's saturation in midcentury culture: "We may assume that everyone by this time knows who T. S.

Eliot is, that it is no longer necessary to testify to his lucidity." "He commands vast influence," according to Kenner, "partly through moral consistency, partly through inscrutability, partly because, in an academic context, his *prose is so quotable*."[57] Moral consistency and inscrutability, maybe. But he's certainly quotable when someone wants to summarize the anxieties of postwar American life, and not just in the academy.

The ease with which Eliot's name takes on meanings in *Time* and *Life* rubs against the grain of the gravitas in his work and professional carriage. The 1950 *Time* cover story gestures toward this incongruity by, of all things, quoting Eliot's early poetry. It reprints the most famous of Eliot's "Five-Finger Exercises," which begins:

> How unpleasant to meet Mr. Eliot!
> With his features of clerical cut,
> And his brow so grim
> And his mouth so prim
> And his conversation, so nicely
> Restricted to What Precisely
> And If and Perhaps and But.

The levity of this quotation starkly contrasts those enjambed lines from *The Waste Land* that *Time* reprinted in 1923, but this selection also suggests that the site of Eliot's obscurity has shifted. The "exercise" of the poem finds Eliot ironizing his own public image, the interpretive leap from Eliot as author of "Prufrock" to Eliot *as* Prufrock that both enables and limits the poet's reputation. The *Time* author explains that there are "many different Mr Eliots—the shy and the friendly, the sad and the serene." Readers know him as "an expatriate, obscurely highbrow poet who wrote an unreadable poem called *The Waste Land* and fathered a catch-phrase about the world ending not with a bang but a whimper." Now, "thanks to a Broadway hit called *The Cocktail Party* (*Time*, Jan. 30), his name at last was beginning to be more frequently encountered." And in his new popularity, "Mr. Eliot" is only the most recognizable of his many poetic personae.[58] Notice, though, that "his name" comes up and not his poems or his work. Eliot the person has replaced his poems as the uninterpretable artifact. Kenner formulates this point in slightly different terms, defining Eliot's poetic masks—Prufrock in particular—as "a name plus a Voice" or a "pseudo-person"; he writes that Eliot "can give, for readers and interviewers alike, consummate *imitations* of the Archdeacon, the Publisher, the Clubman, the Man of Letters in Europe, the Aged Eagle, the Wag, and the Public-Spirited Citizen. . . . The only role he refuses to play is the Poet."[59] Yet for all the self-fashioning that Kenner lays out, Eliot's "Five-Finger Exercise" reinforces the caricature of Eliot-as-Prufrock rather than deflates it; it finds Eliot playing up his carica- tured persona. The playful Edward Lear style extends the quotation-based composition model that helped create the image of Eliot as a bookish and bloodless killjoy that Farrar lambasted in the first place. Rather than com- posing poetry that footnotes other poets, he quotes his own public image, "Mr. Eliot," who originates at the intersection of Eliot's poetry and his extrapoetic circulation in the printed words of others.

As his biographer Peter Ackroyd summarizes, around this time Eliot "wonder[ed] if his fame meant that his writing had only a contemporary appeal . . . he complained that people now thought of him as a celebrity rather than a poet." In a 1948 *New York Times* interview, Eliot responded to his untethered cultural circulation in the impersonal mood: "one seems to have become a myth, a fabulous creature that doesn't exist." Perhaps Eliot's concern over fading into myth refers to the strange inconsistencies that occur when the words he wrote in the 1920s outlive their original context and override his later work. Or, even worse, that he "had ceased to be a poet and had become an institution."[60]

When Eliot voices his concern over becoming an institution, or of fad- ing into myth, perhaps he refers to the interpretive slippage and strange inconsistencies that can occur when words and symbols outlive the inten- tionality of their original context. He suggests as much in a 1956 lecture, "The Frontiers of Criticism," delivered in front of 14,000 people at the University of Minnesota. It was part of the Gideon D. Seymour Memorial Lecture Series, established to honor a famous Minneapolis journalist by convening once a year to discuss the overlap between journalism and an adjacent discipline. For Eliot, that discipline is literary criticism; two years later Archibald MacLeish will talk about poetry. Ironically, the minority culture that T. S. Eliot, F. R. Leavis, and others hoped to create through their work was unprecedentedly large in the postwar period: Allen Tate described Eliot's crowd as "surely the largest audience ever assembled to hear a discourse on literary criticism."[61] Though Eliot had never been more popular, he opens his talk by lamenting that the last thirty-five years of his work had been reduced to "a few notorious phrases which have had a truly embarrassing success in the world" (7). Even worse, when he tries to recapture the harried tone of an early essay, "The Function of Criticism," Eliot says he "found it impossible to recall to mind the background of my outburst" (3). He was "rather bewildered, wondering what all the fuss was about," because he could "not recall a single book or essay, or the name of a single critic" that inspired the essay, which text or name at the time he apparently found so offensive (3). Part of this calculated befuddlement could very well be an enactment of his earlier piece's success. That is, he cannot remember the names of those functionless critics because he and his followers thoroughly scoured them from the literary field. His own method of reading and writing about literature bludgeoned all contenders into nonexistence; now they neither exist in his mind nor in the archive. While this is at least partially true, this literary cleansing seems also to have taken his own pre-"Function" memory along with it. In fact, he has a hard time remembering anything he wrote or thought. In the space of a single paragraph he says, "I turned to see what I had said," "I must have thought well of this essay ten years later," "I was merely rather bewildered," "I found it impossible to recall," "it would seem that I must have had in mind," "but I cannot recall." He summarizes his self-contextualization by giving up: "I did not, on rereading, find it at all helpful" (3). There's an irony in this obliqueness: even if the audience is familiar with work that made Eliot someone worth listening to, he is unfamiliar with himself. Moreover, Eliot's "embarrassing success" is embarrassing only in so far as it reenacts the very cultural forgetting that he rails against: for half a century he championed an artist's familiarity with Tradition, and when he becomes a tradition he finds himself decoupled from his own history. Eliot is quotable because of his circulation in magazines like *Time* and *Life*, but he fears, perhaps correctly, that no one actually reads or understands him anymore.

What is the point of all this circumlocution? What can we say about this strange scene of T. S. Eliot, the great authority on Culture, standing in the center of a mid-1950s American sports stadium unable to remember exactly what authoritative positions he held in the past that made people want to listen to him? Finally, what connects the inverted trajectories of Eliot's growing public image and more circumscribed readership? To begin his lecture this way bespeaks the peculiar place he occupies at this time—as a poet, a critic, and cultural authority but also as the living embodiment of a newly canonical, newly historical, literary movement.

More than likely, the large crowd was familiar with the Eliot who began gracing the covers of mass-market periodicals in the immediate post-war period. An *Atlantic Monthly* cover from 1951 seems to foreshadow this very scene, overlaying Eliot's head in front of a giant, empty Greek theater—a theater that shares a passing resemblance to the stadium Eliot will fill in a couple years. Eliot seems aware of the fact that his fame might have taken on a ritualistic dimension rather than being tied to his specific literary work; it would explain why he found it necessary to give a short summary of his earlier critical project while mocking its youthful vitriol. His postwar ambition to establish himself as a popular dramatist and to develop what he called a "public speech" could only exacerbate the trend, for it entirely does away with the necessity to read his work at all. It is fairly easy to conjecture what he thought about being more read about—when one of his "few notorious phrases" is quoted out of context in a magazine or newspaper—than studied. Several years before in a cover story for the *University of Chicago Magazine*, he bemoaned the "new illiteracy" that finds an increasing "part of the population which has had its elementary schooling but has become illiterate through lack of occasion to use what it has been taught." The "new phenomenon . . . is aggravated by the effect of radio and cinema, and by the replacement, in popular periodicals, of words by pictures." The media-damaged readers "can be classified by the size of type to which they can give attention." He goes on: "There is a large number who can read a few paragraphs, if the type is large enough. There is an increasing proportion of the population which can only read headlines."[62] For thirty years Eliot had provided the content of those headlines that are ruining the intellectual capacity of readers. And, ironically, the mass media appropriates those "notorious phrases" that bring Eliot such embarrassment as catchphrases to describe the exact social ills that Eliot describes above. In this way, the "frontiers" that he hopes to establish metaphorically cordon off the places that criticism should not tread—that is, his own past—as well as limit the use of his own name and words. Or put another way, he couples the frontiers of criticism to the limits of his own literary reputation.

* * *

What is lost and what is gained by concentrating so closely on what appear to be outlandish readings of Eliot and *The Waste Land* rather than attending to the poem itself? Especially because of the robust critical tradition of not reading the poem that I invoked at the beginning of the chapter, it might be worth pausing to consider what it means, for literary-critical practice, once again not to read the poem. The repercussions of not reading seem especially pressing after uncovering the history of Eliot in the big magazines because in some ways Time Inc.'s inattention to the complexities of *The Waste Land* produced the wholly implausible mid-century Americanization of Eliot and, more broadly, modernism. At the most basic level, Time Inc.'s version of *The Waste Land* fails because casting Eliot as Americanist means reading *The Waste Land* as a failure. That is, reading the poem as simply documenting or reflecting the growing unrest and depravity of modern life ignores the parts of the poem that complicate, question, repair, or even transcend that decline narrative. The most telling single example of this can be found near the poem's conclusion: "These fragments I have shored against my ruins." In 1923 *Time* reproduced this line to exemplify Eliot's opaqueness, but this is the *single line* they should have been able to read: it is the only one of the last eight lines in plain English. To ignore its explicit positioning of the fragments as "shored up" against the encroaching ruins purposefully evades a reading of the poem that accounts for its multifaceted representation of a complex, international culture. In the earliest handwritten draft of the poem, the line read, "These fragments I have spelt into my ruins," indicating a more pessimistic vision of personal and historical collapse: it transcribes, or spells out, the crumbling world.[63] But Eliot immediately changed the line in the typed draft to augment the tone, thus emphasizing an attempt to stave off personal, social, or poetic failure. When *Time* evades the possibility that the poem ends ambivalently rather than in ruin, it ignores the inconvenience of reading closely. More than this, the inattentive reading exemplifies the same evasion of multiplicity that lets *Time* and *Life* ship a monochromatic, undifferentiated version of "The American Century" to an international audience, which also turns out to be a terrible misreading of the cultural moment inside the United States. The GI Bill, an expanding middle class, and the judicial cases leading up to the 1954 Supreme Court decision in *Brown v. Board of Education* are only the tip of the iceberg in what became the era of civil rights and cultural pluralism.

The content of this line—present from the beginning of *Time*'s long and complex relationship with this poem—ensures that *The Waste Land* is not "mere poetic journalism," but for different reasons than *Time* puts forward in 1948. The magazine's understanding of *The Waste Land* as a realistic document of the fall of European civilization presupposes that the "fragments shored against my ruins" do not actually fend off the "falling towers" from Jerusalem to London. Which is true, in that a poem cannot save the world; it can't even keep itself from being read by *Time* as a justification for Cold War expansionism. Yet that doesn't mean Eliot wasn't trying to create some kind of internal unity in *The Waste Land* that might establish, or write into existence, the kind of reader and, by extension, culture he pined for: one that wouldn't need him to explain his own importance, one that would pay attention to the complex relationship between the internal structure of *The Waste Land* and its print circulation outside of Eliot's control—the very complexity that *Time* conveniently overlooks.

CHAPTER 5

Hemingway's Disappearing Style

Paying for *Pilar*

Two years after T. S. Eliot graced the cover of *Time*, his face
wedged between a cross and a cocktail glass and his poetry touted as the
answer to the problems of the American Century, Ernest Hemingway was
given the same honor—only he had to share it with a giant fish. This was
the second time the magazine led with an image of Hemingway. The first,
for the publication of *To Have and Have Not* in 1937, also featured him
fishing, though the accompanying article tempered its praise by claiming that Hemingway's "Spartan books" and masculine strut "had begun
to seem a little dated." "The consensus," the article explains, was that
Hemingway had written himself into a corner, exhausted his material,
and, in short, "was rapidly becoming as dead as his subject matter."[1] In
contrast, the 1952 cover, occasioned by *The Old Man and the Sea*, signaled the revival of Hemingway's reputation after the roundly panned
Across the River and Into the Trees (1950), a novel many read as the cul-
mination of his style's slide into either anachronism or self-parody. It was
not just slack prose that motivated this assessment; critics also felt that
Hemingway's books had begun to repeat or perhaps even cannibalize

themselves and that their main topic was the author's own reputation as an author. As one critic put it, late Hemingway evidenced him "succumbing to his own myth."[2]

Hemingway's reputation, as well as the reputation of his famously terse style, suffers something of a recurring death in the critical literature. There are several possible reasons for this, the most prominent being the sheer quantity of material that he put in circulation during his lifetime. Beginning in the 1930s, his reputation as an author had become inextricable from a more general celebrity status. He had begun selling his outsized personality, what Michael North calls "a signboard for himself," as part and parcel with his literary achievements.[3] As we saw in the previous chapter, in the late 1940s the popular press reverses its consensus about T. S. Eliot's poetry from the 1920s, that his difficult poetry provides a smokescreen for his easily discernible literary motivations, to claim his poetry as straightforward but his persona as inscrutable. Something similar happens to Hemingway in the 1930s, as critics begin to treat the author as interchangeable with the characters in his fiction, with the assumption that Hemingway himself is the unstated subject of all his writing.[4] This transubstantiation of art into biography was exacerbated by his relationships with magazine publishers and editors hoping to take advantage of his name. For example, when Arnold Gingrich decided to complement his successful trade-oriented quarterly magazine *Apparel Arts* with another aimed at consumers, one of the first things he did was buy a boat for Hemingway. It was meant to seal a deal between *Esquire*, as Gingrich's fashion magazine for men would be called, and Hemingway, whom Gingrich had been courting for a series of columns he hoped would set the tone of his new magazine: refined, stylish, evocative of cosmopolitan artistic circles, but with "ample hair on its chest and adequate cojones."[5] When Hemingway explained his fee policy to Gingrich—"Make all commercial magazines pay the top rate they have ever paid anybody. This makes them love and appreciate your stuff and realize what a fine writer you are"—Gingrich obliged.[6] Along with sending Hemingway some of the sample clothes from *Apparel Arts*, Gingrich contributed $3,000 toward the purchase of the *Pilar*, which would provide a vessel on which Hemingway could craft adventures and *Esquire* columns.

At least in part, the gesture sought to reassure *Esquire*'s biggest contributor that it would be around long enough to publish his letters from Cuba and the African savannah. After all, this was the heart of the Great

Depression, which meant Gingrich would be marketing fashionable leisure activities like hunting, shooting, and alpine skiing to untold numbers of the unemployed, who probably would not refer to their copious free time as "leisure." Paying for *Pilar* was a sign of Gingrich's confidence in his ability to bridge the imaginative, if not economic, divide between the upper class and those that aspired to it, but it was something else, too: an investment in Hemingway's brand. It provided his star writer with the means to undertake the deep-sea fishing and adventure stories Gingrich hired him for; likewise, the stories themselves reframed the relatively passive acts of reading and writing as homologous to the masculine efforts that Hemingway took part in. All told, Hemingway contributed twenty-five columns and six short stories to *Esquire* between its first issue and February 1939, which helped bring *Esquire* into the national spotlight as the decade's premier men's magazine. Hemingway's participation assisted Gingrich in attracting an almost entirely male cast of contributors: cultural critics such as H. L. Mencken, George Jean Nathan, and Gilbert Seldes; European intellectuals including Bertrand Russell, Knut Hamsun, and Thomas Mann; and American writers such as John Dos Passos, Ezra Pound, John Steinbeck, Langston Hughes, Chester Himes, and, significantly, F. Scott Fitzgerald, whose three-part series "The Crack-Up," published in the spring of 1936, helped resuscitate Fitzgerald's reputation. Between Hemingway's first column in the fall of 1933 and Fitzgerald's last installment of "The Crack-Up," *Esquire*'s circulation exploded from one hundred thousand to 550,000 copies per month. *Esquire* was the periodical embodiment of fashionable masculine culture, and it struck its mold from Hemingway's reputation in more ways than one. Along with paying top dollar for his contributions, the journal's mascot, "Esky," created by the cartoonist E. Simms Campbell, bore a striking resemblance to the author.[7] Esky, a barrel-chested and mustachioed clay figure, appeared on every cover from the 1930s except the very first, and from month to month he was shown taking part in all those feats of stylized manliness that the magazine valorized: fishing, drinking, hunting, flying a plane, piloting a boat, wooing women. Though Esky was supposed to be the source of the magazine's editorial voice, he only ever appeared in still images, making it hard to hear what, exactly, he had to say. For that, one could simply turn to Hemingway's travel stories and fiction, which represented the same type of experiences depicted on the cover in the terse, descriptive prose that Gingrich hired Hemingway to write.

Esquire ended up with Hemingway and a Hemingwayesque mascot, but the relationship paid dividends for the author, too. It gave him reliable access to one of the largest, most sustained readerships of any American author in the twentieth century. And his willingness to contribute frequently and unashamedly to a big magazine was one source for the critical backlash he experienced in the 1940s.[8] Pairing with *Esquire* alters his reputation, but it also indelibly marks the content of his later fiction. His "Letters from the Gulf Stream" romanticized the quiet integrity of hunters and fishermen whose solitary, expertly executed work was noble and underpaid. The first, "Marlin off the Morro: A Cuban Letter," was sent from Havana and published in the inaugural issue. Along with explaining how to choose a hotel and whether to eat breakfast (there's two schools of thought on the issue, he explains), he introduces Carlos Gutierrez, the old fisherman from whom he "first heard about the big marlin that run off Cuba," and describes the migratory patterns of marlin and how to catch them in extraordinary detail.[9] After incubating for twenty years, Gutierrez would become the model for Santiago, the old man of *The Old Man and the Sea*, which won the Pulitzer Prize for fiction in 1953. When Hemingway won the Nobel Prize for Literature in 1954, the prize committee cited the strength of Hemingway's most recent novel and his impact on "contemporary style."[10]

So *Old Man* originates in an *Esquire* column, the popular context that sullied Hemingway's critical reputation in the first place, and then its publication twenty years later overturns that assessment, both in critical and popular circles. Hemingway called the novel an "epilogue to all his writing and to all he had learned, or tried to learn, while writing and trying to live."[11] For the rest of this chapter, I'd like be hard-headedly literal about the *Old Man* as an epilogue to Hemingway's writing and to "all he had learned"; that is, I take the novel, the last published during his lifetime, as both an endpoint and a self-conscious summary of his biography as a writer. It is hard not to read Santiago's plight—his long dry spell, his noble battle with the big fish, his quiet integrity in defeat—as, on one level, an allegory of Hemingway's own tempestuous career and the mercurial reception of his work. At the same time, *Old Man* exemplifies the final transformation in what we might call the biography of his literary style: the development and codification of verbal patterns and themes that make a sentence recognizable as Hemingway's. By the early 1950s, this was increasingly hard to do. Hemingway's writing was so popular, so abundant, and so often imitated that it became hard to distinguish where the real thing stopped and the "Hemingwayesque"— or the tendency for the "contemporary style" to imitate Hemingway's prose—began. Along with the enormous amount of text published under his own name, there were "bad Hemingway" writing contests that amplified his terseness and bravado into caricature, advertisements written in his style to sell international travel and luxury goods, and any number of literary followers influenced by his early writing. Contemplating the depth and reach of Hemingway's cultural influence, one critic surmises, "it was as if Hemingway's inimitable style had been so long under the gaze that there was little left of it beyond its imitability."[12] This problem reaches a peak in the publication of *Old Man*, or, to be more accurate, in its double publication in *Life* and as a standalone novella by Scribners. Hemingway and his critics imagined these print forms in competition, and the respective affordances of periodicals and books that turn up in the discussions of *Old Man* map onto the competing interpretations of his legacy during the last stage of his working career. And, finally, they highlight the changing relationship between modernism and popular print culture in the 1950s.

Picturing the Old Man

In many ways, the Time Inc.–Hemingway text of *The Old Man and the Sea* provides a perfect capstone to the creeping interpenetration of American modernism and big magazines that my book has been tracking, not least because its immediate popularity served both Hemingway's and Time Inc.'s reputations. The issue of *Life* containing *Old Man* sold 5,318,650 copies within forty-eight hours, and the novel received almost unanimously positive reviews in both mainstream and academic circles. Though it is a critical commonplace to read Hemingway's biography, as well as his bibliography, as following a tragic arc in which celebrity eventually trumps literary craft, the earliest reviews of *Old Man* strike a different note. They emphasize different aspects of the novel's appeal, but there is general consensus that it succeeds because, unlike everything from *To Have and Have Not* to *Across the River*, it does not include Hemingway's public persona. Writing in the *Atlantic*, Edward Weeks hails it as a masterpiece in part because it "suffers not a single intrusion by the author or any personage who might be Hemingway." One critic called it a "short and simple story" and a "parable," another "a natural parable." Some say it has both "romantic and sentimental language"; others praise that it has "everything to do with reality and concreteness."[13] Despite competing reasons for celebrating the novel, none of the early readers ventures the possibility that it is about its author. Instead, early responses interpret the novel as being about itself or, more specifically, about its own form. The calm, undulating descriptions of sea life in *Old Man* mirror their nautical setting and reflect the simplicity of the plot, its telescoping of Santiago's life into a single trip out and back. As one early reviewer summed up, *Old Man* is "at once both superbly placid and superbly exciting, with something of the irresistible sub-surface power that one can always sense beneath the long swells of a calm tropical sea."[14] The narrative form perfectly melds to the plot, both of which hint at but never verbalize the intentions or deeper meanings submerged under Hemingway's prose as it appears on the page.

In this way the early reception of *Old Man* in the back pages of magazines and books pages of newspapers resonates with the evaluative criteria of the New Critics, especially Cleanth Brooks and Robert Penn Warren, whose textbooks *Understanding Poetry* (1938) and *Understanding Fiction* (1943) helped codify a reading method attuned to formal closure and aesthetic unity. This is not to say that periodical pages were full of New Critics; in fact, academia and professors repeatedly turn up in these essays as the exemplars of bad—which is to say biographical—reading. Maybe for good reason: Hemingway's disagreements with Philip Young's and Max Geismer's psychobiographical approaches to his work were well known. Finding correlations between the surface story and deeper meanings, what Hemingway will famously denounce as untoward "symbolysm,"[15] is a task "better left to the professors," according to one reviewer. "The wiser reader," he goes on, "must take it on its own spare terms and let its meanings become as large and as manifold as he can sense them."[16] This insistence at the moment of first publication on the novel's referential self-enclosure, that its meaning must be taken on its own terms, can sound a little odd for a number of reasons: *Old Man*'s long prehistory in magazine columns; its author's devotion to real-life adventures and, at least up until this point, the near conflation of his autobiography and literary work; and its status as a monument of the middlebrow, inaugurated by Dwight Macdonald's critique of its flabby prose and "constant editorializing."[17] Most strikingly, these statements about formal closure surface in popular periodicals, not in academic articles, and their authors are mostly book reviewers and journalists, not professors.

This inversion of the evaluative methods usually associated with academic and journalistic venues looks even odder when one considers that most of these early reviewers first read *Old Man* as "an extra dividend" in *Life* rather than in its book format. *Life* sent out over six hundred review copies in advance of its publication of the novel, and the magazine version came out one week before the Scribners hardcover edition. Many critics timed their reviews to coincide with the *Life* issue rather than the book release, and several even explicitly mention that they are reviewing the *Life* version rather than the Scribners one.[18] For example, *Publisher's Weekly* devotes more space to explaining what *Old Man* does for the relationship between magazine and book readerships than to the novel's content or its relationship to Hemingway's career.

> Here we have a book that has been brought dramatically into focus for millions of readers, the mass-market that ordinarily only a segment of the industry taps. . . . When the final figures are added up, there will, of course, be no way of determining how many more copies of the book would have been sold through bookstores had *Life* not published it first. But we suspect that the Hemingway fans will buy the book anyway and that a good many non-bookbuyers who read the novel in *Life* for 20 cents will even dig down for the $3 the book is worth to preserve for themselves and share with others, in enduring form, a deeply moving experience.[19]

The cost of a magazine versus a book and the relative number of "book-buyers" to nonbookbuyers quickly morphs into a statement of cultural value and preservation. *Old Man*–as-book both indexes and in a material way embodies the "enduring form" of the prose it contains, matching the "deeply moving experience" held between its pages in a way that magazines cannot. To read the novel in *Life* is to take part in the zeitgeist— "for once, the public has been introduced to a book, rather than a book to the public"[20]—but *only* to read it in the *Life* edition is to shirk one's responsibility as literary-cultural archivist and to read it in a form unequal to the content.

Hemingway's stories and novels circulated in magazines throughout his career—*Across the River and Into the Trees* had been serialized in *Collier's* just two years before *Old Man*—and the format specificity of periodical and book informs his early struggles with Max Perkins over censorship in his first novels.[21] Perkins hoped to convince Hemingway that removing the "dirty words" would help him gain a foothold in the literary market without altering the spirit of the text, so he argued that the revision was not really censorship because it was for a magazine serialization and not "the real thing":

> Now this serialization is not the real thing, as the book is. If we considered "A Farewell to Arms" only in respect to its intrinsic quality, and refused to regard the question from any practical point of view, we would all be dead against serialization. It is an incidental and outside thing, and the best reason for it, to my mind, was on account of the practical aspects of it in widening your public, and in making you understandable to a great many more people, and generally in helping you to gain complete recognition. It is in view of all this that I think—as I judge you do by your letter today—that cuts can be philosophically made, for if we can keep people from being diverted from the qualities of the material itself, by words and passages which have on account of *conventions*, an astonishingly exaggerated importance to them, a great thing will have been done.[22]

The magazine version is "an incidental and outside thing" when considering the novel's "intrinsic quality," but it is key to the more "practical aspects" of making Hemingway's work "understandable to a great many more people," whose "conventions" he must meet halfway. This is why it can be chopped up and spread out over a dozen issues of *Scribners* without harming the "material itself," which is somehow both entirely immaterial—it is the idea of the novel rather than its embodiment on the page—and closely aligned with its appearance "as the book," a specific format for publishing that is opposed to the pseudopublication in a periodical.[23]

Selling a novel to *Life*, though, was a special coup both for Hemingway and for the status of modernism in popular culture. Before *Old Man*, the magazine had never published short stories or poetry, let alone a full novel. At the time, it was one of the most widely circulated magazines in the world, part of the largest print-media corporation ever to exist, and its editorial mission was roundly antilinguistic. Its goal was to present a continuous, pictorial experience of the world, making words—especially fictional words—largely obsolete in its representational mission. Despite its lack of literature, though, *Life* often published photo essays about authors, and it took a Hemingwayesque approach to the *mot juste*, claiming "a photograph, supplemented by exactly the *right* words, can often communicate a situation to the reader faster, more accurately and more vividly than any other means."[24] Hemingway frequently showed up as the content of these captioned photographs: he either contributed to or was the subject of at least sixteen *Life* photo essays over the course of his career. The magazine published everything from a review of *The Fifth Column* (1940) to a biographical article by Malcolm Cowley to Hemingway's schmaltzy paean to Marlene Dietrich, "A Tribute to Mamma, from Papa." The tone of such coverage varies widely, but it is at its strangest in a 1941 piece on *For Whom the Bell Tolls* when it attempts to rewrite Hemingway prose as a *Life* photo essay. The article was part of a longer, multipage spread devoted to all things Ernest: his recent marriage to Martha Gellhorn, hunting and bird shooting in Idaho, sales figures for the novel (over four hundred thousand copies in the United States, moving at a rate of fifty thousand copies a week), and, last but certainly not least, "his style, so terse and clean, yet vivid and rich." The absence of a literary-specific modifier before "style" suggests that the marriage, honeymoon in Idaho, and sales figures are just as much a part of Hemingway's style as anything written in his most recent novel. In this vein, the section on *For Whom the Bell Tolls* ends up being more about the production of Paramount Pictures' adaptation than about the novel itself, particularly how the company could translate his prose into images. To get at that problem, the *Life* photographer Robert Capa, the cofounder with Henri Cartier-Bresson of the news photo agency Magnum Photos, followed Hemingway around Spain and photographed places named in the novel. One photo shows Hemingway and Capa sitting together with a copy of *For Whom the Bell Tolls* between them as they choose photographs for the *Life* article. The novel only shows up in the second half of the article: excerpts serve as photo captions for eighteen portraits that attempt "to outline for Paramount the type of country, the type of people" to be found in *For Whom the Bell Tolls*. Hemingway's and Capa's photo text produces something like a storyboard for the studio, complete with headshot-style photographs of locals that could be used to cast the novel's main characters.[25]

The page design here positions Hemingway as something like a coauthor of the photographic version of his novel, and it aligns with John Raeburn's claim that Hemingway "authored" his celebrity as much as his fiction from the 1930s forward in mass print media.[26] For Raeburn, this is endemic of Hemingway's decline into artifice, but it can also look like the natural extension of a feature that was always part of his prose. Hugh Kenner early on claimed that Hemingway's paratactic style was "cinematic in principle," and the best passages stick with the reader primarily because they "would be intelligible and exciting in a sequence of movie shots."[27] *Life*'s coverage, from this perspective, simply makes explicit that Hemingway's best work is a series of screenplays masquerading as novels. However, the article's explicit reference to "his style, so terse and clean, yet vivid and rich," and the felt need to anchor its coverage of film rights and honeymoons with a pictorialization of the novel, also makes it clear that Hemingway's fiction—the settings, verbal patterns, and themes that make it identifiable *as* Hemingway's—is crucial to the interpretation of the larger cultural persona.[28] In the end, *Life* offers a telling caveat to the representational clarity of its photo essay. "Paramount is warned that [the photographs] must be checked against the precision of Hemingway's book," it concludes. While it demotes *For Whom the Bell Tolls* from novel to photo caption, it also suggests Hemingway's "*right* words" are more accurate than any pictures.

This insistence on the supraphotographic quality of Hemingway's prose carries over into *Life*'s presentation of *Old Man*. It assures readers "it will be one of the most *pictorial* experiences" they will ever have, as it "photograph[s] the poignant paintings of the human spirit."[29] Unlike the words in *For Whom the Bell Tolls*, which perfectly capture specific moments of the Spanish Civil War, *Old Man* is a photograph doubly removed from the real world: it captures one medium of representation, painting, in yet another, language. Add to that its rather abstract content, "the human spirit," and it becomes clear that if *Life* is trying to translate Hemingway's late-career prose into its own photojournalistic style, it does so with an enormous amount of strain. The editorial headnote to the *Life* issue containing *Old Man* explains the magazine's decision to break with its photographic journalism by publishing prose fiction: "once in a while words alone can paint pictures in the reader's mind that the camera cannot capture," which, in its conflation of writing and painting, does not so much separate the visual from the literary as cordon off two modes of representation (writing and painting) from a third—the camera. This becomes even more evident with the presentation of *Old Man* in the magazine: it has no photographs, and it unfolds completely uninterrupted by advertisements, photographs, or content breaks (when a magazine continues an article after other, unrelated content). Though *Life* sent Alfred Eisenstaedt to Cuba so that it could have accompanying photographs, it chose not to run them and instead included several simple, hand-drawn illustrations. The only photographs are of Hemingway himself, one on the cover and one directly before the novel begins. The decision to present *Old Man* in *Life* but not to make it look like *Life* was not lost on the reviewers. "*Life* has every reason to be proud of the excellence of its presentation of the novel," one critic wrote, because the layout was "achieved with imagination and good taste, and disappointing only to those who predicted that readers would be put off by having to stalk the story along a circuitous paperchase between columns of advertising."[30] "Imagination and good taste," here, seem to be synonymous with attempting to make the novel look as much like a book shoehorned into the middle of a magazine as possible. The other contents of *Life* do not intrude into the literary space of *Old Man*, allowing it to maintain the illusion of being an aesthetic object unto itself. By borrowing the aesthetic of a book, *Life* brings together the serialized popularity of magazines with the prestige of literature—and because of Hemingway, of a retrofitted version of literary modernism that is defined by its stubborn refusal of informational clarity. Thus, *Old Man* is "an extra dividend" in more ways than one. Most obviously, *Life*'s publication of the novel, and its decision to present it as if it were a book, lend the intellectual heft of literature to the biggest of big magazines. It melds the chosen print media of serious authors and those that write for work, but it does not flatten them. Instead, it insists on an epistemological difference between Hemingway's approach to representation and its own, and then it isolates that difference in its presentation of *Old Man*.

The Myth of Hemingwayese

Of course, other writers of the 1920s, such as T. S. Eliot, surfaced in postwar magazines as the face of a newly domesticated expatriate modernism as well as the vessel through which a postwar "American internationalism" would be exported to an expanding print market. Certainly, by this point in the century, and by this point in these writers' careers, it seems fair to ask if we are still talking about modernism at all. John Dos Passos worked as a war correspondent for *Life* in 1945 and 1946, where he wrote on the effects of the war in the United States and abroad.[31] Gertrude Stein serialized *The Autobiography of Alice B. Toklas* in *The Atlantic* in 1933 and then, after World War II, wrote a German travelogue for *Life*. A callout box assures "Stein's admirers . . . that both her literary style and her shrewd insight have survived the war undamaged," even if Paris, her adopted hometown, did not. Stein's experience talking to the recently defeated German nationals taught her "Germans should learn to be disobedient."[32] These examples attest to the expanded name recognition of modernists, but even more they signal a change in the late style of modernist writers. The straightforward prose of *Old Man*, the verse drama of T. S. Eliot's *The Cocktail Party*, or even Stein's travelogue from Germany are so much less alienating than *In Our Time*, *The Waste Land*, or *Tender Buttons*. Eliot's, Hemingway's, and Stein's midcentury work seems fundamentally different from their 1920s writing. Hemingway accounts for this change by claiming that *Old Man* is free from the "inevitable awkwardness" of his earlier fiction, which recasts the difficulty of his earlier work as unintentional—the growing pains of a young writer unsure of what he wanted of his prose. In this way, the style of and expanded audience for *Old Man* are linked by its very lateness both in Hemingway's individual career and in relation to literary modernism more generally. Along with Eliot, who migrated to the center of mainstream American culture in the late 1940s, these authors underwent what Loren Glass refers to as "the signature career arc" of modernist writers "from the restricted elite audience of urban bohemia and 'little magazines' to the mass audience of the U.S. Middlebrow,"[33] which the combination of *Life* and *The Old Man and the Sea* epitomizes.

Hemingway provides a somewhat unique case of this crossover, if only because his artistic production and print circulation falls into both the camp of poet-reporters and into that of postwar symbols of mainstream culture. Here, it's worth acknowledging that the more obvious place for Hemingway to fit in my book would be much earlier, say, between the chapters on Willa Cather at *McClure's* and W. E. B. Du Bois and Jessie Fauset at *The Crisis* or as prelude to Time Inc.'s perfection of corporate voice. More than any other writer in the first half of the twentieth century— and unlike Cather, Du Bois, Fauset, or Agee—Hemingway's style is commonly attributed to his time as a reporter. As the story goes, Hemingway's short sentences, simple words, and general lack of adjectival fluff can be traced back to his internalization of the now-legendary 110 rules of writing that he encountered in 1917 at the *Kansas City Star* and, later, the forced compression that resulted from sending stories from Europe to the Toronto newsroom via telegraph. These stylistic and technological constraints exert at least as much influence on Hemingway's terseness as does Ezra Pound's imagism.[34] Nesting Hemingway's modernism within the editorial offices of Kansas City and the technological innovations of telegraphed composition would combine my attention to Cather's office life in chapter 1 and Du Bois's interest in printing and copying machines in chapter 2. There's even a preexisting term that alludes to this connection: *cablese*, a language that erupts from the staccato bursts of electronic communication. Hemingway is full of stories about its influence on him. "Cablese," Hemingway apparently told Lincoln Steffens after covering the Genoa Conference, "is a new language."[35] In a 1934 *Esquire* column, "Old Newsman Writes," he contrasts his recent move to the column format, where "columnists were allowed to write about themselves," with his origins as "an old newspaper man" whose work was "copyrighted by Monumental News Service" and whose "output would be something on this order: KEMAL INSWARDS UNBURNED SMYRNA GUILTY GREEKS."[36] Hemingway's prose, here, is modernist insofar as it emerges out of this organizational and technological depersonalization of writing— not just the cable but also the news service, which smothers the reporter's individual voice with its own "monumental" corporate style. Thus, by way of Hemingway's cablese, another strand of modernist experimentation can be traced to innovations in editorial practice.

But that isn't where Hemingway fits in this book because that story falls apart in at least two places. First, the technological shock of the telegraph and commentary on its "new language" was quite old by the 1920s. Steffens's response to Hemingway's thoughts on cablese does not survive, but it is hard to imagine he would agree. Telegraphed news had been around for at least a generation: both Steffens and Willa Cather, who worked together at *McClure's*, got their start in periodicals in the 1890s and had been either writing or receiving cabled stories for at least twenty years. In fact, one of Cather's first jobs when she moved to Pittsburgh from Nebraska in 1896 was at the telegraph desk of the Pittsburgh *Leader*, where she translated the electronic pulses of that "new language" back into newspaper English, twenty years before Hemingway set foot in an editorial office. Second, it is hard to square the developmental narrative of Hemingway's "cablese" with the tone of his early journalism, which is surprisingly chatty. It is certainly possible that examples like the one he invents for *Esquire* might exist somewhere, unattributed to Hemingway and puffed out by a rewrite man. However, the pieces that can be linked to him are already quite puffy in their own right. Take, for instance, the opening of "A Free Shave," from a 1920 issue of the *Toronto Star Weekly*, which repurposes the closing lines of "The Star Spangled Banner" to discuss a haircut: "The true home of the free and the brave is the barber college. Everything is free there. And you have to be brave. If you want to save $5.60 a month on shaves and hair cuts go to the barber college, but take your courage with you."[37] Or this one, which appeared in the *Toronto Star Weekly* a month before Hemingway would begin covering the Genoa Conference, the site of his conversation about cablese with Lincoln Steffens:

> Switzerland is a small, steep country, much more up and down than side-ways, and is all stuck over with large brown hotels built on the cuckoo clock style of architecture. . . . The fashionable hotels of Switzerland are scattered over the country, like bill-boards along the right of way of a railroad and in winter are filled with utterly charming young men, with rolling white sweaters and smoothly brushed hair, who make a good living playing bridge. . . . The Swiss make no distinction between Canadians and citizens of the United States. I wondered about this, and asked a hotelkeeper if he didn't notice any difference between the people from the two countries.
>
> "Monsieur," he said, "Canadians speak English and always stay two days longer at any place than Americans do." So there you are.[38]

The full article dedicates more than six hundred words to the interaction rituals of bridge-playing bachelors, wealthy dowagers, and visiting French aristocrats—content, if not style, more at home in Henry James than in a Nick Adams story. More to the point, neither this nor "A Free Shave" is the kind of material that the *Toronto Daily Star* would have paid three dollars a word to telegraph for the morning edition, and they certainly are not written in the hypercompressed prose that Hemingway remembers adopting for his dispatches. Yet, in the morgue of his early journalism, this is the norm, and for good reason: it was the norm of weekly supplements like the *Toronto Star Weekly*, which were far more like magazines than newspapers. Thus, his breezy prose style suits the place that it was published. Which isn't to say Hemingway was a bad journalist, only that he is not quite the kind of journalist that he is often assumed to be.[39]

Perhaps even more striking than the content of these early articles, though, is the mode of address. They routinely invoke the same collo-quial, inclusive "you" as his *Esquire* columns from the 1930s and, as we'll see later, the advertisements from the 1950s for beer and airlines that will use both Hemingway's face and signature literary style to market an updated version of modernist iconoclasm in magazines like *Life* and *Holiday*. Rather than delimiting the objective world into imagistic bursts of cablese, like he says the "old newsman" does, or even providing some-thing like a precursor to the experiential or immersive New Journalism of the 1960s, which would at crucial moments adopt second-person address, Hemingway's knowing "you" finds his early journalism striking the tone of a casual companion; he's a fellow commuter passing the time, giving you his unbidden opinion. Or, to keep this within the world of print pub-lication, he comes close to the tone of 1920s advertising, which as Roland Marchand has convincingly shown, was beginning to take the form of novelistic "socio-dramas."[40]

According to Arnold Gingrich, modernist prose and modern adver-tising could be quite similar in their approach to verbal compression. Gingrich had some experience connecting the two, because along with being an extraordinarily successful magazine editor, he also saw himself as a misunderstood artist. He wrote several novels while overseeing *Esquire*, the strangest and most interesting being *Cast Down the Laurel* (1935), which was published by Alfred Knopf, the same house that put out the works of Willa Cather, H. L. Mencken, and Jack London. The book's reflexive narrative structure conflates the intellectual work of writing and selling novels by breaking the story into three parts: the first a conversa-tion between a bestselling author and a dejected ad man about an idea for a novel called *Apollo's Young Widow*, the second the aforementioned novel, and the third the ad man's response to the book within the book. The advertising writer positively links the "forty-wording" that he does in the office to the task of writing a novel, chastising his novelist friend for failing to "understand what a luxury it is to be able to rattle along at the rate of a hundred words where one, or none, would do as well." He tells the novelist that the forced compression of advertising writing, where "you spend your days . . . trying to cram everything into forty words—including ten for a long company name and sales and factory address," is the exact kind of lesson in writing that the overly wordy—and extraordinarily successful—novelist needs to regain his bearings.[41]

Gingrich's conjecture that modernist compression might have some affinity with the "forty-wording" of commercial advertising can help highlight two different aspects of Hemingway's relationship to the development of periodical culture. Hemingway is not modern for his terse cablese, but he is modern in the way that magazines are: overabundance. As much as his bibliography can make it look like there are long dry spells, he was prolific and ever-present from his earliest moment on the American literary scene. By the end of 1926, he had published three books in just over a year, all of which were reviewed in major journals. While Leslie Fiedler describes Hemingway's style as "near-silence," in fact, when one looks at his appearances in and contributions to magazines, it's far more accurate to fault him for refusing to keep quiet.[42] Yet he accomplishes this double feat—constantly talking about and publishing accounts of his own terseness—by playing off the changing environment of big magazines, which are becoming more visual, aggressively commercial, and interested in "culture," a category in which literary modernism carves out a major role for itself. If Arnold Gingrich can justify paying Hemingway top dollar and at the same time publish his own fractured, self-reflexive novels about art and homosocial bonding and the market, then maybe we can rethink the decline narrative of midcentury middlebrow as something more akin to mass modernism, where modernist difficulty is no longer difficult because it is everywhere. Perhaps Hemingway's later style is not a slide into the commercial—it was always commercial—but a response to his own widespread influence, maybe even its obviousness. It's not that Hemingway reads like an advertisement (or not just that) but that advertisements read like Hemingway.

The Spread of Hemingwayesque

One of the many fascinating aspects about *The Old Man and the Sea* hinted at in this brief history of its origin in another magazine is how, despite *Life*'s presentation of the novel as a standalone book and critics' assertion that it only refers to itself, its content seems to leak out in all directions. In the run-up to publishing *Old Man*, *Life* ran a series of ads claiming that the novel is "so compellingly good," so full of "wonder and excitement," that it "bursts out of Hemingway's letters to us . . . and fills the mind of everyone who has seen the manuscript." In an accompanying puff piece, Hemingway attests to the quality not just of the novel but also of its appearance in *Life*, which he claims makes him "much happier than to have a Nobel Prize"—a statement that hindsight fills with dramatic irony.[43] *Life* then writes a response to Hemingway's letter, frankly stating that "we are not in the fiction business" but that *Old Man* is part of their mission to "publish a round account of what goes on in the world," urging its audience to find "time to read it during the last long weekend of the summer."[44] In the next issue, Hemingway writes his own introduction to *Old Man*, then writes an explanatory piece in the following issue ensuring that there are no symbols, then he gets a cover story and review in *Time* the next week. If, as Catherine Turner argues, in the 1920s Hemingway's publisher allied the "monotonous style and penchant for profanity" of *The Sun Also Rises* with changing definitions of literary quality based on honesty and authentic experience, then the publication of *Old Man* may serve as signpost for another epoch, one in which modernism has saturated the print market and in which Hemingway's "near-silence" floods out into any number of formats other than his own stories.[45]

The style of the novel expands outward, too. It appears in a Ballantine Ale advertisement that Hemingway endorses in the issue of *Life* immediately after its publication of *Old Man*. Here, next to a photograph of the author, a letter teaches the reader the proper way to drink:

> You have to work hard to deserve to drink it. But I would rather have a bottle of Ballantine Ale than any other drink after fighting a really big fish. . . .
> You are tired all the way through. The fish is landed untouched by sharks and you have a bottle of Ballantine cold in your hand and drink it cool, light, and full-bodied, so it tastes good long after you have swallowed it.[46]

Gingrich's co-location of modernist style and "forty wording" comes full circle here. Most clearly, this ad closes the already miniscule gap between Hemingway's status as a courageous fisherman and his status as a novelist of folksy "big fish" stories. However, the advertisement also points to the uneasy fit between the plot *of* Hemingway writing *Old Man* and the plot actually contained *within* the text. To read the novel as "an allegory of its own history"[47] is to erase the basic tone of the novel as well as the context of its reception. The Ballantine ad, intentionally or not, makes this apparent. That is, while the ad clearly invests in the correspondence between Santiago's plight in the novel and Hemingway's adventures on *Pilar*, it also differentiates Hemingway from his fictional character. Unlike Santiago, who returns home with a moral victory (but not a material one) over the sharks, in the advertisement Papa brings the marlin in "untouched." And with this, the ad's recasting of *Old Man* as self-referential allegory ends up undercutting itself. For the allegory to work—Santiago as author, fish as novel, etc.—*Old Man* could be a symbol of courage and stamina, but it could not also exist as an intact piece of successful writing. Santiago arrives back on shore with a carcass: if he's an author, he does not reel in a pristine novel. Or, if the fish is supposed to be the novel, then *Old Man* is a totem of failed work. It broadcasts Hemingway's inability to snag a fully realized, aesthetically pleasing, *and* financially successful novel.

Old Man is not alone among Hemingway's novels to receive this reworking by other print genres. A 1950 *Time* article, "'Hemingway Is Bitter About Nobody'—But His Colonel Is," consists of a series of questions the magazine posed to the writer about the tepid critical response to the recently serialized *Across the River and Into the Trees.* The Hemingway questionnaire was almost a genre of its own by this point, with *Partisan Review*, the *New York Review of Books*, the *New York Tribune, transition*, an earlier *Time* article, and the *Saturday Review*, among others, making a game out of asking Hemingway questions about his writing and the world at large. Hemingway agreed to this specific interview, according to the article, on the condition that *Time* prints his response, which he cabled from Cuba, "in full or not at all"—a point he takes care to mention multiple times, along with explicitly putting a figure on the twenty-five dollars he spent sending the telegram. Throughout he refers to himself in the third person, as "Hemingway," and organizes his letter in the terse "cablese" of a news report. He begins by laying out his bodily ailments as well as his bona fides as a world traveler attuned to the terminological differences that characterize America and Europe:

> Hemingway was ill with erysipelas, streptococcus, staphylococcus, and anthrax infections in Cortina d'Ampezzo and in hospital in Padova. English spelling Padua. Received 13 million units of penicillin and 3,000,000 more later in Cortina.

His credo is to write as well as he can about things that he knows and feels deeply about. . . . The novel was written in Cortina d'Ampezzo; at Finca Vigia, San Francisco de Paula, Cuba; and in Paris and Venice.

It is the best novel that Hemingway can write, and he has tried to make a distillation in it of what he knows about the above subjects ["love, death, happiness, and sorrow," and "the city of Venice and the Veneto"] plus one other subject, which is war.[48]

So many unnecessary verbs and conjunctions make it difficult to take seriously either the time or fiscal constraints of this telegram. The small bits of terseness ("English spelling Padua") and the attention to the costly transmission of information are done more to acknowledge Hemingway's own reputation for directness than because of necessity, and they only highlight the effort exerted to make this read like "Hemingway style." He is hamming it up for an audience attuned to his monosyllabic stories, not trying to save their time and money. The litany of subjects that he claims to address in *Across the River* (with the supplemental "plus one") and the exotic locations where he composed it successfully evoke the experiences of a world traveler, but they also suggest that Hemingway's "distillation" of the scattered themes and places into a unified whole in *Across the River* did not quite achieve its stated goal. Hemingway's prose has always been characterized by its paratactic leveling of sensation, but in the above passage there is a connection between his hypermasculine body and literary corpus: just as his body ails, the prose of *Across the River* (as well as the telegram) slackens and loses focus, too. This reflexive connection becomes clearer about halfway through the article, when Hemingway explicitly takes on the awkwardness of his cablese. "H. believes he did a marvelous job in organizing the invasion, if he was actually the man who organized it. H. means Hemingway, which I am tired of writing, and *he* in the above sentence means Eisenhower. . . . In the last war, Hemingway, a word I'm getting sick of, was at sea on various projects . . ." (107). Toward the end he begins calling himself "Hemingstein" and alternating between the third-person and first-person plural: "About what he will concede [on the quality of *Across the River*]: we concede nothing, and what we take we hold" (108). When asked elsewhere about the influence of his most recent novels, he responded, "Hemingway influence only a certain clarification of the language which is now in the public domain."[49] However, in Hemingway's claim about the reach of his own style, the referent is unclear: is it the "language" or the "Hemingway influence" that exists in the public domain?

The marker of what constitutes the "Hemingway influence" has passed from a specific body of texts to a general style of writing and, lastly, to a general set of tropes and themes associated with the writer. For example, a 1956 Pan American World Airways ad in *Holiday* not only shows a picture of him; it also mimics the paratactic sentence structures found in his novels and interviews: "After the old Key West-Miami-Havana-Bahamas early days, there was the Pacific when you took a day to Midway—another to Wake—one more to Guam—one to Manila—and Hongkong." The syntactical juxtaposition of place names mirrors the iterative path of the modernist exile, and it lets the reader follow in Hemingway's hardscrabble journey from America to the Far East. "Flying in China you had to sweat out many things," the advertisement informs the reader, but the one thing "you" don't have to worry about is getting to Europe safely and cheaply. The headline of the two-page advertisement explicitly situates the postwar reader as a descendent of Hemingway's Parisian past, stating that now any American can and should lay claim to the Lost Generation's legacy. "*Ernest Hemingway says*: Each generation of Americans has to *Re-Discover* Europe . . . Why? Because you'll see your own country's destiny more clearly if you spend your next vacation abroad."[50] The advertisement expands the range of what constitutes Hemingway's influence to a cluster of topics: the glory of the "early days," transnational travel, and the place of the United States in the world. Each of these concerns formerly marked Hemingway as exceptional in some way, but now they are normalized as the general experience of postwar American culture. Everyone now feels like an outsider or at least wants to have the option of self-exile—and cheap intercontinental transportation has made that dream possible. Both the Grand Tour and Caribbean adventure have descended from the rarified air of Boston Brahmins and bohemian writers and settled in the middle of an audience of popular magazines. It is now a national duty to take part in "your own country's destiny" by spending time abroad: the middle class now models itself on the style of modernism.

What is intriguing about the reduction of Hemingway's fiction to memoir and of Hemingway the novelist into Hemingway the celebrity is that there is something compellingly literary about its articulation in the pages of big magazines. Consider several instances of just how pervasive—but also vague—discussions of Hemingway's style were in describing a wider cultural experience in the 1950s. And not just in advertisements but in Hemingway's own comments. In a 1954 *Time* article he exhorted the importance of style:

> "The right way to do it—style—is not an idle concept," he says. "It is simply the way to get done what is supposed to be done. The fact that the right way also looks beautiful when it's done is just incidental."
>
> This feeling about style, perhaps more than anything else, has always been Hemingway's credo—whether it concerned the right way to kill a bull, track a wildebeest, serve Valpolicella or blow up a bridge. And it was usually the redeeming feature and ultimate triumph of his characters: they might die, but they died with style.[51]

Style as the "right way" to do something—anything, it seems—but also "simply the way to get done what is supposed to be done." "Hemingway's credo," as the article calls it, applies equally to his own actions and those of the characters in his texts. The result is that Hemingway transforms into a literary character himself. As one reviewer put it, "From Paris bistros to Chicago saloons, he is known as a character—not the sallow, writing type with an indoor soul" but the kind of person other people want to imitate.[52] In one of the first extended biographical treatments of Hemingway, Malcolm Cowley marvels at how anyone who spends any time around him "starts speaking in Hemingway's style" and that his greatest contribution is that he "gave the young people attitudes to strike and patterns of conduct to follow."[53] In all of this, literary style expands outside of its original print form—a magazine story or a book—and into other cultural registers: advertisements, of course, but also more generally an ethos, a way of carrying oneself. This slow slide of Hemingway's style off the page offers a different path to popularity than the antiliterary decline narrative so often presented, as it isn't the absence of the literary but instead its spread into all aspects of his "influence." Hemingway is a character born out of his fiction, and the affectless monotone that characterizes Hemingway's fiction—but not his journalism and nonfiction writing—becomes a widely circulating cultural style.

As the peculiarities of Hemingway's prose begin to move out of his novels and into any number of other types of communication that no longer depend upon an actual Hemingway text, it can begin to feel like his literary style is at once everywhere and nowhere. Compare Cowley's vision of total cultural saturation with his later description of Hemingway's place in the canon, "Mr. Papa and the Parricides" (1967). The essay, first published in *Esquire*, offers something like a literature review of popular treatments of Hemingway, and it fears that no one actually reads the modernists, especially Hemingway, anymore. It tracks a gradual slimming down of what should be considered the author's greatest hits. Quoting passages from Leslie Fiedler, Stanley Edgar Hyman, Dwight Macdonald, John Thompson, and Vance Bourjaily, Cowley finds that since Hemingway's death the critical consensus keeps pushing more and more of his work out of circulation every year. First, Cowley says, Hemingway was admired for everything up to *For Whom the Bell Tolls*, then it was everything up to *The Green Hills of Africa*, then it was *The Sun Also Rises* and all of the short stories, then the novels are chopped all together. "The fact is Hemingway is a short-story writer and not a novelist," he quotes from Dwight Macdonald. "In a novel he gets lost, wandering aimlessly in a circle as lost people are said to do, and the alive parts are really short stories."[54] Cowley realized just how dire the situation had become when he, along with a number of other critics, began putting together an anthology of American literature. As the group began discussing which Hemingway to include, Cowley relays a fellow anthologizer's argument that they should "omit any reference to his novels" at all, focusing just on his stories. Over the course of the conversation, the group narrows even that criteria, referencing only "Hemingway's two or three best stories." Then they winnow the ever-shrinking list down to a single example, "Big Two-Hearted River," which encapsulates all of Hemingway's strongest features. Cowley, flummoxed, follows this out to its logical conclusion: "The next step would be to chip that story down to a single paragraph, presented by critics as the only true essence of his work, from which they could infer the rest of it much in the fashion that paleontologists reconstruct the skeleton of an extinct animal from a single bone" (25). "Does nothing survive of the work but a few short stories? Why not toss them out with the novels and finally reduce the Hemingway canon to a blank page?" he concludes (32). Ever mindful of his literary generation's legacy, he predicts all of modernism being put out to pasture. "Of course," he reasons, "the ultimate goal of the operation is the whole age group of which Hemingway was a member": Faulkner, Fitzgerald, Dos Passos, and Wolfe are all named as examples. Without buying into the Freudian, or maybe more accurately, Bloomian overtones of Cowley's grand theory of generational slaughter—he calls it "the ritual murder of the literary fathers"—this article still indexes a feeling in the 1960s that something has irrevocably changed in Hemingway's and modernism's literary standings. Within ten years of *Old Man* in *Life* and Hemingway's Nobel, and less than fifteen years after Cowley himself wrote that the entire nation was enraptured with "the Hemingway style," it can now feel like the actual fiction that evidences that style is disappearing.

The Surface of the Sea

What we are faced with, then, if we can keep this double picture of Hemingway Everywhere and Hemingway Nowhere in mind, is a situation in which modernism as a cultural signifier is so widely recognized that it is almost too obvious, and no one feels the need actually to read it. Rather than being cordoned off on the periphery of both literary and popular cultures, traveling through coterie circles in little magazines, modernism is now common, available to anyone with twenty cents and access to a newsstand. Hemingway seems to have anticipated this very moment of critical winnowing, though not with quite the same emphasis. In a letter from 1933, Hemingway explained that during his lifetime a writer is judged by the sum total and average of his work but that after he died only the best mattered.[55] In fact, the simultaneous outward expansion of the reading public's knowledge of modernism and disappearance of actual texts can look inevitable from the point of view of Hemingway's own philosophy of composition. It is exactly how he describes the logic of the "iceberg theory" when he explains how he wrote *The Old Man and the Sea*:

> [The novel] could have been over a thousand pages long and had every character in the village in it and all the processes of how they made their living, were born, educated, bore children etc. That is done excellently and well by other writers. In writing you are limited by what has already been done satisfactorily. So I have tried to learn to do something else. First I have tried to eliminate everything unnecessary to conveying experience to the reader so that after he or she has read something it will become a part of his or her experience and seem actually to have happened. This is very hard to do and I've worked at it very hard. . . .
>
> I've seen the marlin mate and know about that. So I leave that out. I've seen a school (or pod) of more than fifty sperm whales in that same

stretch of water and once harpooned one nearly sixty feet in length and lost him. So I left that out. All the stories I know from the fishing village I leave out. But the knowledge is what makes the underwater part of the iceberg.[56]

He describes a gradual shuttling of what one "knows" about the subject from the inside to the outside of the text, or from the surface of the page to below it, "the underwater part." Once he has seen or experienced something, it no longer has a place in the novel. Because both the reader and writer know what has been "done excellently and well by other writers," his own writing is limited to that which has not been accomplished or known before. Of course, he intends for these limitations to apply to the writer, who "should know too much"[57] about the subject so that the inevitable excisions do not leave any holes. But Hemingway intended his simple and straight style to stand up to multiple readings; he claims to have read *Old Man* "over 200 times, and everytime it does something to me."[58] So we also might imagine a hypothetical version of the iceberg theory that applies not just to the writer but to the reader, too—not just to literary production but also to reception. As the story begins "conveying experience to the reader," as it becomes "a part of his or her experience and seem actually to have happened," the text's shuttling of "the knowledge" it contains inevitably changes the text itself. As more of the narrative innovations contained in the story move from "unknown" to "known," the content would be continuously emptied out.

The possibility of an all-encompassing readerly knowledge that would disperse the particulars of a text into the cultural "sub-surface" is hinted at not just in how *Old Man* travels outside of its own pages but also in the various identifications made in the novel between Santiago and his environment. Santiago is constantly trying, and failing to find, symbols that can make sense of what is happening below the surface of the world he inhabits. Throughout the story he is characterized by his knowledge of the sea and his acclimation to its patterns, but he repeatedly encounters phenomena that he doesn't know how to interpret. He is confused by the general movement of fish around his boat: "They are working far out and fast. Everything that shows on the surface today travels very fast and to the north-east. Can that be the time of day? Or is it some sign of weather that I do not know?" As the old man fishes—"that which I was born for," he says—he contemplates the same problems of surface and depth that readers of the story also face: how to make sense of what is going on below from the signs that are visible above the water. And the problem seems to be, both for the fisherman and the reader, that it's hard to tell where the surface gives way to something else. Just below his description of "everything that shows on the surface," he makes it clear that "surface" is a tricky thing to define: "The sea was very dark and the light made prisms in the water. The myriad flecks of plankton were annulled now by the high sun and it was only the great deep prisms in the blue water that the old man saw now with his lines going straight down into the water that was a mile deep."[59] The light is "in" the water, not "on" it; the "great deep prisms" seem to be both inside and on top of the ocean; his fishing lines, which also correspond to the repeated references to the lines on his face, distend from the boat through the surface to "a mile deep." This single passage, which is not remarkable or particularly different from the rest of the novel, pushes against the idea that there is a knowable surface that can be separated out from beneath and above. The exposed part of the iceberg, the part that we don't know yet, constantly keeps moving.

Not only this, but the surfaces described in the text seem endlessly to feed back into their surroundings, so that the difference between above, on, in, or below becomes less and less familiar. In other sections of the novel, this takes on an added interpretive weight because everything is described as exactly like everything else. The old man is repeatedly compared to the sea, to the fish, to the sharks, to an older version of the young boy, to the sky, and, like the lines that both cross his face and travel down into the water, to the tools of his trade. The "Hemingway style" of *Old Man* is one he says he "had been working for all [his] life,"[60] and what that seems to entail is a representational world so flat and homogenous that characters, objects, and landscape all dissolve into one another. In this way, it perfectly recreates what had been happening to his reputation since the 1930s. *Old Man* may be a booklike material artifact in the middle of *Life*, a totem to literary permanence in the center of mass print culture, but the "Hemingway influence" has also spread out over the cultural landscape, effacing the distinctions that previously marked Hemingway as unique.

If this seems a strange proposition, consider how Hemingway treats a similar kind of literary departicularization in "The Snows of Kilimanjaro," which first appeared in *Esquire* in 1936. The narrator, a mildly successful writer who nevertheless sees himself as a failure, laments "all the stories that he meant to write" but never had the chance. The story cuts between his present situation, where he slowly succumbs to gangrene on an African safari, and italicized memories of his youth in bohemian Paris, witnessing the Greco-Turkish War, and visiting Constantinople. These are the previously untold stories that he should have devoted himself to, and he imagines how he would write it all down: "There wasn't time, of course, although it seemed as though it telescoped so that you might put it all into one paragraph if you could get it right."[61] The well-lived life reworked as a well-written story can and should be reduced to a couple sentences, according to Harry. And even though Hemingway devotes one of his longest pieces of magazine fiction to Harry's lyrical remembrances and regrets—which could sound a lot like Hemingway's own: "he had never written of Paris!" Harry thinks to himself—in the story world none of it actually gets recorded. His wife cannot take dictation, so his one great paragraph dies with him. That the paragraph remains unknown is a minor tragedy, but if placed in the context of the iceberg theory, then to record it would have been redundant anyway: Harry already knew it, so he didn't need to write it down. In this way, the paragraph's lack of transcription and circulation is also presented, allegorically, as a moral triumph, as the one piece of artistry that cannot become common knowledge. As Harry's disembodied consciousness looks down at its dying body on the mountain, the blinding white snow at the top of Kilimanjaro, like the sheet of paper that Harry left storyless, remains pure and chaste. More than that, the totalizing view from the top of the mountain, where Harry can place his tragedy in perspective, is only available in his hallucination after he stops worrying about writing it down and fades completely out of existence. Even that single, telescoped paragraph proves too much information to share.

The problem with the reader-centered version of the iceberg theory, in which the known part of a story would eventually recede into the unseen portions of the iceberg, is that the published story, in its very status as a published story, ossifies and cannot change in the same way as Harry's projected writing or Hemingway's twenty-year run-up to *Old Man*. But Hemingway does come close to projecting a situation in which it could. This happens during a little-known legal skirmish with *Esquire* in 1958. The fight entailed three stories that Hemingway published in *Esquire* in the 1930s, all of which were set during the Spanish Civil War and thematically linked via references to Chicote's Café. Arnold Gingrich was compiling an anthology of *Esquire* pieces, to be called *The Armchair* *Esquire* (1958), and, as he had reprint rights for the stories, he planned to include them in the anthology. Hemingway objected to this reprinting, and the briefing that Hemingway's lawyer submitted as part of his injunction makes it clear that the inside of literary texts, under certain pressures, are malleable. "The passage of time can affect the writings of authors either favorably or unfavorably," the document asserts. Hemingway's politics in the 1930s are the primary issue; the three stories are quite openly pro-Loyalist, which he feels makes for less-than-convincing literature outside of their original time period. However, he also attributes their ephemerality to their medium of publication. "Sometimes I correct a story forty or fifty times," he explains. "I don't consider something published unless it is in a book. . . . When I looked over those *Esquire* stories I told myself, 'I can write better than that!'"[62] What "better" means is condensation. Only "The Butterfly and the Tank" survives the transition from *Esquire* the magazine to *The Armchair* Esquire book, an excision that puts Hemingway in the same camp as those that Cowley despises for pruning his corpus of the works that are not absolutely necessary.

* * *

To focus solely on Hemingway's slow fade into the cultural ether would miss how magazines like *Esquire*, *Time*, and *Life* questioned their own staying power in the 1950s, as the media culture around them drastically shifted toward the television. When Gingrich reworks old *Esquire* material into book form in the 1950s, he implicitly registers how much the division of labor between print formats had changed since Arthur Kimball explained the respective roles of newspapers, magazines, and books in 1900.[63] Gingrich's preface to *The Armchair* Esquire invokes the fear that the big magazine, which can at the same time be stylistically unique and commercially successful, is on the wane.

> American magazines, like American automobiles, seem to be increasingly characterized by their resemblances rather than their differences. Looking at the older examples, you may feel inclined to say, "They don't build 'em like that any more." But don't forget, what you're looking at today is the survivor. The overwhelming success of a few makers, of magazines as well as automobiles, results in an increasing conformism to success patterns,

and a resultant killing off of the hindmost. The off beat, the irregular, the unorthodox, seem to be acquiring an unenviable scarcity value.[64]

Gingrich attributes the stylistic conformity of midcentury magazines to "success patterns," but something else was "killing off the hindmost" of periodicals, too. In 1948, when T. S. Eliot won the Nobel, less than 1 percent of American households owned televisions. When Hemingway wins in 1954, over 50 percent do, and by 1958, when *The Armchair Esquire* is published, that number is over 80 percent. Print had always competed with other media, especially film and radio. And Time Inc.'s newsreel business, as well as the use of the telegraph to dispatch quickly stories from the field to the editorial office, show that these other media could supplement just as much as impede upon print's efficacy in reaching an audience. However, publishers, writers, and cultural critics see television as a completely different beast. Unlike film, it moved into people's houses, occupying the domestic space that books and magazines formally dominated. Radios could live in the home, too, but they lacked the visual possibilities of print. Television was capable of showing moving pictures and, maybe worst of all, it had the potential always to be on. Though it would be decades until local stations actually developed round-the-clock programming, the low hum of electronic communication had no maximum page count and no monthly, weekly, or even daily lag between event and coverage. By the mid-1960s, *Look*, *Holiday*, and many other popular magazines closed up shop; even *Life* would fall in 1973.

The rise of television changes the relationship between modernist writers and American mass-market magazines, particularly the place of big magazines at the center of American mass culture.[65] Yet there is a more subtle change that happens, too, as postwar novelists deeply indebted to modernist experimentation come under the purview of the newly shrunken magazines. For example, Ralph Ellison's *Invisible Man* (1952), which won the National Book Award in the same year that *Old Man* won the Pulitzer Prize, showed up in *Life* alongside *Old Man*, but it was represented in a much different style. The August 25 issue of *Life* contained an advertisement for Hemingway's novel, which would appear in the next issue, but it displayed far more prominently a photo essay inspired by Ellison's novel by Gordon Parks, *Life*'s first African American photographer, titled "The Man Becomes Invisible." Parks' photo essay gives the reader Ellison's *Invisible Man* "translated into picture," a project resembling that of Capa's treatment of *For Whom the Bell Tolls*.[66] But the visual enactment of that translation is far more arresting: a man emerging from a sewer cover, his face submerged below the pavement; an extreme closeup of an eye floating in a mason jar, with the background blurred in harsh chiaroscuro; a man in shirtsleeves sitting in a chair between two turntables, surrounded by light bulbs that resemble a circuit board, with the New York skyline superimposed above it. Parks's photographs imitate the disjointed plot of *Invisible Man*, much like Capa's photographs took for granted the primacy of Hemingway's words. But unlike Capa's clearly photographed faces, framed like Hollywood headshots, or even Alfred Eisenstadt's photo of Hemingway for *Old Man*, Parks either obstructs or blurs the faces in his photographs, undermining *Life*'s visual style and its mission of clearly representing the world. Parks would also contribute the photos for Hemingway's "Paris Sketches" in 1964, creating another link, however tentative, between Ellison's and Hemingway's visual presentation in the magazines. The presence of Ellison's first novel in the pages of *Life* alongside one of Hemingway's last, and the African American photographer Gordon Parks as a mediator between the two, can help attune us to the overlap between an increasingly normalized modernism of the 1920s and the invigorating literary experiments that it influenced but that also will supersede it. While the title of Park's photo essay, "A Man Becomes Invisible," works in a number of ways, perhaps the most subtle, and certainly the farthest afield of the actual content of his remarkable photographs, is the disappearing Hemingway in the back pages of this issue.

Keeping the big magazine's recession in the late 1950s in mind could help us make sense of a novel such as Robert Coover's *The Public Burning* (1970), which declares the magazine *Time* to be poet laureate of the United States. It also provides capsule biographies of Time Inc., the media corporation, and *Time* and *Life* magazines, as if they were characters in the novel, much like the biographies of famous Americans in John Dos Passos's *U.S.A.* trilogy. We could also turn to Norman Mailer's *The Armies of the Night* (1968), his endlessly self-referential diptych on the 1967 march on the Pentagon. Mailer, who perhaps takes the Hemingway model of self-advertisement further than anyone else, begins his foray into literary nonfiction by quoting *Time*'s coverage of his own drunken speech at the Ambassador Theater that began the surreal political theater that ends with a group of protestors attempting to levitate the Pentagon. "Now may we leave *Time* in order to find out what happened," he begins, incorporating the empty center of *Time* style into his own account.[67] In the twenty-first century, it would be hard to imagine anyone claiming that a single periodical is so well known and culturally important that it could serve as the national representative of letters or could justify being included at the beginning of an experimental novel. However, in the middle decades of the twentieth century Coover grew up learning about Hemingway and Eliot in *Time*, and Mailer was just as much a journalist for new hybrids of the big and little magazines like *Rolling Stone* as he was as a novelist. When Coover and Mailer flatten the character of *Time* into their experimental novels, they also look back, perhaps nostalgically, to a moment when mass culture could convincingly be conceived of as a primarily print-based enterprise—and one that could be metonymically represented by a single, all-encompassing title.

Working from Home

Journalistically speaking . . .
—DAVID FOSTER WALLACE, "Federer Both Flesh and Not"

T HIS BOOK HAS MADE A CASE FOR THE CENTRALITY OF
journalism—its office cultures, professional protocols, and print
media—in the development and reception of literary modernism in the United States over the first half of the twentieth century. It
has tracked the two fields' codependence from the migration of the
staff system out of the newspapers and into muckraking magazines like
McClure's, where Willa Cather reimagined artistic production as editorial
effacement, to *Life*'s publication of Ernest Hemingway's *The Old Man
and the Sea*, where the style of the little magazine amplified into mass
modernism, on the one hand, and the big magazines reimagined themselves as a modernist form, on the other.

Mass modernism as an actual social condition may initially seem far-
fetched, yet this seems to be the situation that Chad Harbach has in mind
in his recent campus novel *The Art of Fielding* (2011), when the character Guert Affenlight offers an impromptu cultural history of postwar ano-
mie. Affenlight, a Melville scholar–cum–college president, comes up with
his idea while watching the Westish College Harpooners baseball team,
particularly the shortstop, Henry Skrimshander. Henry is on the verge
of setting a record for most games without an error when he contracts

what baseball players call "the yips": he can no longer complete mindless, routine tasks like throwing the ball to first base. As Affenlight surveys the baseball diamond, pondering Henry's problem, he offers something like a trickle-down theory of modernist influence. Wondering where exactly it all went wrong, for Henry and everyone else, he thinks:

> Nineteen seventy-three. In the public imagination it was as fraught a year as you could name: Watergate, *Roe v. Wade*, withdrawal from Vietnam. *Gravity's Rainbow*. Was it also the year that Prufrockian paralysis went mainstream—the year it entered baseball? It made sense that a psychic condition sensed by artists of one generation—the Modernists of the First World War—would take a while to reveal itself through the population. And if that psychic condition happened to be a profound failure of confidence in the significance of individual human action, then the condition became an epidemic when it entered the realm of utmost confidence in the same: the realm of professional sports. In fact, that might make for a workable definition of the postmodernist era: an era when even the athletes were anguished Modernists, in which case the American postmodern began in spring 1973, when a pitcher named Steve Blass lost his arm.
>   *Do I dare, and do I dare?*[1]

According to the novel, Henry's yips are a symptom of modernism's spread into the general population, and it offers the baseball player Steve Blass as patient zero for the epidemic. After forty years of increasing exposure, "Prufrockian paralysis," the repetitive and obsessional self-questioning epitomized by *"Do I dare, and do I dare?"* becomes the default position of modern life: "even the athletes," Affenlight thinks. If nothing else this certainly provides a sense of teleology to the twentieth century, and, ever the Melvillean, Affenlight looks for a cosmic connection between T. S. Eliot's poetry, Vietnam, *Gravity's Rainbow*, the cultural revolutions of the 1970s, and the unlucky fall into self-reflexivity of his college's shortstop. The theory of cultural change he arrives at is mostly a thematic reading of modernism, which is surprising not only because it claims that twentieth-century American culture should be read through a modernist poem but also because it ignores the academic emphasis on literary form, on difficulty, that "Prufrock"'s author helped inaugurate and that guided so much scholarship over the same period that Affenlight surveys. In fact,

Affenlight's thematic understanding of Eliot's real significance—that he accurately describes an affective position that was once restricted to a small group of expatriates but that eventually spreads to the general American population—sounds similar to the reading of Eliot provided by Henry Luce and *Time* magazine after World War II: modernist irony reread as American realism.

The vehicle of Eliot's cultural saturation remains unclear in the above passage, as the "psychic condition" of modernism is said to "reveal itself." And while in some ways it befits Eliot and "Prufrock" for the novel to imagine mass modernism happening of its own accord—Ezra Pound famously told Harriet Monroe that Eliot "has actually trained himself AND modernized himself ON HIS OWN"—I have been keying into the big magazines' role in that process.[2] The primary culprits in recent histories of postwar literature, however, have been universities like the one that employs Affenlight, where literature departments schooled undergraduates, including student-athletes like Henry, on the finer points of Eliot and Joyce. In the college classroom, the counterpublic sphere of the expatriate avant-garde normalized into what Mark McGurl convincingly calls institutionalized modernism, which takes "the product of urban coteries, circulating in the tiny sphere of little magazines," and relocates them "helpfully on the syllabus as objects of study."[3] This transformation is one part of "the program era," which takes the creative-writing program as exemplary of postwar fiction's combination of individual ingenuity and systematic discipline. The establishment and extraordinary proliferation of these programs allowed a growing number of poet-professors and writers in residence to find employment and instruct students on how to internalize a formalist version of modernism and then replicate its attention to craft in their own writing.

In many ways *The Art of Fielding* can look like the "program novel" par excellence: Harbach began it as part of his MFA degree at the University of Virginia; it takes place on a college campus, with the competitive camaraderie of the baseball team standing in for the writing seminar; and it bears the mark of self-reflexivity endemic to institutionalized modernism by incorporating a baseball self-help manual also called *The Art of Fielding* into its plot. With this ammunition, *The Art of Fielding*'s none-too-subtle analogy between athletic performance and artistic practice—Harbach considers "athletes as artists of a pretty serious variety" who, like novelists, exert "the dedication to produce that grace"[4]—slides over into allegory:

Henry's Prufrockian paralysis is also Harbach's, who spent ten years rewriting the manuscript before finally getting an agent then a publisher to invest in it. Thus, alongside Affenlight's bit of armchair cultural history (presented by Harbach with the straightest of faces), Harbach's and Henry's shared plight looks like McGurl's university-sponsored institutionalized modernism in a dark mirror, where a generation learns the pathologies of modernism without inheriting the fringe benefits of elevated taste or cultural prestige. The Art of Fielding's plot-driven and character-based narrative form, along with its embrace of Americana, might be seen as pushing back against the assumption that literary innovation means formal difficulty. After all, if mass modernism really is so readily available, then realism might now be the difficult genre to make sense of.

Harbach's other work, though, in the magazines, helps provide another context for The Art of Fielding's interest in the slow creep of modernism, one that points to some of the contemporary implications for thinking about modernism and mass print culture together. After attending Harvard and moving to New York, he cofounded a contrarian magazine, n+1, modeled on forebears like The Baffler and The Partisan Review. Though not a big magazine by any stretch of the imagination, its existence is predicated on the history of and current state of periodical culture. Even though a manifesto against exercise was the most widely read essay in n+1's first issue, published in the summer of 2004, the more representative content was a number of "state-of-the-field" articles on magazines: a thinkpiece on the postmodern neoconservatism of The Weekly Standard, a critique of The New Republic's staid literary taste and regressive politics, and two articles on the author Dave Eggers and his San Francisco–based magazines McSweeney's and The Believer. The editors at n+1 called out Eggers and the "Eggersards" for believing that they could save print from the digital world by combining overt sentimentality with a nostalgia for "an era when ink-fingered printers actually set metal type."[5] It's hard not to see n+1 as invested in the same sincere revival of print culture as McSweeney's and The Believer, even if its editors do so with more attention to intellectual history than page design; for example, the final words of the first issue are "say what you mean," and Harbach's coeditor Marc Grief claims that the journal's end goal is "creating a long print archive in an era of the short sound bite."[6]

This consciously new magazine dedicated to resuscitating an older era of periodicals, fiction, and print culture more generally is the institutional space that Harbach occupied while revising and rerevising *The Art of Fielding*. Thus, the novel's obvious callbacks to nineteenth-century narrative genres—its regionalism, its family plot, its obsession with Melville—might be seen as an extension of *n+1*'s twin missions of saving intellectual inquiry from insulation in the academy and helping longform narrative prose fend off the Internet. Harbach seems to think that, right now, the novel is a more capable venue than a magazine for disseminating that worldview, because *The Art of Fielding*'s user-friendly form and recognizably all-American themes actively try to bring those topics to a larger reading base than the intentionally small community of *n+1*. It is the opposite attitude toward the potential audiences of journalism and literature held by early writers such as Cather, Du Bois, and Agee as well as that of more recent novelist-reporters such as David Foster Wallace. In fact, given Harbach's public ardor for Wallace—his sole contribution to the first issue of *n+1* is forthrightly titled "David Foster Wallace!"—his double life as a populist novel writer and little-magazine worker can look like an inversion of Wallace's career, which toggled between that of an aggressively difficult novelist and an extraordinarily lucid journalist for periodicals such as *Harper's* and the *New York Times*.

Granted, referring to an editor of *n+1* as a little-magazine *worker* might be a misnomer. Harbach and his fellow editors "spent six months working full-time, or close to full-time for free," and early on their complimentary office space in Brooklyn was taken away and given to paying customers.[7] Unlike James Agee, Kenneth Fearing, and Dwight Macdonald, whose salaried work at big magazines made them unsure of what to call their personal writing, Harbach and his colleagues could not exactly call their editorial work a job because they did not get paid for it. Harbach, for example, eked out enough money to pay his bills by temping at law offices. It's a much different experience of writing and work than that presented in the former *Newsweek* editor Michael M. Hastings's posthumous novel, *The Last Magazine* (2014), whose protagonist makes it clear early on that "I make more working at *The Magazine* than writing a memoir about working for a newsmagazine." Along with serving as a minimally fictionalized expose of the big-magazine newsroom circa 2002, Hastings's novel is also something of a digital-age kunstlerroman, telling in miniature the drastic changes to both the work life of writers and the office life of a big magazine that is in the process of realizing its own mortality. Hastings narrates the travails of an aspiring journalist, also named Michael Hastings, as he rises from unpaid intern to temporary hire at a large news weekly that faces increasing pressure from news and culture websites, such as Wretched.com, which hires the fictional Hastings as a pseudonymously credited weekend editor. The reason for the fake name—and at least part of the reason why Hastings did not publish the highly autobiographical novel during his lifetime—is made explicit in a disclaimer on the book's first page: "My magazine has a policy, a little item in the fifty-seven-page Human Resources manual called the 'outside activities clause.' It prevents employees from publishing journalism without the magazine's permission. That could apply to writing books like this one. So I want to say right now: This is fiction, it's all made up."[8] Hastings's assurance that his fiction is a categorically different kind of writing than what he does for *Newsweek* has a clear legal bent here, but it offers a contemporary version of the modernist anxiety about the generic implications of magazine work.

The source of that anxiety, though, appears to be on the way out, even if a new one is replacing it. As the title of *The Last Magazine* boldly asserts, the institutions that created and enforced those policies for their poet-reporters do not hold sway like they did before. When Hastings writes, "maybe the genre is corporate *betrayal*," it is unclear whether he refers to his own tell-all or the ensuing layoffs. Hastings's own employer, *Newsweek*, announced in 2012 that it would stop print publication and make deep cuts to its editorial staff. In early 2013, TimeWarner spun off its print holdings, *Time* and *Life* among them, along with $1.3 billion of debt, into a standalone company called, with plenty of historical irony, Time Inc. These are only the largest examples of the sea change that mass-market periodicals experienced when the first generation of news-aggregation websites such as *The Huffington Post* began to take up more of the market share. These corporate-scale changes have affected the experience of editors and writers, of course: for example, Michael Massing begins his study of contemporary journalist practice by recounting the coerced retirement of Steven Greenhouse, a longtime labor reporter at the *New York Times*, which he and others interpreted as a bellwether of the "fear and insecurity that has gripped traditional news organizations in the digital era." In surveying the "impact that technology has had on the actual practice of journalism," Massing finds that "the distinctive properties of the internet—speed, immediacy, interactivity, boundless capacity, global reach—provide tremendous new opportunities for the gathering an presentation of news and information," even if the content of that medium has not delivered on its capabilities.[9]

The fictional Michael M. Hastings's precarious professional positions, first at a print-based news weekly and then at a culture website, offer an example of how the uneasy state of contemporary magazines, printed and digital, impacts the employment opportunities for writers. Instead of the staff system's shared office spaces and generous paychecks, Hastings describes a piecemeal collection of one-off contributions by moonlighters and part-timers—some of which are paid, some not. While Hastings's novel primarily has been discussed in terms of the barely concealed media personalities that fill out its character list, the more interesting aspect of it for me is how it depicts the casualization of labor as fundamental to both journalistic and literary culture. Though the dissolution of steady, salaried employment goes by many names—the *Harvard Business Review* has called it the freelance economy, workforce casualization, and the rise of the supertemp—it seems telling that a journalist has coined the most prevalent term: the gig economy. Tina Brown, a former editor of *Vanity Fair* and founder and editor of the news website *The Daily Beast*, uses the term to describe a situation newly common among her highly educated, upper-middle-class, white-collar acquaintances who make ends meet by way of "free-floating projects, consultancies, and part-time bits and pieces." At first, Brown says, people acted as if the "flexibility" and "freedom" were the antidote to the bureaucracy and repetitiveness of full-time work, the same wide-open space for the entrepreneurial spirit that William H. Whyte pined for in *The Organization Man*. "Twelve months later," Brown says, "nobody bothers with that cover story anymore. Everyone knows what it actually feels like, this penny-ante slog of working three times as hard for the same amount of money (if you're lucky)."[10]

The local effect of the gig economy on would-be writers is the world that informs Hastings's novel and Harbach's magazine work, though it is perhaps best described in Colson Whitehead's *John Henry Days* (2001), which is deeply concerned with how work has changed over the course of the twentieth century. Whitehead's protagonist, the freelance journalist J. Sutter, starts his career as an unpaid intern at an ironically "downright corporate" alternative weekly, which bears a striking resemblance to *The Village Voice*, where Whitehead worked as a pop-culture critic in the early 1990s before becoming a novelist.[11] However, Sutter is now one of a group of "junketeers," journalists who travel the country at the bequest

of advertising and public-relations firms and, only as a secondary motivation, write up the events for a seemingly endless number of magazines and
weekly newspaper supplements. The novel begins as the junketeers land in
Talcott, West Virginia, to cover the first annual John Henry Days festival,
a celebration of the American folk hero inspired by the announcement
of an official John Henry postage stamp, which the town also hopes will
pump tourist dollars into the dead local economy. Sutter has convinced
a new travel website to buy his story, and as the other junketeers discuss
whom they might sell their work to, the narrator considers how their precarious employment produces a certain foxhole mentality:

> They encounter each other on the newsstands, they chafe against one an-
> other in the contributors' notes of glossy magazines, but primarily they
> meet like this, on the eve of war, hungry, sniffing comps and gratis, these
> things like smoke from a freebie battlefield on the other side of morning.
> At stake: the primal American right of free speech, the freedom, without
> fear of censor, to beguile, confuse and otherwise distract the people into
> plodding obeisance of pop. Their ideals: the holy inviolability of the re-
> ceipt, two dollars a word, travel expenses. The junketeers are soldiers, and
> they hail each other.[12]

There is a link being made between the forgotten wage slavery that
underwrites the legend of John Henry—he is "testament to the strength
of the human spirit," as one character puts it, rather than a casualty of
atrocious working conditions—and the intensification of hyperbolic, sen-
timentalized reporting that comes with battling your ex-colleagues for
assignments. Without romanticizing the heyday of mass print culture,
we can read the junketeers' cynicism and sensationalism as symptoms of
what Daniel Pink calls "free agent nation," with writers encountering one
another in print, rather than in person, and fighting for reasonable pay-
by-word rates.[13]

Cutting back and forth in time between John Henry's hammer swing-
ing and J. Sutter's hack writing, Whitehead's novel sets up a comparison
between the unique indignities of industrial and postindustrial labor. One
of Sutter's fellow junketeers makes this explicit, highlighting "the industrial age–information age angle" of the John Henry Days festival, which
advertises Henry's courageous stand against mechanization—his folk-
hero status rests on winning a race against a steam-powered drill, only to

collapse and die shortly after—by way of the immaterial labor of the culture industry.[14] What's more striking than the novel's moralistic critique of consumer culture and "the plodding obeisance of pop," though, is how presciently it ties the narrative form of new media with writers' working conditions. After nearly choking to death during the buffet dinner of the festival's opening ceremonies, Sutter muses on the extraordinarily lax protocols of his profession:

> He figures he'll write the piece in the airport on Sunday and email it to the editor at the website. A bloodless edit will follow, emails lob back and forth, and one day an electronic burp with his byline will float up into the web morass, a little bubble of content he will never see. Fart in a bathtub. The new innovation of the internet, its expansion of the already deep abstraction of his job, appeals to him. He files and a check arrives. . . . He gets assignments. He is a successful freelancer.[15]

Sutter is depersonalized from the "little bubble of content" that he produces for the travel website, but in a quite different way than staff-system employees experienced the anonymity of their writing. Instead of effacing his own input, like Cather, or having it effaced by corporate style, like Agee and Fearing, or encoding it as racialized work, like Du Bois, the new media journalist simply stops reading his own content. James Wood finds the tonal imbalance between the mock-heroic war metaphors and the puerile humor above, with its "fart in a bathtub," to be a weakness of *John Henry Days*, a symptom of its neurotic attempt to be and say everything.[16] However, when read with only the smallest amount of faith in Whitehead's abilities as a novelist, the "bloodless edit" that Sutter anticipates for his John Henry Days piece can be seen as intentionally informing the style of the present-day sections of *John Henry Days*, which are full of the redundancies, tonal shifts, and repetitions of a first draft. Or, more accurately, Sutter's sections of the novel mimic the narrative style of undercooked thinkpieces that are native to travel and culture websites like the one that contracted him to cover the John Henry festival. Yes, Wood is right that the Sutter sections of *John Henry Days* could benefit from the editorial acumen of a modern-day Cather or Du Bois, but he also misses how that formal tic fits into the historical point that Whitehead makes when parodying the style of web-based culture writing. Sutter's writing style fits into the other historical and media-specific forms that the novel incorporates: 1870s work songs, Tin Pan Alley sheet music, oral histories from the 1930s, and what Daniel Grausam calls the postpostal genre of the commemorative stamp, which is meant to be archived rather than used.[17] While Sutter sees the "new innovation of the internet" as unprecedented in its commodification of everything, its capacity to be infinitely and immediately updated, and its devaluation of quality writing for poorly paid content, *John Henry Days* situates the narrative forms of digital culture within a much longer history of work and artistic production.

Not that the opposite couldn't also be said about the effect of "the digital" on writing. Web journalism is just as much characterized by the surface noise of microblogging, listicles, and thematic slideshows as the slow burn of what's become known as "long form." This is the métier of another character, Pamela, also a temp worker, when she starts at a "content driven interactive information provider." Though her lofty title is "ontologist," her day-to-day activity looks a lot like what *Time* editors were doing in the 1920s. "The ontologists," her new boss tells her, "classify websites into root categories such as Entertainment, News, and Health, categories recognizable to many from the real world, and write descriptions of no more than thirty-five words." The promise of endless space for writing produces the need for a new profession of aggregators and an intense focus on genre, both of which were also key features of the big magazines. And, following the line of argument that the plight of the magazining modernist is now everyone's plight, it is only fitting that when Pamela tells J. Sutter what her job consists of—"Typing and filing, usually. They call you up and you head out"—he identifies with it: "Just like me," he tells her.[18]

Given that Whitehead got his start in print journalism at *The Village Voice* as a fact checker and pop-culture critic, a job he says "taught him how to sit down for five hours and not get distracted," his turn to web-based journalism after writing six novels can look like an enactment of J. Sutter's fictional dip into the form, and it provides another way to bring the paired histories of modernism and big magazines into the present.[19] The now-defunct sports-culture website *Grantland* assigned him to cover the 2012 Olympics in London, ostensibly under its "College Sports" banner, and then staked his entry into the World Series of Poker in Las Vegas in exchange for a serialized first-person account of the experience. The appeal of such an assignment, according to Whitehead, is that it is manageable work, occupying several days instead of the two years it takes him to write a novel. One can only assume that *Grantland*'s reputation for paying its contributors well—it was a property of ESPN, which in turn is owned by Disney—is another motivator, along with the fact that it averaged over six million unique visitors every month, a readership that even a well-known author of literary fiction could not hope to touch with his novels. *Grantland* also claimed that it wanted to provide a place for high-quality writing on the Internet, to "prove long-form content still [has] a place online," and to bring in the "strongest writers" for the "strongest topics."[20] Here, it is worth noting the echoes of S. S. McClure and Arnold Gingrich, who also responded to the felt oversupply of information with an intense focus on the style of their content, which they bought from authors who had proven themselves in the literary field. Which is only to say that the double life of modernism and big magazines does not end when the long tail of modernist formal experimentation gives way to other narrative preoccupations, nor does it end when big magazines reorganize their offices and mastheads while trying to acclimatize to digital culture. To make a positive claim for the creative sparks engendered by the double life of a writer—which, for what it's worth, is what I hope to have accomplished with this book—is not to look back nostalgically at a golden age of magazines, nor is it to romanticize the poverty of underpaid and overworked writers for whom such employment rarely exists. Instead, learning a thing from big magazines, it is to acknowledge that aesthetic experimentation can be its own occupation and that given enough time and support it can circulate in unexpected ways.

NOTES

Introduction: Making Modernism Big

1. F. Scott Fitzgerald, "This Is a Magazine," *Vanity Fair* (December 1920): 71; reprinted in *F. Scott Fitzgerald, In His Own Time: A Miscellany*, ed. Matthew Bruccoli and Jackson R. Bryer (Kent, Ohio: Kent State University Press, 1971), 227–230. Further references will be cited parenthetically in the text.

2. W. E. B. Du Bois, "Books," *The Horizon* 1, no. 4 (April 1907): 5–6.

3. Willa Cather, "On the Art of Fiction," in *On Writing* (New York: Knopf, 1949), 101.

4. Matthew Bruccoli, "A Brief Life of Fitzgerald," in F. Scott Fitzgerald, *A Life in Letters*, ed. Matthew Bruccoli (New York: Simon & Schuster, 1994), xx.

5. F. Scott Fitzgerald, *A Life in Letters*, ed. Matthew Bruccoli (New York: Simon & Schuster, 1994), 40–41.

6. Clement Greenberg, "Avant-Garde and Kitsch," in *Art and Culture: The Critical Essays* (Boston: Beacon, 1961), 3–21; Dwight MacDonald, "Masscult and Midcult," in *Against the American Grain* (New York: Random House, 1962), 3–78; Paul Goodman, "Reflections on Literature as a Minor Art," in *The Paul Goodman Reader*, ed. Taylor Stoehr (Oakland, Calif.: PM, 2001), 216–219.

7. Richard Ohmann, *Selling Culture: Magazines, Markets, and Class* (London: Verso, 1996); and Roland Marchand, *Advertising the American Dream: Making Way for Modernity, 1920–1940* (Berkeley: University of California Press, 1985), are the most important studies of the general-interest magazine's role in the birth of

consumer capitalism. My summary of the genre's innovations is indebted to their work. However, for the most part Ohmann and Marchand completely ignore the editorial content of the magazines they study, which is justified by the centrality of advertising in the financial structure of the periodical industry.

8. Shelly Fisher Fishkin, *From Fact to Fiction: Journalism and Imaginative Writing in America* (New York: Oxford, 1985), shows how canonical writers from Twain and Whitman to Hemingway and Dos Passos were both journalists and literary authors. She develops an "apprenticeship model" that filters Philip Rahv's theory of American literature as a "cult of experience" through these writers' experiences in reportage and news writing. Besides the problem that her account is exclusively of white male writers, thus universalizing the experience of a fairly standard type, it also flattens journalistic practice into a set of standard attitudes toward reality—distrust hearsay, experience for yourself, etc.—that pays little attention to the variety of publication types and editorial styles that fall under "journalism." In this way, Fishkin represents a common approach to the literature/journalism question that either begins with the question and ends with the assertion of the inherent "literariness" of certain pieces of journalism or suggests that certain pieces of literature display a "journalistic" investment in objectivity and the authenticity of facts. That is, these studies are interested primarily in genre and the instability and slipperiness of categorical markers, in questions of objectivity versus subjectivity, or fact versus fiction. One need only glance at several titles to see this: Barbara Foley's *Telling the Truth: The Theory and Practice of Documentary Fiction* (1986); Phyllis Frus's *The Politics and Poetics of Journalistic Narrative* (1994); John Russel's *Reciprocities of the Nonfiction Novel* (2000). My aim is not primarily to deconstruct genre or to argue that literary scholars should take journalism's aesthetic merits more seriously. In fact, this study rather crassly ignores the question of these aesthetic subcategories in favor of an approach that emphasizes the importance of "company time." That is, all the work published by the magazining modernists recursively accounts for its own production or its institutional affiliation. My interest, therefore, is not in generic divisions between the news article and the poem or novel or between ontological categories of truth and fiction. Instead, I claim that the house style of magazines reaches beyond its pages and into the works that are produced ostensibly in rebellion against or ancillary to them.

9. Willa Cather, *The Professor's House* (1925; New York: Vintage, 1990), 114. David M. Earle, *Re-Covering Modernism: Pulps, Paperbacks, and the Prejudice of Form* (Burlington, Vt.: Ashgate, 2009), addresses the thematic presence of mass-market magazines then turns to the "smarts" and paperback-book industry for print history. On representations of news in modernist fiction, see David Rando, *Modernist Fiction and the News: Representing Experience in the Early Twentieth Century* (London: Palgrave, 2011).

10. Sean Latham and Robert Scholes, "The Rise of Periodical Studies," *PMLA* 121, no. 2 (2006): 517–531; Scholes and Wulfman, *Modernism in the Magazines*, 3. The *Journal of Modernist Periodical Studies*, founded in 2010, along with the Modernist Journals Project (founded in 1995), which digitizes mostly little

magazines published before 1923, evince the growing institutionalization of modernist periodical studies.

11. A notable exception to this focus on little magazines is Patrick Collier, *Modernism on Fleet Street* (Burlington, Vt.: Ashgate, 2006). Robert Scholes and Cliford Wulfman, *Modernism in the Magazines: An Introduction* (New Haven, Conn.: Yale University Press, 2010), briefly discusses how large-circulation magazines helped spread the popularity of modernist artists, such as when *Scribner's* reproduced works by Paul Cézanne.

12. Mark Morrisson, *The Public Face of Modernism: Little Magazines, Audiences, and Reception, 1905–1920* (Madison: University of Wisconsin Press, 2001). Morrisson provides an invaluable treatment of how modernist little magazines productively engage with the "crisis of publicity" inaugurated by the print revolution of the late nineteenth century. Even while mass print culture provided Ford Madox Ford, T. S. Eliot, Ezra Pound, Marianne Moore, Harold Monro, and others a "rhetorical enemy" (9) against which to distinguish their own forays into publishing, Morrisson shows how editors of little magazines appropriated certain design strategies and promotional materials developed in the commercial press to buoy their largely unprofitable endeavors. *On Company Time* complements Morrisson in two ways: first, it extends his story, which ends in 1920, through the late 1950s, when the mass adoption of television radically changed popular culture by dethroning magazines. It also focuses more fully on American writers and magazines. There are several reasons for this decision: for practical purposes, limiting examples to American magazines helps provide narrative coherence over the longer time frame. A more compelling reason, though, is that journalism as a profession developed quite differently in the United States than in England in terms of style, funding, genres, audience, etc. Also, while Morrisson's study looks at how little magazines appropriate the marketing strategies of the commercial press, he actually has little to say about that commercial press, most notably the wide range of modernists who worked for, were published in, and circulated as editorial content in mass-market magazines. For the British "slow print" movement in the late nineteenth century, see Elizabeth Carolyn Miller, *Slow Print: Literary Radicalism and Late Victorian Print Culture* (Stanford, Calif.: Stanford University Press, 2014).

13. Lawrence Rainey, *Institutions of Modernism: Literary Elites and Public Culture* (New Haven, Conn.: Yale University Press, 1998), 5.

14. Ibid., 78.

15. Matthew Schneirov, *The Dream of a New Social Order: Popular Magazines in America, 1893–1914* (New York: Columbia University Press, 1994), 6.

16. In this way, Rainey's story about modernism's construction of its own, autonomous "contrived corridors" can look like a slightly expanded version of the New Critics' autotelic, or self-contained and self-defining, texts, with the autonomous aesthetic object (the *inside* of the poem) transferred to an insulated coterie of culture mongers on the outside of it.

17. Frank Luther Mott, *A History of American Magazines*, vol. 4, *1885–1905* (Cambridge, Mass.: Belknap, 1957), 3–10.

18. Ezra Pound, "Small Magazines," *The English Journal* 19, no. 9 (November 1930): 689; hereafter cited parenthetically in the text.

19. Harold S. Wilson, *McClure's Magazine and the Muckrakers* (Princeton, N.J.: Princeton University Press, 1970), 197–200.

20. Ezra Pound, *ABC of Reading* (New York: New Directions, 1930), 29; Tristan Tzara, in *Seven Dada Manifestoes and Lampisteries*, trans. Barbara Wright (Surrey: One World, 2011), 3, 10.

21. T. S. Eliot, introduction to *Nightwood*, by Djuna Barnes (New York: New Directions, 1937), xviii.

22. Alfred Kazin, *Starting Out in the Thirties* (Boston: Little, Brown, 1962), 103.

23. Christopher P. Wilson, *The Labor of Words: Literary Professionalism in the Progressive Era* (Athens: University of Georgia Press, 1985), 57. Historians of journalism also claim the late nineteenth century as a pivotal period in the commercialization of the news as well as in the standardization of journalistic objectivity as a central feature of the field's professional identity. See Gerald J. Baldasty, *The Commercialization of the News in the Nineteenth Century* (Madison: University of Wisconsin Press, 1992); Richard Kaplan, *Politics and the American Press: The Rise of Objectivity, 1865–1920* (Cambridge: Cambridge University Press, 2002). Histories of journalistic professionalism tend to foreground the editorial culture of newspapers rather than the changes that occur in magazines.

24. Ibid., 17.

25. Wilson's otherwise powerful account fully neglects how this "masculinization" of writing affected the careers of the many women authors in the period as well as how the increasing number of women in the editorial workplace contributed to the hypermasculine version of authorship he associates with naturalism and muckraking. According to Susan Coultrap-McQuin, *Doing Literary Business: American Women Writers in the Nineteenth Century* (Chapel Hill: University of North Carolina Press, 1990), women faced a similar definition of authorship that focused on market orientation and masculine publicity. Jennifer Fleissner, *Women, Compulsion, Modernity* (Chicago: University of Chicago Press, 2004), argues that fundamental shifts in the division of labor allow one to read naturalism as invested in feminist concerns.

26. On the professionalization of journalism in the United States, see Michael Schudson, *Discovering the News: A Social History of American Newspapers* (New York: Basic Books, 1981); Michael Schudson, *The Sociology of the News*, 2nd ed. (New York: Norton, 2011), esp. chap. 4; Stephen A. Banning, "The Professionalization of Journalism: A Nineteenth-Century Beginning," *Journalism History* 24 (1998–1999): 157–163.

27. On the history of journalism education, see Christopher B. Daly, *Covering America: A Narrative History of the Nation's Journalism* (Amherst: University of Massachusetts Press, 2012) 150–155; Frank Luther Mott, *American Journalism: A History: 1690–1960*, 3rd. ed. (New York: Macmillan, 1962), 600–605; on the founding of the University of Missouri School of Journalism, see Betty Houchin Winfield,

ed., *Journalism 1908: The Birth of a Profession* (Columbia: University of Missouri Press, 2008).

28. The most prominent debate took place in a series of *North American Review* articles after the announcement of Pulitzer's endowment at Columbia. See Horace White, "The School of Journalism," *The North American Review* (January 1904): 25–32; and Joseph Pulitzer's reply, "The College of Journalism," *The North American Review* (May 1904): 641–680.

29. Qtd. in Daly, *Covering America*, 152.

30. The definitive account of the creative-writing program and its effect on American literature is Mark McGurl, *The Program Era: Postwar Fiction and the Rise of Creative Writing* (Cambridge, Mass.: Harvard University Press, 2009).

31. John Macy, "Journalism," in *Civilization in the United States: An Inquiry by Thirty Americans*, ed. Harold E. Stearns (New York: Harcourt, Brace, and Co., 1922), 34.

32. Archibald MacLeish, *Poetry and Journalism: A Lecture Delivered at Northrop Memorial Auditorium*, The Gideon Seymour Memorial Lecture (Minneapolis: University of Minneapolis Press, 1958), 3.

33. Thomas Strychacz, *Modernism, Mass Culture, and Professionalism* (Cambridge: Cambridge University Press, 1993), 25.

34. Michael Denning, *The Cultural Front: The Laboring of American Culture in the Twentieth Century* (London: Verso, 1997), xvi.

35. Qtd. in ibid., 102–103.

36. Jared Gardner, *The Rise and Fall of Early American Magazine Culture* (Urbana: University of Illinois Press, 2012), x. Gardner sees the early magazine's understanding of a participatory audience as analogous to the twenty-first-century emphasis on user-generated content. Gardner is specifically talking about the magazines of the early republic and how they differ from modern, i.e., twentieth-century magazines, but the characterization holds through at least until the end of the Civil War.

37. Malcolm Cowley, *Exile's Return: A Literary Odyssey of the 1920s* (New York: Penguin, 1994), 214, 289.

38. MacLeish, *Poetry and Journalism*, 3.

39. Archibald MacLeish, "The First Nine Years," in *Writing for* Fortune (New York: Time Inc., 1980), 10.

40. Two other obvious career paths were moving to Hollywood to work in the studio system, most famously satirized in Nathanael West's *The Day of the Locust* (1939), or getting a job in one of the New Deal arts programs, such as the Federal Writers Project. Each presented its own set of problems for young artists. On the studios, see Thomas Schatz, *The Genius of the System: Hollywood Filmmaking in the Studio Era* (New York: Holt, 1988); and Jerome Christensen, *America's Corporate Art: The Studio Authorship of Hollywood Pictures* (Stanford, Calif.: Stanford University Press, 2012). On the federal arts programs, see Michael Szalay, *New Deal Modernism: American Literature and the Invention of the Welfare State* (Durham, N.C.: Duke University Press, 2000); and Jeff Allred, *American Modernism and Depression Documentary* (New York: Oxford University Press, 2010).

41. Bernard Lahire, *The Plural Actor* (Cambridge: Polity, 2011); Bernard Lahire, "The Double Life of Writers," trans. Gwendolyn Wells, *New Literary History* 41 (2010): 443–465. Lahire's sociology is clearly indebted to that of Pierre Bourdieu. Lahire alters Bourdieu's theory of the restricted fields of cultural production by emphasizing a field's points of intersection with other adjacent fields. That is, for Lahire, an individual's position in one field—as well as the habitus—depends on its relationship to and overlapping identification with other fields. Whereas Bourdieu is interested in explaining how a social field is structured and how authors' definitions of authorship (and the types of recognition that constitute economic or symbolic capital) are structured by the preexisting conditions that they must enter, Lahire turns his attention to the ways that nonliterary social fields influence symbolic capital as well as how those fields can produce the idiosyncrasies that we see between two writers with relatively similar backgrounds.

42. Lahire, "Double Life," 445.

43. *Time*, "Books" (March 6, 1923): 13.

44. See Elisabeth Majeras, "Determined and Bigoted Feminists: Women, Magazines, and Popular Modernism," in *Modernism*, vol. 1, ed. Astradur Eysteinsson and Vivian Liska (Amsterdam: Johns Benjamins, 2007), 619–636.

45. "Dogma, Science," *Time* (March 17, 1923).

46. "Sterile Modernism," *Time* (March 10, 1930).

47. Macdonald, "Masscult and Midcult," 54.

48. Ibid., 68–69.

49. Ibid., 51.

50. For an overview of the effect of this new archival superabundance as it relates to literary studies, see Carrie Hyde and Jospeh Rezek, "Introduction: The Aesthetics of Archival Evidence," *J19: The Journal of Nineteenth-Century Americanists* 2 (2014): 155–162; for an entry point into textuality and digitization, see Jerome McGann, *The Textual Condition* (Princeton, N.J.: Princeton University Press, 1991); and Matthew K. Gold, ed., *Debates in the Digital Humanities* (Minneapolis: University of Minnesota Press, 2012).

51. Qtd. in Clay Shirky, *Here Comes Everybody: The Power of Organizing Without Organizations* (New York: Penguin, 2009), 7. Of course, amateurization is not endemic only to journalism as it is one aspect of an increased emphasis on "flexibility" in postindustrial labor markets. Virno describes the gradual replacement of specialization with a performative, "virtuosic" understanding of work as integral to post-Fordist capitalism. See Paolo Virno, *A Grammar of the Multitude*, trans. Isabella Bertoletti, James Cascaito, and Andrea Casson (Los Angeles: Semiotext[e], 2004).

1. Willa Cather's Promiscuous Fiction

1. Willa Cather, *The Professor's House* (1925; repr. New York: Vintage, 1990), 114. Subsequent references appear parenthetically in the text.

2. Willa Cather, "On *The Professor's House*," in *On Writing: Critical Studies on Writing as an Art* (New York: Knopf, 1949), 31–32.

3. Leon Edel, "A Cave of One's Own," in *Critical Essays on Willa Cather*, ed. John J. Murphy (Boston: G. K. Hall, 1984), 205.

4. The most famous account of the relationship between periodicals and the nation-state is Benedict Anderson, *Imagined Communities: Reflections on the Origin and Spread of Nationalism*, rev. ed. (London: Verso, 2006). For railroads, see Wolfgang Schivelbusch, *The Railway Journey: The Industrialization of Time and Space in the Twentieth Century* (1977; repr. Berkeley: University of California Press, 2014). Schivelbusch claims that in the United States railroads, along with steamships, were a "producer of territories" and a "means of gaining a new civilization from a hitherto worthless (because inaccessible) wilderness" (91).

5. James Woodress, "The Pre-Eminent Magazine Genius: S. S. McClure," in *Essays Mostly on Periodical Publishing in America*, ed. James Woodress (Durham, N.C.: Duke University Press, 1973), 171.

6. Edith Lewis, *Willa Cather Living: A Personal Record by Edith Lewis* (New York: Knopf, 1953), 42. Though there are many accounts of Cather's journalism as "apprenticeship," of particular note are M. Catherine Downs, *Becoming Modern: Willa Cather's Journalism* (Selingsgrove, Penn.: Susquehanna University Press, 1999), as it treats the journalism as interesting in its own right; and Joseph A. Urgo, "Willa Cather's Political Apprenticeship at *McClure's* Magazine," in *Willa Cather's New York: New Essays on Cather in the City*, ed. Merril Macguire Skaggs (Madison, N.J.: Farleigh Dickinson University Press, 2000), 60–74, because it finds that, contrary to most histories of *McClure's*, that the magazine actually gets more political after Cather takes over.

7. Willa Cather to E. H. Anderson, November 24, 1922. In Willa Cather, *The Selected Letters of Willa Cather*, ed. Andrew Jewell and Janis Stout (New York: Knopf, 2013), 330–331.

8. James Woodress, *Willa Cather: A Literary Life* (Lincoln: University of Nebraska Press, 1989), 89.

9. Willa Cather to H. L. Mencken, in *Selected Letters*, 309.

10. Christopher P. Wilson, *The Labor of Words: Literary Professionalism in the Progressive Era* (Athens: University of Georgia Press, 1985), provides the canonical account of this process.

11. Henry Adams, *The Education of Henry Adams* (1918; repr. New York: Modern Library, 1931), 384. See Francesca Sawaya, *Modern Women, Modern Work: Domesticity, Professionalism, and American Writing, 1890–1950* (Philadelphia: University of Pennsylvania Press, 2004); Carol J. Batker, *Reforming Fictions: Native, African, and Jewish American Women's Literature and Journalism in the Progressive Era* (New York: Columbia University Press, 2000). A foundational study of late nineteenth-century female authorship is Susan Coultrap-McQuin, *Doing Literary Business: American Women Writers in the Nineteenth Century* (Chapel Hill: University of North Carolina Press, 1990).

12. Willa Cather, "Escapism," in *On Writing*, 23–24.

13. Willa Cather, "On the Art of Fiction," in *On Writing*, 101.

14. Fanny Butcher, "Willa Cather Tells Purpose of New Novel," *Chicago Tribune* (September 12, 1925). Reprinted in *Willa Cather: The Contemporary Reviews*, ed. Margaret Anne O'Connor (Cambridge: Cambridge University Press, 2001), 237–238. The presentational differences between the *Collier's* serialization and the first book edition by Knopf are thoroughly explored in Charles Johanningsmeier, "Determining How Readers Responded to Cather's Fiction: The Cultural Work of *The Professor's House* in *Collier's Weekly*," *American Periodicals* 20, no. 1 (2010): 68–96.

15. Cather to Dorothy Canfield Fisher, in *Selected Letters*, 313.

16. Willa Cather, "The Novel Démeublé," *New Republic* (April 12, 1922): 5–6. Reprinted in *Not Under Forty* (New York: Knopf, 1936).

17. Lewis, *Willa Cather Living*, 60.

18. For the central role of women editors in little magazines, see Jayne Marek, *Women Editing Modernism: "Little" Magazines and Literary History* (Lexington: University of Kentucky Press, 1995).

19. Howells's influence on the literary world was so great that Alfred Kazin began his classic study of modern American literature by locating that subject's birth in Howell's nearly unsuccessful move from belletristic Boston to commercial New York in 1891 to edit *Cosmopolitan*. Alfred Kazin, *On Native Grounds: An Interpretation of Modern American Prose Literature* (1942; repr. New York: Harcourt, 1970), 3–4.

20. On the rhetoric of James's New York Edition prefaces as editing, see Thomas M. Leitch, "The Editor as Hero: Henry James and the New York Edition," *Henry James Review* 3, no. 1 (1981): 24–32.

21. In this vein, her attention to the 1937 Autograph Edition of her collected novels might be seen as springing from her unhappy experience of leasing the movie rights for *A Lost Lady* as well as a one-time lease of her novel *Death Comes for the Archbishop* to the Modern Library. She subsequently regretted both of these decisions, the latter especially, because it made for "cheaper editions" that circulated so widely that readers young and old, rich and poor, might feel "compelled to read her." To make sure this would not happen again, her will stipulated that her novels and stories could not be made into movies, nor could they be used for television or radio scenarios, and, though her estate eventually rescinded, she originally banned her work from being included in anthologies or reprinted in paperback, even though (or perhaps because) both would bring down the cost of publication and spread her work across a much wider reading public.

22. Lise Jaillant, *Modernism, Middlebrow, and the Literary Canon: The Modern Library Series, 1916–1955* (London: Pickering and Chatto, 2014).

23. Lewis, *Willa Cather Living*, 61.

24. See Urgo, "Willa Cather's Political Apprenticeship," for more on how *McClure's* changed under Cather's direction.

25. Sarah Blackwood, "Editing as Carework: The Gendered Labor of Public Intellectuals," *Avidly* (June 6, 2014), http://avidly.lareviewofbooks.org; Kay-Wilmers quoted in Elizabeth Day, "Is the LRB the Best Magazine in the World?," *Guardian* (March 8, 2014). Blackwood offers carework as a counterpoint to other models of

editing, such as mastery, connoisseurship, and curation, with whom she aligns James, Howells, and Pound, respectively.

26. Qtd. in Woodress, "Pre-Eminent Magazine Genius," 182–183.

27. Woodress, "Pre-Eminent Magazine Genius," 184.

28. Qtd. in Wilson, *McClure's*, 104.

29. Ibid., 81.

30. Steffens, *Autobiography*, 358.

31. Historians of American journalism strongly associate the ethos of objectivity with newspapers rather than with magazines. See Steven Maras, *Objectivity in Journalism* (Malden, Mass.: Polity, 2013); Richard Kaplan, "The Origins of Objectivity in American Journalism," in *The Routledge Companion to News and Journalism*, ed. Stuart Allen (New York: Routledge, 2010): 25–37.

32. Arthur Kimball Reed, "The Invasion of Journalism," *Atlantic Monthly* 86 (July 1900): 122.

33. Richard Ohmann, *Selling Culture: Magazines, Markets, and Class* (London: Verso, 1995), 8.

34. Wilson, *McClure's*, 197–200.

35. For a more in-depth study of nineteenth-century periodical genres, see Matthew Schneirov, *The Dream of a New Social Order: Popular Magazines in America, 1893–1914* (New York: Columbia University Press, 1994), 4–12.

36. In Frank L. Mott, *A History of American Magazines*, vol. 4: *1885–1905* (Cambridge, Mass.: Belknap, 1957), 7.

37. Lincoln Steffens, *Autobiography of Lincoln Steffens* (New York: Houghton, 1931), 364.

38. Lewis, *Willa Cather Living*, 62.

39. Cather, "Escapism," 20–21. For an example of Cather's waning reputation in the 1930s, see Granville Hicks, "The Case Against Willa Cather," *English Journal* 22, no. 9 (1933): 703–710.

40. Ellen Gruber Garvey, " 'Important, Responsible Work': Willa Cather's Office Stories and Her Necessary Editorial Career," *Studies in American Fiction* 36, no. 2 (2008): 171.

41. Edwin Llewelyn Schuman, *Practical Journalism: A Complete Manual on the Best Newspaper Methods* (New York: D. Appleton, 1910), xi.

42. Willa Cather, *The World and the Parish: Willa Cather's Articles and Reviews*, vol. 1: *1893–1902*, ed. William Curtin (Lincoln: University of Nebraska Press, 1970), 273.

43. Ibid., 274.

44. Cather, "Miss Jewett," in *Not Under Forty*, 81.

45. Ibid., 79.

46. Cather, "On the Art of Fiction," 101.

47. Cather, *World and Parish*, 273–274.

48. Ibid., 273, 276.

49. Henry James, *Letters*, vol. 4: *1895–1916* (Cambridge, Mass.: Belknap, 1984), 395.

50. Henry James, *Literary Criticism: Essays on Literature, American Writers, English Writers* (New York: Library of America, 1984), 100–101.

51. Cather, "My First Two Novels (There Were Two)," in *On Writing*, 93, 95.

52. Willa Cather, *O Pioneers!* (1913; repr. Lincoln: University of Nebraska Press, 1992), 53.

53. Jonathan Flatley, "Like: Collecting and Collectivity," *October* 132 (2010): 73.

54. Willa Cather, "Ardessa," in *Stories, Poems, and Other Writings* (New York: Library of America, 1992), 169. Hereafter cited parenthetically in the text.

55. Willa Cather, "The Willing Muse," in *The Collected Short Fiction*, vol. 1, ed. Mildred R. Bennett (Lincoln: University of Nebraska Press, 1965), 113. Hereafter cited parenthetically in the text.

56. Willa Cather, *The Song of the Lark* (1915; repr. Lincoln: University of Nebraska Press, 2012), 128.

57. This recalls a similar scene in Bram Stoker's *Dracula* (1897), in which Jonathan Harker and his fiancée Mina Murray furiously type behind closed doors as a room full of people listen.

58. See Mark Seltzer, *Bodies and Machines* (New York: Routledge, 1992), for a broader discussion of the "body-machine complex" as a guiding methodological precondition of naturalism.

59. Jennifer Fleissner, "The Biological Clock: Edith Wharton, Naturalism, and the Temporality of Womanhood," *American Literature* 78, no. 3 (2006): 519–549.

60. Willa Cather, *My Ántonia* (1918; repr. Lincoln: University of Nebraska Press, 1994), xiii.

61. Cather, "On the Art of Fiction," 101.

62. Lewis, *Willa Cather Living*, 139.

63. Qtd. in David Stouck, "Historical Essay," in *O Pioneers!* (Lincoln: University of Nebraska Press, 1992), 285.

64. Willa Cather, *Alexander's Bridge* (1912; repr. New York: Houghton, 1922), 11.

65. Cather, *Song of the Lark*, 162–163, 182.

66. Eve Kosofsky Sedgwick, "Willa Cather and Others," in *Tendencies* (Durham, N.C.: Duke University Press, 1993), 174.

67. Mark McGurl, *The Novel Art: Elevations of American Fiction After Henry James* (Princeton, N.J.: Princeton University Press, 2001), 31.

2. Printing the Color Line in *The Crisis*

1. Theodore P. Greene, *America's Heroes: The Changing Models of Success in American Magazines* (New York: Oxford University Press, 1970), 288.

2. David Levering Lewis, *W. E. B Du Bois: The Biography of a Race, 1868–1919* (New York: Holt, 2000), 408.

3. W. E. B. Du Bois to Joel Spingarn, October 28, 1914, in *Correspondence of W. E. B. Du Bois*, vol. 1: *1877–1934*, ed. Herbert Aptheker (Amherst: University of Massachusetts Press, 1973), 203–207.

4. Lewis, *Biography of a Race*, 477.

5. W. E. B. Du Bois, "Dr. Du Bois Resigns," in *Writings*, ed. Nathan Huggins (New York: Library of America, 1986), 1259–1263.

6. W. E. B. Du Bois, "Books," *The Horizon* 1, no. 4(April 1907): 5. Du Bois felt strongly enough about this that he would reuse most of this article in his column for the *Chicago Defender* in September 1945.

7. Lewis, *Biography of a Race*, 409.

8. A similar logic occurs with the genre-magazine boom of the 1920s, where formulaic "pulp fiction" takes its name from the cheap paper stock on which it is printed. In both cases, the respective qualities of physical and literary material are imagined as coextensive.

9. F. H. M. Murray, "Magazinelets," *Horizon* (April 1908): 22–23.

10. Du Bois, "Books," 5–6.

11. See Frances Smith Foster, "A Narrative of the Interesting Origins and (Somewhat) Surprising Developments of African-American Print Culture," *American Literary History* (2005): 714–740; and Frances Smith Foster, "Genealogies of Our Concerns, Early (African) American Print Culture, and Transcending Tough Times," *American Literary History* 22 (2010): 368–380.

12. Jessica Pressman, "The Aesthetic of Bookishness in Twenty-First-Century Literature," *Michigan Quarterly Review* (Fall 2009): 465–483.

13. W. E. B. Du Bois, "Editorial," *The Crisis* (November 1910): 10.

14. Ann Ardis, "Staging the Public Sphere: Magazine Dialogism and the Prosthetics of Authorship at the Turn of the Twentieth Century," in *Transatlantic Print Culture, 1880–1940*, ed. Ann Ardis and Patrick Collier (London: Palgrave, 2008), 30.

15. Christopher B. Daly, *Covering America: A Narrative History of the Nation's Journalism* (Amherst: University of Massachusetts Press, 2012), 151–152.

16. In *Dusk of Dawn*, Du Bois implies that Washington's influence affected his ability to find support for his earlier efforts, especially *The Moon*. See W. E. B. Du Bois, *Dusk of Dawn* (1940; repr. New York: Oxford University Press, 2007), 46–47.

17. There are a couple common figures for the highest circulation numbers of *The Crisis*. Cheryl A. Wall claims that in June 1919, they sold 104,000 copies. In a 1930 letter to the NAACP Board of Directors, Du Bois says the "average net paid monthly subscription" for 1919 was 94,908, which means that when newsstand and other nonsubscription sales are included, it is quite possible that Wall's number is correct. See Cheryl A. Wall, *Woman of the Harlem Renaissance* (Bloomington: Indiana University Press, 1995), 45; "W. E. B. Du Bois to the National Association for the Advancement of Colored People" (July 11, 1930), W. E. B. Du Bois Papers (MS 312), University of Massachusetts Amherst Special Collections.

18. See Robert T. Elson, *Time Inc.: The Intimate History of a Publishing Enterprise, 1923–1941* (New York: Atheneum, 1968), 328, 339.

19. Du Bois, *Correspondence*, 206.

20. See Eric Sundquist's introduction to the *Oxford W. E. B. Du Bois Reader* (New York: Oxford University Press, 1996) for an argument that Du Bois was a constructivist. Daylanne English argues that Du Bois, like many advocates for social

equality at the time, held latently essentialist ideas about the biological, even physio-logical, sources of racial difference. See Daylanne English, "W. E. B. Du Bois' Family *Crisis*," *American Literature* 72 (2000): 291–319.

21. For an exemplary study of *The New Negro* anthology's place in the Harlem Renaissance, see Brent Hayes Edwards, *The Practice of Diaspora: Literature, Translation, and the Rise of Black Internationalism* (Cambridge, Mass.: Harvard University Press, 2003); on *The New Negro* as a modernist anthology precisely because of the questions it raises about the anthology form, see Jeremy Braddock, *Collecting as Modernist Practice* (Baltimore, Md.: Johns Hopkins University Press, 2013).

22. Katherine Biers, "Syncope Fever: James Weldon Johnson and the Black Phonographic Voice," *Representations* 96 (Fall 2006): 99. Studies of the New Negro movement and Harlem Renaissance often begin by connecting the expansion of racial types available in mass media with this expansion of print culture and tech-nological innovation. Some form of this position about the relationship between technological and formal innovations in print culture and about new methods and forums for documenting (or projecting) the rise of the New Negro can be found in most studies of the period. See Anne Elizabeth Carroll, *Word, Image, and the New Negro: Representation and Identity in the Harlem Renaissance* (Bloomington: Indiana University Press, 2005), 89; Russ Castronovo, "Beauty Along the Color Line: Lynching, Aesthetics, and the *Crisis*," *PMLA* 121, no. 5 (2006): 1443–1459. For an insightful critique of the structural positioning of African Americans outside of print culture, see Madhu Dubhey, *Signs and Cities: Black Literary Postmodernism* (Chicago: University of Chicago Press, 2003), 1–12.

23. Ann Ducille, "Blue Notes on Black Sexuality: Sex and the Texts of Jessie Fauset and Nella Larson," *Journal of the History of Sexuality* 3, no. 3 (1993): 419.

24. Fred Moten, *In the Break: The Aesthetics of the Black Radical Tradition* (Minneapolis: University of Minnesota Press, 2003), 32.

25. Both are central terms in Henry Louis Gates's landmark study *The Signifying Monkey: A Theory of African American Literary Criticism* (New York: Oxford University Press, 1988). For an account of how material-culture studies and book history force a reconsideration of these tropes, see Leon Jackson, "The Talking Book and the Talking Book Historian: African American Cultures of Print—The State of the Discipline," *Book History* 13 (2010): 251–308.

26. Charles W. Chesnutt, *Marrow of Tradition*, ed. Nancy Bentley and Sandra Gunning (1901; repr. New York: Bedford, 2002), 75. Hereafter cited parentheti-cally in the text.

27. Richard Yarborough, "Violence, Manhood, and Black Heroism: The Wilmington Riot in Two Turn-of-the-Century African American Novels," in *Democracy Betrayed: The Wilmington Race Riot of 1898 and Its Legacy*, ed. David S. Cecelski and Timothy B. Tyson (Chapel Hill: University of North Carolina Press, 1998), 225–252.

28. Chesnutt to Du Bois, 1903, in *Correspondence*, 56.

29. W. E. B. Du Bois, "Criteria of Negro Art," *The Crisis* (October 1926): 290–297. Reprinted in *The Emerging Thought of W. E. B. Du Bois: Essays and Editorials from* The Crisis, ed. Henry Lee Moon (New York: Simon and Schuster, 1972), 367.

30. Ibid., 367.

31. Ibid., 367.

32. Martha Jane Nadell, *Enter the New Negroes: Images of Race in American Culture* (Cambridge, Mass.: Harvard University Press, 2004), 23–24.

33. Edwards, *The Practice of Diaspora*, 44.

34. W. E. B. Du Bois, "A Proposed Negro Journal," in *Against Racism: Unpublished Essays, Papers, Addresses, 1887–1961*, ed. Herbert Aptheker (Amherst: University of Massachusetts Press, 1985), 77.

35. Ibid., 79.

36. Ibid., 78–80.

37. Du Bois, *Correspondence*, 109.

38. "Annual Report of the Director of Publicity and Research for the Fiscal Year 1912," W. E. B. Du Bois Papers, University of Massachusetts Amherst Special Collections.

39. Du Bois, "Proposed Negro Journal," 79.

40. "Annual Report of the Director of Publicity and Research for the Fiscal Year 1912."

41. "Balance Sheet, 1913, for *The Crisis*," Microfilm of W. E. B. Du Bois Papers, University of Memphis Library, Reel 4, Slide 5-7043.

42. Du Bois, *Correspondence*, 203.

43. "Annual Report of the Director of Publicity Research for the Fiscal Year 1913," Microfilm of W. E. B. Du Bois Papers, University of Memphis, Reel 4, Slide 554. This particular report clearly is a response to Villard's multiple attempts to take over *The Crisis*.

44. Du Bois, *Correspondence*, 203–204.

45. W. E. B. Du Bois, "Photography," *The Crisis* (October 1923): 249.

46. W. E. B. Du Bois, "In Black," *The Crisis* (October 1920): 263.

47. Ibid., 263, 265.

48. See Anne Cheng, *Second Skin: Josephine Baker and the Modern Surface* (New York: Oxford, 2011), which analyzes representations of and discourses around black skin, particularly of Josephine Baker's, in the context of racialized female celebrity and modernist form.

49. W. E. B. Du Bois, "Editing *The Crisis*," in *The* Crisis *Reader: Stories, Poetry, and Essays from the N.A.A.C.P.'s* Crisis *Magazine*, ed. Sondra Kathryn Wilson (New York: Modern Library, 1999), xxix.

50. The title of George Hutchinson's *The Harlem Renaissance in Black and White* (Cambridge, Mass.: Belknap, 1995) alludes to this connection between print and race. However, it is much more interested in the connections between white and African American cultural institutions in the Harlem Renaissance than with the implications of ink and page color.

51. For treatments of modernism and photography, see Michael North, *Camera Works: Photography and the Twentieth-Century Word* (New York: Oxford University Press, 2005); Stuart Burrows, *A Familiar Strangeness: American Fiction and the Language of Photography, 1839–1945* (Athens: University of Georgia Press, 2008). For photography and the Harlem Renaissance, see Sara Blair, *Harlem Crossroads: Black*

Writers and the Photograph in the Twentieth Century (Princeton, N.J.: Princeton University Press, 2007).

52. Edwards, *The Practice of Diaspora*, 8.

53. Jonathan Flatley, *Affective Mapping: Melancholia and the Politics of Modernism* (Cambridge, Mass.: Harvard University Press, 2008), 128–130. In the mid-1920s Du Bois served as a board member of Black Swan Records, which historians often refer to as the first black-owned record label. Though they initially pressed and advertised classical music—they turned away Bessie Smith because she did not fit their recording roster—they quickly began recording ragtime and spirituals as sung by African Americans. Black Swan advertisements often appeared in *The Crisis*.

54. W. E. B. Du Bois, "Our Book Shelf," *The Crisis* (November 1925): 31.

55. Ibid.

56. Ibid.

57. Henry Louis Gates Jr., "The Trope of a New Negro and the Reconstruction of the Image of the Black," *Representations* 24 (Fall 1988): 129.

58. For the tension between realism and romance in diasporic literature, see Yogita Goyal, *Romance, Diaspora, and Black Atlantic Literature* (Cambridge: Cambridge University Press, 2010).

59. For his conservatism, see Caroline Goesser, *Picturing the New Negro: Harlem Renaissance Print Culture and Modern Black Identity* (Lawrence: University of Kansas Press, 2007). For Du Bois's unconscious embrace of early twentieth-century eugenic discourse, see Daylanne English, *Unnatural Selections: Eugenics in American Modernism and the Harlem Renaissance* (Chapel Hill, N.C.: University of North Carolina Press, 2004).

60.   Rhonda L. Reymond, "Looking In: Albert A. Smith's Use of *Repoussoir* in Cover Illustrations for *The Crisis* and *Opportunity*," *American Periodicals* 20, no. 2 (2010): 216.

61. Garret Stewart, "Painted Readers, Narrative Regress." *Narrative* 11, no. 2 (2003): 135.

62. Michael Fried, *Theatricality and Absorption: Painting and Beholder in the Age of Diderot* (Berkeley: University of California Press, 1980), 69.

63. Du Bois, "In Black," 263.

64. Rebecca Zurier, *Art for the Masses: A Radical Magazine and Its Graphics, 1911–1917* (Philadelphia: Temple University Press, 1999), 182–183. Zurier solely deals with his *The Masses* covers. Mark Morrisson, *The Public Face of Modernism: Little Magazines, Audiences, and Reception, 1905–1920* (Madison: University of Wisconsin Press, 2001), uses a Walts pastel from *Masses* for its cover, but he has little to say about Walts's work.

65. Fried describes the competing impulses to hide or broadcast the two-dimensionality of the painting canvas as "illusionism" and "literalism," the first aligned with modernist painting that attempts to transcend its material existence and the second with what he calls the "art of objecthood" that hopes to disassociate itself with art and literalize its relationship to the space outside the field of representation.

See Michael Fried, "Art and Objecthood," in *Art and Objecthood: Essays and Reviews* (Chicago: University of Chicago Press, 1998), 148–172.

66. Nadell, *Enter the New Negroes*, 48.

67. Qtd. in Goesser, *Picturing the New Negro*, 2.

68. Ibid., 21.

69. Nadell, *Enter the New Negroes*, 76.

70. For a synopsis of Du Bois's attitudes toward the younger generation of artists, see David Levering Lewis, *When Harlem Was in Vogue* (New York: Penguin, 1997), 120–125.

71. For an overview of Fauset's career as a journalist, see Carol J. Batker, *Reforming Fictions: Native, African, and Jewish American Women's Literature and Journalism in the Progressive Era* (New York: Columbia University Press, 2000). Elizabeth Ammons, "Black Anxiety About Immigration and Jessie Fauset's 'Sleeper Wakes,'" *African American Review* 42 (2008): 461–476, provides the only substantial critical account of "Sleeper Wakes."

72. Chesnutt's novel was not published until 1998, but it was composed from 1919–1920. Ovington and Chesnutt are the two most obvious precursors because of the historical proximity of their composition to "The Sleeper Wakes" and the institutional affiliation of the authors with *The Crisis*. Ovington was a board member of the NAACP, and Chesnutt was a judge for the Spingarn medal and then, beginning in 1927, namesake of the magazine's literary prize.

73. Jessie Fauset, "The Sleeper Wakes," *The Crisis* (August 1920): 172. "The Sleeper Wakes" was serialized in three issues, from August 1920 to October 1920. Hereafter cited parenthetically in the text with the issue and page number.

74. W. E. B. Du Bois, "Paper," *The Crisis* (June 1920): 72.

75. "Governments and Newspapers," *New York Times* (May 15, 1920): 14.

76. Lewis, *When Harlem Was in Vogue*, 124.

77. For instance, see Abby Arthur Johnson and Ronald Maberry Johnson, *Propaganda and Aesthetics: The Literary Politics of African-American Magazines in the Twentieth Century* (1979; Amherst: University of Massachusetts Press, 1991), 36.

78. Headnote to "The Horizon," *The Crisis* (January 1922).

79. Qtd. in Johnson, *Propaganda and Aesthetics*, 32.

80. Qtd. in ibid., 36.

81. W. E. B. Du Bois, "The New *Crisis*," *The Crisis* (May 1925): 7–9.

3. On the Clock: Rewriting Literary Work at Time Inc.

1. Laurence Bergreen, *James Agee: A Life* (New York: Penguin, 1985), 103–06.

2. Ibid., 103.

3. Qtd. in Robert T. Elson, *Time Inc.: The Intimate History of a Publishing Enterprise, 1923–1941* (New York: Atheneum, 1968), 5.

4. Rita Gunther McGrath, "15 Years Later, Lessons from the Failed AOL–Time Warner Merger," *Fortune* (January 10, 2015), http://fortune.com/2015/01/10/15-years-later-lessons-from-the-failed-aol-time-warner-merger.

5. Joseph J. Firebaugh, "The Vocabulary of *Time* Magazine," *American Speech* 15, no. 3 (1940): 232.

6. The development of an objective and dispassionate reportorial voice in the late nineteenth century has been discussed thoroughly in Michael Schudson, *Discovering the News: A Social History of American Newspapers* (New York: Basic, 1981).

7. For a more complete list of these portmanteaus, see Firebaugh, "The Vocabulary of *Time* Magazine"; Norris Yates, "The Vocabulary of *Time* Magazine Revisited," *American Speech* 56, no. 1 (1981): 53–63.

8. Walcott Gibbs, "*Time . . . Fortune . . . Life . . .* Luce," *New Yorker* 12, no. 41 (1936): 21.

9. For the impact of federal programs on literature, see Michael Szalay, *New Deal Modernism: American Literature and the Invention of the Welfare State* (Durham, N.C.: Duke University Press, 2000); for the Hollywood studios, see Jerome Christensen, *America's Corporate Art: The Studio Authorship of Hollywood Pictures* (Stanford, Calif.: Stanford University Press, 2012).

10. On the Great Depression's impact on literature and photography, see Jeff Allred, *American Modernism and Depression Documentary* (New York: Oxford, 2010). On the ways that AOL Time Warner still shapes artistic practice, see Michael Szalay, "HBO's Flexible Gold," *Representations* 1, no. 126 (2014): 112–134; on the AOL Time Warner merger as it related to the post–studio era film industry, see J. D. Connor, *The Studios After the Studios: Neo-Classical Hollywood, 1970–2010* (Palo Alto, Calif.: Stanford University Press, 2015).

11. Szalay, *New Deal Modernism*, 20.

12. Several recent studies attend to the relationship between modernism and American foreign policy. See Greg Barnhisel, *Cold War Modernists: Art, Literature, and American Cultural Diplomacy* (New York: Columbia University Press, 2015); William J. Maxwell, *FB Eyes: How J. Edgar Hoover's Ghostreaders Framed African American Literature* (Princeton, N.J.: Princeton University Press, 2015); Erin G. Carlston, "Modern Literature Under Surveillance: American Writers, State Espionage, and the Cultural Cold War," *American Literary History* 22, no. 3 (2010): 615–625; *Modernism on File: Writers, Artists, and the FBI, 1920–1950*, ed. Claire A. Culleton and Katherine Leick (New York: Palgrave, 2008).

13. Alfred Kazin, *Starting Out in the Thirties* (Boston: Little, Brown, 1962), 104.

14. Archibald MacLeish, *Poetry and Journalism: A Lecture Delivered at Northrop Memorial Auditorium*, The Gideon Seymour Memorial Lecture (Minneapolis: University of Minneapolis Press, 1958), 3.

15. Jeff Allred, "Boring from Within: James Agee and Walker Evans at Time Inc.," *Criticism* 52 (2010): 43; Robert Vanderlan, *Intellectuals Incorporated: Politics, Art, and Ideas Inside Henry Luce's Media Empire* (Philadelphia: University of Pennsylvania Press, 2012).

16. Bergreen, *James Agee*, 108.

17. Archibald MacLeish, "The First Nine Years," in *Writing for Fortune* (New York: Time Inc., 1980), 10.

18. Kazin, *Starting Out*, 105.

19. "The Great Trial," *Time* (July 20, 1925): 17ff.

20. James Agee, "Tennessee Valley Authority," in *Film Writing and Selected Journalism*, ed. Michael Sragow (New York: Library of America, 2005), 634–635.

21. James Agee, *Letters of James Agee to Father Flye* (New York: George Braziller, 1962), 66.

22. Agee, "Tennessee Valley Authority," 635.

23. Robert Fitzgerald, "A Memoir," in *The Collected Short Prose of James Agee* (New York: Ballantine Books, 1970), 51; Alfred Kazin, "Writing for Magazines," in *Contemporaries* (Boston: Little, Brown, 1962), 473.

24. Elson, *Time Inc.*, 6.

25. Richard Poirier, "The Difficulties of Modernism and the Modernism of Difficulty," in *Images and Ideas in American Culture*, ed. Arthur Edelstein (Hanover, N.H.: Brandeis University Press, 1979), 126.

26. "Shantih Shantih Shantih," *Time* (March 6, 1923): 12.

27. For more on this see Roland Marchand, *Advertising the American Dream: Making Way for Modernity, 1920–1940* (Berkeley: University of California Press, 1985).

28. Alan Brinkley, *The Publisher: Henry Luce and His American Century* (New York: Knopf, 2010), 136.

29. Niklas Luhmann, *Observations on Modernity*, trans. by William Whobrey (Stanford, Calif.: Stanford University Press, 1998), 85.

30. For two contemporaneous examples, see F. R. Leavis, *Mass Civilization and Minority Culture* (Cambridge: Minority, 1930); and John Macy, "Journalism," in *Civilization in the United States*, ed. Harold E. Stearns (New York: Harcourt Brace, 1922), 35–52.

31. F. R. Leavis, *New Bearings on English Poetry* (1932; repr. Ann Arbor: University of Michigan Press, 1964), 107.

32. Aaron Jaffe, *Modernism and the Culture of Celebrity* (Cambridge: Cambridge University Press, 2005), 8.

33. Qtd. in Frank Luther Mott, *History of American Magazines*, vol. 5: *1905–1930* (Cambridge, Mass.: Harvard University Press, 1968), 295.

34. Qtd. in Elson, *Time Inc.*, 129, 197.

35. Qtd. in Brinkley, *The Publisher*, 128.

36. Qtd. in Elson, *Time Inc.*, 84.

37. T. S. Eliot, *The Frontiers of Criticism* (Minneapolis: University of Minnesota Press, 1956), 9.

38. T. S. Eliot, "Tradition and the Individual Talent," in *The Sacred Wood* (1920; repr. London: Methuen, 1960), 57, 59.

39. See Jaffe, *Modernism and the Culture of Celebrity*, 1–14.

40. James Agee, "Comedy's Greatest Era," *Life* (September 5, 1949): 70–71. For an in-depth discussion of *Life*'s visual style see Allred, *American Modernism*.

41. Agee, *Letters*, 56.

42. Kenneth Fearing, *The Big Clock* (1946; repr. London: Orion, 2001), 18. Hereafter cited parenthetically in the text.

43. For a discussion of Fearing's poetry, see Rita Barnard, *The Great Depression and the Culture of Abundance* (Cambridge, Mass.: Cambridge University Press, 1995).

44. Funding highbrow endeavors with popular projects certainly is not unique to Fearing. In fact, during this period it is fairly close to the norm. One might read it as analogous to H. L. Mencken subsidizing *The Smart Set* with *Black Mask*.

45. Qtd. in Robert M. Ryley, "Introduction," in *Complete Poems of Kenneth Fearing* (Orono, Maine: National Poetry Foundation, 1994), xiii.

46. Kenneth Fearing, *New and Selected Poems* (Bloomington: Indiana University Press, 1956), xvi.

47. Dwight MacDonald, *Against the American Grain* (New York: Random House, 1952), 33; interpolation in original.

48. Andrew Ross, "The Mental Labor Problem," *Social Text* 18, no. 2 (2000): 1–31.

49. Andrew Richard Anderson, "Fear Ruled Them All: Kenneth Fearing's Literature of Corporate Conspiracy," Ph.D. diss., Purdue University (December 1989), 164.

50. James Agee, *James Agee Rediscovered: The Journals of* Let Us Now Praise Famous Men *and Other New Manuscripts*, ed. Michael A. Lofaro and Hugh Davis (Knoxville: University of Tennessee Press, 2005), 14.

51. Ibid., 12.

52. For more on *Famous Men*'s path from Harpers to Houghton Mifflin, see ibid., 44. Though Agee's original submission was thought to be lost, an early draft has been published as James Agee, *Cotton Tenants: Three Families* (Brooklyn: Melville House, 2013).

53. James Agee, "Plans for Work: October 1937," in *The Collected Short Prose of James Agee*, ed. Robert Fitzgerald (Boston: Houghton Mifflin, 1968), 150.

54. James Agee and Walker Evans, *Let Us Now Praise Famous Men* (1941; repr. New York: Houghton-Mifflin, 2001), 13. Hereafter cited parenthetically in the text.

55. Agee, *Rediscovered*, 13.

56. Barnard, *The Great Depression*, 6.

57. Agee, *Rediscovered*, 21.

58. Paula Rabinowitz, "Voyeurism and Class Consciousness: James Agee and Walker Evans, *Let Us Now Praise Famous Men*," *Cultural Critique* 21 (1992): 161–162.

59. Bruce Jackson, "The Deceptive Anarchy of *Let Us Now Praise Famous Men*," *Antioch Review* 57, no. 1 (1999): 47.

60. See Alan Spiegel, *James Agee and the Legend of Himself: A Critical Study* (Columbia: University of Missouri, 1998), for a breakdown of appropriations of Agee. Spiegel's text shows that even the compilation of Agee's affiliations can now be considered a scholarly task. Also see T. V. Reed, "Unimagined Existence and

the Fiction of the Real: Postmodern Realism in *Let Us Now Praise Famous Men*," *Representations* 24 (1988): 156–176, who names Agee's aesthetic "postmodern realism," suggesting that each category also has a combinatorial power that, in theory, would allow Agee arcana to proliferate infinitely.

61. "In Love and Anger," *Time* (September 26, 1960): 112.

62. William H. Whyte, *The Organization Man* (1956; repr. Philadelphia: University of Pennsylvania Press, 2002), 78.

63. William H. Whyte, "How to Back Into a *Fortune* Story," in *Writing for Fortune* (New York: Time Inc., 1980), 191.

64. Ibid., 191.

65. Scribners published both *The Organization Man* and Sloan Wilson's novel about the edges of corporate life, *The Man in the Gray Flannel Suit*, months apart. For the connection between their publications, see Evan Brier, *A Novel Marketplace: Mass Culture, the Book Trade, and Postwar American Fiction* (Philadelphia: University of Pennsylvania Press, 2010), which argues that *The Man in the Gray Flannel Suit* was part of an advertising strategy for Whyte's book.

66. Whyte, "*Fortune* Story," 189.

4. Our Eliot: Mass Modernism and the American Century

1. "Shantih Shantih Shantih," *Time* (March 6, 1923): 12. Hereafter cited parenthetically in the text.

2. In 1939, Burton Rascoe will emend his praise of Eliot and write a relatively well-known takedown in *Newsweek*. Burton Rascoe, "Shreds and Tatters," *Newsweek* (April 3, 1939): 40.

3. James English, *The Economy of Prestige: Prizes, Awards, and the Circulation of Cultural Value* (Cambridge, Mass.: Harvard University Press, 2005).

4. John Chipman Farrar, "To an Intellectualist," *Forgotten Shrines* (New Haven, Conn.: Yale University Press, 1919), 42.

5. I take "academicism" and "avant-gardism" from Dwight Macdonald, "A Theory of Mass Culture," in *Mass Culture: The Popular Arts in America*, ed. Bernard Rosenberg and David M. White (New York: Free Press, 1957): 59–73. Karen Leick, *Gertrude Stein and the Making of an American Celebrity* (New York: Routledge, 2009), looks in depth at how much an American reader could have known about modernism in the 1920s, citing 1933–1934 as the "moment when modernist writers became truly popular" (2). This coincides with Gertrude Stein's *Autobiography of Alice B. Toklas* being chosen as a Book-of-the-Month Club selection in October 1933 as well as with the conclusion of the *Ulysses* obscenity trials in the United States and that novel's first American publication in 1934. For more on how modernism's American reception was colored, if not outright defined, by obscenity trials, see Loren Glass, "#$%^&*!?: Modernism and Dirty Words," *Modernism/modernity* 14, no. 2 (2007): 209–223. For a brilliant history of the poetry that was actually

234 4. Our Eliot: Mass Modernism And The American Century

popular in the first half of the twentieth century, see Mike Chasar, *Everyday Reading: Poetry and Popular Culture in Modern America* (New York: Columbia University Press, 2012).

6. Russell Kirk, *Eliot and His Age: T. S. Eliot's Moral Imagination in the Twentieth Century* (New York: Random House, 1971).

7. Ezra Pound, "Small Magazines," *The English Journal* 19, no. 9 (November 1930): 691.

8. "Books," *Time* (March 6, 1923): 13.

9. "Books," *Time* (Jan. 21, 1924). The 1937 article, "Modernist Miracle," *Time* (November 1, 1937), reviews the forgotten novel *The Gardener Who Saw God*, by Edward James, the style of which has a "methodological madness suggesting nothing so much as a cross between Evelyn Waugh and Marcel Proust," in that it bares the "same chillingly precise appreciation of high-flown decadence" as those two writers.

10. See Michael Levenson, *The Genealogy of Modernism: A Study of English Literary Doctrine, 1908–1922* (Cambridge: Cambridge University Press, 1984). I focus on the definition of modernism in the United States, but others have compared the literary history of modernism in the United States to its reception elsewhere. For example, see William Marx, "Two Modernisms: T. S. Eliot and *La Nouvelle Revue Française*," in *The International Reception of T. S. Eliot*, ed. Elisabeth Däumer and Shyamal Bagchee (New York: Continuum, 2007): 25–35.

11. Lionel Trilling, *Beyond Culture* (New York: Viking, 1965), 4, 12. Trilling calls such a pedagogical method "polemical," claiming that it "went against the grain. It went against my personal grain. It went against the grain of the classroom situation. . . . And it went against the grain of the authors themselves" (13).

12. Serge Guilbault, *How New York Stole the Idea of Modern Art: Abstract Expressionism, Freedom, and the Cold War*, trans. Arthur Goldhammer (Chicago: University of Chicago Press, 1985), 200–201.

13. Daniel Tiffany, *My Silver Planet: A Secret History of Poetry and Kitsch* (Baltimore, Md.: Johns Hopkins University Press, 2014); Sianne Ngai, *Our Aesthetic Categories: Zany, Cute, Interesting* (Cambridge, Mass.: Harvard University Press, 2012). Ngai makes the case that cuteness is closely related to kitsch for contemporary artistic practice.

14. Macdonald, "Theory of Mass Culture," 60.

15. Dwight Macdonald, "Masscult and Midcult," in *Against the American Grain* (New York: Random House, 1952), 49.

16. Foundational studies of middlebrow culture include Joan Shelley Rubin, *The Making of Middlebrow Culture* (Chapel Hill: University of North Carolina Press, 1992); Janice A. Radway, *A Feeling for Books: The Book-of-the-Month Club, Literary Taste, and Middle-Class Desire* (Chapel Hill: University of North Carolina Press, 1997); Gordon Hutner, *What America Read: Taste, Class, and the Novel, 1920–1960* (Chapel Hill: University of North Carolina Press, 2009). In regards to modernism and the middlebrow, see Catherine Turner, *Marketing Modernism Between the Two World Wars* (Amherst: University of Massachusetts Press, 2003); *Middlebrow Moderns: Popular American Women Writers of the 1920s*, ed. Lisa Botshon and

Meredith Goldsmith (Boston: Northeastern University Press, 2003); Katherine Keyser, *Playing Smart: New York Women Writers and Modern Magazine Culture* (New Brunswick, N.J.: Rutgers University Press, 2010).

17. Macdonald, "Masscult and Midcult," 50–51.

18. Ibid., 50–51.

19. Levenson, *Genealogy of Modernism*, 167.

20. Rebecca Walkowitz, *Cosmopolitan Style: Modernism Beyond the Nation* (New York: Columbia University Press, 2006), 2.

21. John Wiener, *How We Forgot About the Cold War: A Historical Journey Across America* (Berkeley: University of California Press, 2012).

22. "1,000 Lost Golf Balls," *Time* (November 15, 1948): 32.

23. Lawrence Rainey, *Institutions of Modernism: Literary Elites and Public Culture* (New Haven, Conn.: Yale University Press, 1998), 106.

24. Rainey's painstaking recreation of who read *The Waste Land* and when they read it has been published and updated several times, most recently in *Revisiting* The Waste Land (New Haven, Conn.: Yale University Press, 2005).

25. Rainey, *Revisiting*, 128. Rainey, in this volume, does suggest that something "immense. Magnificent. Terrible." is contained inside the poem.

26. "Free for All?" *Time* (April 28, 1923): 11.

27. Qtd. in Michael North, *Reading 1922: A Return to the Scene of the Modern* (New York: Oxford University Press, 1999), 142.

28. "Free for All?," 11.

29. Ibid.

30. Qtd. in Robert T. Elson, *Time Inc.: The Intimate History of a Publishing Enterprise, 1923–1941* (New York: Atheneum, 1968), 5.

31. Jerome McGann, *Black Riders: The Visible Language of Modernism* (Princeton, N.J.: Princeton University Press, 1993), 1–12.

32. "Shantih Shantih Shantih," 12.

33. "From Tom to T.S.," *Time* (January 2, 1939): 35.

34. This conflation of Eliot's psychological alienation with his personal and family histories is common in both scholarly and popular biographical treatments. See Peter Ackroyd, *T. S. Eliot: A Life* (New York: Simon & Schuster, 1984); A. D. Moody, "T. S. Eliot: The American Strain," In *Placing T. S. Eliot*. ed. Jewel Spears Brooker (Columbia: University of Missouri Press, 1991), 77–89.

35. "From Tom to T. S.," 35.

36. I compiled this chart by reading every issue of *Time* from 1923 to 1964 and tracking every reference to T. S. Eliot in each issue. If any article mentioned him by name, I counted it once, so a passing reference to him in an article on, say, 1960s children's literature counts the same as a six-page feature profile. I included the *Time*'s "Letters" section, as well as the listings for television, theater, and cinema, though these are not articles in the strictest sense. From 1923 to 1964, Eliot is mentioned in 425 articles, compared to 505 for Ernest Hemingway, 252 for William Faulkner, and 218 for Gertrude Stein. Though Hemingway has the most references overall, Eliot has both the single most popular year (in 1950, he is mentioned in

35 articles) and the highest five-year sum (between 1947 and 1952 he is mentioned 137 times). Eliot is also the first author of those listed above who is mentioned in the magazine.

37. Eliot's *The Criterion*, which lasted until 1939 with funding from his employer Faber & Gwyer, is an exception.

38. See Alan Brinkley, *The Publisher: Henry Luce and His American Century* (New York: Knopf, 2010), 223, 282.

39. T. S. Matthews, "T. S. Eliot Turns to Comedy," *Life* (February 1, 1954): 56, 54.

40. "1,000 Lost Golf Balls," 32.

41. The artist, Boris Artzybasheff, created more than two hundred *Time* covers between 1941 and 1965 as well as advertisements for dozens of American corporations.

42. T. S. Eliot, *The Waste Land*, ed. Michael North (New York: Norton, 2000), ll. 19–20.

43. "Reflections," *Time* (March 6, 1950): 22. Hereafter cited parenthetically in the text.

44. "Kaleidoscopic mirror" is one of many descriptions lifted from uncited sources; here, the phrase seems to originate in Louis Untermeyer, "Delusion vs. Dogma," *Freeman* (January 7, 1923): 453.

45. See Moody, "T. S. Eliot: The American Strain," who brings to light a number of instances in the 1940s and 1950s when Eliot claims that imagery from "The Love Song of J. Alfred Prufrock" and *The Waste Land* were inspired by his early life in St. Louis.

46. Matthews, "T. S. Eliot Turns to Comedy," 58.

47. Henry Luce, "The American Century," *Life* (February 17, 1941): 63. Hereafter cited parenthetically in the text.

48. "The world as one city" predates McLuhan's more lasting formulation of "the global village," but the former is more relevant here because it describes how the press represents postwar life. See Marshall McLuhan, *The Mechanical Bride: Folklore of Industrial Man* (New York: Vanguard, 1951), which begins with a chapter on a *Time* advertisement.

49. Qtd. in Elson, *Time Inc.*, 168.

50. Brinkley, *The Publisher*, 130.

51. T. S. Eliot, "Banquet Speech," in *Nobel Lectures, Literature 1901–1967*, ed. Horst Frenz (Amsterdam: Elsevier, 1969), 436.

52. Anders Osterling, "Presentation Speech," in *Nobel Lectures, Literature 1901–1967*, ed. Horst Frenz (Amsterdam: Elsevier, 1969), 431, 433.

53. Delmore Schwartz's "T. S. Eliot as International Hero" is an early entry into this reading of Eliot's singularity. As the next chapter makes clear, Ernest Hemingway will also come to signify a similar worldview in the pages of *Time* and *Life*, especially after *Life* publishes *The Old Man and the Sea* in September 1952 and selections from *A Moveable Feast* in April 1964.

54. "People," *Time* (December 13, 1963): 39.

55. "Foreign Relations: That Month," *Time* (April 26, 1963): 21.

56. Russell W. Davenport, "A *Life* Round Table on the Pursuit of Happiness," *Life* (July 12, 1948): 97.

57. Hugh Kenner, *The Invisible Poet: T. S. Eliot* (London: Allen, 1960), ix–x.

58. "Reflections," 22, 23.

59. Kenner, *The Invisible Poet*, 40–41.

60. Qtd. in Ackroyd, *T. S. Eliot*, 284, 289, 300.

61. T. S. Eliot, *The Frontiers of Criticism* (Minneapolis: University of Minnesota Press, 1956), 1. Hereafter cited parenthetically in the text.

62. T. S. Eliot, "Notes . . . from T. S. Eliot," *University of Chicago Magazine* (December 1950): 11.

63. T. S. Eliot, *The Waste Land. A Facsimile and Transcript of the Original Drafts Including the Annotations of Ezra Pound*, ed. Valerie Eliot (New York: Harcourt Brace Jovanovich, 1971), 81. The holograph also has Eliot's own "shored against" written directly over "spelt into"—so even as "spelt into" came first, it was immediately overwritten (but not crossed out) by "shored against."

5. Hemingway's Disappearing Style

1. "All Stones End . . . ," *Time* (October 8, 1937).

2. Melwyn Breen, "Man, Nature and Nothing," *Saturday Night* 67 (September 13, 1952): 26.

3. Michael North, *Camera Works: Photography and the Twentieth-Century Word* (Oxford: Oxford University Press, 2005), 187.

4. For an early, influential essay about the difficulty in separating the artist from the celebrity, see Lionel Trilling, "Hemingway and His Critics," *Partisan Review* 6 (Winter 1939): 52–60.

5. Qtd. in Carlos Baker, *Ernest Hemingway: A Life Story* (New York: Putnam's, 1969), 240.

6. Hemingway to Arnold Gingrich, March 13, 1933, in *Selected Letters, 1917–1961*, ed. Carlos Baker (New York: Scribner, 1981), 383.

7. Campbell was one of the most prominent African American commercial artists of the 1930s. Before specializing in battle of the sexes–style cartoons, though, he contributed the illustrations to Harlem Renaissance books such as Sterling Brown's *Southern Road*.

8. John Raeburn, *Fame Became of Him: Hemingway as Public Writer* (Bloomington: Indiana University Press, 1984), 46.

9. Ernest Hemingway, "Marlin off the Morrow: A Cuban Letter," in *By-Line: Ernest Hemingway*, ed. William White (New York: Scribners, 1967), 138.

10. See Ove G. Svensson, "Ernest Hemingway and the Nobel Prize for Literature," *Hemingway Review* 27 (2008): 118–122. Svensson's is the first published analysis of the recently released documents regarding the 1954 Nobel decision.

11. Qtd. in Baker, *Ernest Hemingway*, 499.

12. Thomas F. Strychacz, *Hemingway's Theaters of Masculinity* (Baton Rouge: Louisiana State University Press, 2003), 3.

13. Edward Weeks, "Hemingway at His Best," *Atlantic* 190 (September 1952): 72; Brendan Gill, "Not to Die," *New Yorker* 28 (September 6, 1952): 104; Carlos Baker, "The Marvel Who Must Die," *Saturday Review* 34 (September 6, 1952): 10–11; Harold C. Gardiner, "Pathetic Fallacy," *American* 87 (September 13, 1952): 569; Harvey Breit, "Hemingway's Old Man," *The Nation* 175 (September 6, 1952): 194–195.

14. Henry Seidel Canby, "An Unforgettable Picture of Man Against the Sea and Man Against Fate," *Book of the Month Club News* (August 1952): 2–3.

15. Hemingway, *Selected Letters*, 780.

16. Gill, "Not to Die," 104.

17. Dwight MacDonald, "Masscult and Midcult," in *Against the American Grain* (New York: Random House, 1962), 43.

18. Orville Prescott, "Books of the Times," *New York Times* (August 28, 1952): 21.

19. P. S. J., " 'The Old Man' and the Book," *Publishers' Weekly* 162 (September 13, 1952): 1011.

20. Ibid.

21. This debate over the proper publishing format of literature has a close relative within the American book trade, which also underwent a crisis in the ontology of the book and the origins of literary value when publishers started offering paperback reprints of the classics. Though paperback publishing goes back at least to the 1830s, the influx of "quality" paperback reprints after World War II reanimated the belief that inexpensive or inelegant printing might devalue literary content. See Kenneth C. Davis, *Two-Bit Culture: The Paperbacking of America* (New York: Mariner, 1984). In regards to how the rise of the paperback specifically relates to modernism, see David M. Earle, *Re-Covering Modernism: Pulps, Paperbacks, and the Prejudice of Form* (Surrey: Ashgate, 2009); Gregory Barnhisel, *James Laughlin, New Directions, and the Re-Making of Ezra Pound* (Amherst: University of Massachusetts Press, 2005); and Paula Rabinowitz, *American Pulp: How Paperbacks Brought Modernism to Main Street* (Princeton, N.J.: Princeton University Press, 2015).

22. Maxwell Perkins to Hemingway, February 19, 1929. In Matthew Bruccoli, ed., *The Only Thing That Counts: The Ernest Hemingway–Maxwell Perkins Correspondence* (New York: Scribner, 1996), 92–93.

23. A treatment of Hemingway and Perkins's dialogue over censorship, as well as a convincing argument that the reputation of Anglophone modernism depends on obscenity, can be found in Loren Glass, "#$%^&*!?: Modernism and Dirty Words," *Modernism/modernity* 14, no. 2 (2007): 209–223.

24. "Images, Verbal and Photographic," *Life* (September 1, 1952): 9.

25. "The Hemingways in Sun Valley," *Life* (January 6, 1941): 49.

26. Raeburn, *Fame Became of Him.*

27. Hugh Kenner, *A Homemade World: The American Modernist Writers* (Baltimore, Md.: Johns Hopkins University Press, 1975), 127.

28. Critics often refer to the combination of Hemingway's writing and persona as "The Hemingway Text," which includes how others wrote about him as an author and celebrity. See Nancy Comley and Robert Scholes, *Hemingway's Genders: Rereading the Hemingway Text* (New Haven, Conn.: Yale University Press, 1994).

29. "Images, Verbal and Photographic," 9. On the tradition of pictorialism in American modernism, see Deborah Schnitzer, *The Pictorial in Modernist Fiction from Stephen Crane to Ernest Hemingway* (Ann Arbor, Mich.: UMI Research Press, 1988).

30. P. S. J., "'The Old Man' and the Book," 1011.

31. The first was John Dos Passos, "State of the Nation," *Life* (September 25, 1944).

32. Gertrude Stein, "Off We All Went to See Germany," *Life* (August 6, 1945): 54.

33. Loren Glass, *Authors Inc: Literary Celebrity in the Modern United States, 1880–1980* (New York: New York University Press, 2004), 6.

34. Hemingway recounts Pound's influence in *A Moveable Feast* (New York: Scribners, 1964), 164.

35. In James R. Mellow, *Ernest Hemingway: A Life Without Consequences* (New York: Houghton Mifflin, 1994), 181.

36. Ernest Hemingway, *By-Line: Ernest Hemingway*, ed. William White (New York: Scribners, 1967), 179.

37. Ibid., 5.

38. Ibid., 18, 19.

39. Michael North and Scott Donaldson are two of the very few critics who have pointed out the problem with attributing Hemingway's narrative style to his journalism.

40. Roland Marchand, *Advertising the American Dream: Making Way for Modernity, 1920–1940* (Berkeley: University of California Press, 1985), 20. North, *Camera Works*, also links Hemingway's prose style to his short time working in advertising.

41. Arnold Gingrich, *Cast Down the Laurel* (New York: Knopf, 1935), 8.

42. Leslie Fiedler, "The Death of the Old Men," in *A New Fiedler Reader* (Amherst, N.Y.: Prometheus, 1999), 183.

43. "From Ernest Hemingway to the Editors of *Life*," *Life* (August 25, 1952): 124.

44. Ibid.

45. Catherine Turner, *Marketing Modernism Between the Two World Wars* (Amherst: University of Massachusetts Press, 2003), 146.

46. Ballantine Ale advertisement, *Life* (September 8, 1952): 57.

47. R. W. B. Lewis, "The Eccentrics' Pilgrammage," *Hudson Review* 6 (Spring 1953): 146–148.

48. In Matthew Bruccoli, ed., *Hemingway and the Mechanism of Fame* (Columbia: University of South Carolina Press, 2006), 106–107. Interview responses hereafter cited parenthetically in the text.

49. Ibid., 93.

50. Advertisement for Pan Am, in *Holiday* (February 1956): 60. Bruccoli, *Hemingway*, 138.

51. "American Storyteller," *Time* (September 6, 1952): 72.

52. Ibid., 70.

53. Malcolm Cowley, "Portrait of Mr. Papa," *Life* (January 10, 1949): 86, 98.

54. Malcolm Cowley, "Mr. Papa and the Parricides," in *—And I Worked at the Writer's Trade: Chapters of Literary History, 1918–1978* (New York: Viking, 1963), 24. Hereafter cited parenthetically in the text.

55. Baker, *Ernest Hemingway*, 238.

56. *Writers at Work: The Paris Review Interviews, Second Series* (New York: Viking, 1963), 235–236.

57. Hemingway, *Letters*, 780.

58. "From Ernest," 124.

59. Ernest Hemingway, *The Old Man and the Sea* (New York: Scribners, 1952), 40.

60. "From Ernest," 124.

61. Ernest Hemingway, "The Snows of Kilimanjaro," in *The First Forty-Nine Stories* (New York: Scribners, 1938): 71, 68.

62. Jerome Beatty Jr., "Who Owns the Past? Hemingway vs. *Esquire*," *Saturday Review* (August 23, 1958): 9, 11.

63. Arthur Kimball, "The Invasion of Journalism," *Atlantic Monthly* (July 1900): 119–125.

64. Arnold Gingrich, preface to *The Armchair* Esquire (New York: Putnam, 1958), 17–18.

65. The best treatment of American literature's response to television is Kathleen Fitzpatrick, *The Anxiety of Obsolescence: The American Novel in the Age of Television* (Nashville, Tenn.: Vanderbilt University Press, 2006).

66. "The Man Becomes Invisible," *Life* (August 25, 1952): 9.

67. Norman Mailer, *The Armies of the Night: History as a Novel, the Novel as History* (1968; repr. New York: Plume, 1994), 3.

Afterword: Working from Home

1. Chad Harbach, *The Art of Fielding* (New York: Little, Brown, 2011), 328. Hereafter cited parenthetically in the text.

2. Ezra Pound to Harriet Monroe, in *The Letters of Ezra Pound, 1907–1941* (New York: Faber and Faber, 1951), 80.

3. Mark McGurl, *The Program Era: Postwar Fiction and the Rise of Creative Writing* (Cambridge, Mass.: Harvard University Press, 2009), 50, 51.

4. Interview with Joshua Lars Weill, "Fielding Questions on *The Art of Fielding*," *GQ*, http://www.gq.com/story/art-fielding-chad-harbach-interview.

5. The Editors, "A Regressive Avant-Garde," *n+1* (Summer 2004), http://nplusonemag.com/issue-1/the-intellectual-situation/regressive-avant-garde/.

6. Qtd. in Susan Hodara, "Intellectual Entrepreneurs," *Harvard Magazine* (January–February 2010): 15–18, 17.

7. Keith Gessen, "On *n+1*," in *The Little Magazine in Contemporary America*, ed. Ian Morris and Joanne Diaz (Chicago: University of Chicago Press, 2015), 44.

8. Michael Hastings, *The Last Magazine* (New York: Blue Rider, 2014).

9. Michael Massing, "Digital Journalism: How Good Is It?" *New York Review of Books* (June 4, 2015): 43.

10. Tina Brown, "The Gig Economy," *Daily Beast* (January 12, 2009), http://www.thedailybeast.com/articles/2009/01/12/the-gig-economy.html.

11. Colson Whitehead, *John Henry Days* (New York: Doubleday, 2001), 169.

12. Ibid., 47.

13. Daniel H. Pink, *Free Agent Nation: The Future of Working for Yourself* (New York: Warner, 2001).

14. Whitehead, *John Henry Days*, 70.

15. Ibid., 135.

16. James Wood, "Virtual Prose," *New Republic* (August 6, 2001): 30. Wood sees this as a problem of multiplotted, multicultural novels in general, a genre he names "hysterical realism" in a review of Zadie Smith that appeared the same month as his review of *John Henry Days*. See James Wood, "Human, All Too Human," *New Republic* (August 30, 2001): 28.

17. Daniel Grausam, "After the Post-al," *American Literary History* 23, no. 3 (2011): 625–642.

18. Whitehead, *John Henry Days*, 185.

19. Colson Whitehead interview with Nancy Smith, *The Rumpus* (July 17, 2012), http://therumpus.net/2012/07/the-rumpus-interview-with-colson-whitehead/.

20. Jason Del Rey, "As *Grantland* Grows Up, It Looks to *New York Magazine* as a Model," *Advertising Age* (January 10, 2013), http://adage.com/article/digital/grantland-grows-york-magazine-a-model/239098/.

"1,000 Lost Golf Balls." *Time* (November 15, 1948): 32.

Ackroyd, Peter. *T. S. Eliot: A Life*. New York: Simon & Schuster, 1984.

Acocella, Joan. *Willa Cather and the Politics of Criticism*. Lincoln: University of Nebraska Press, 2000.

Adams, Henry. *The Education of Henry Adams*. 1918. New York: Modern Library, 1931.

Agee, James. "Comedy's Greatest Era." *Life* (September 5, 1949): 70–88.

——. *Cotton Tenants: Three Families*. Brooklyn: Melville House, 2013.

——. *Letters of James Agee to Father Flye*. New York: George Braziller, 1962.

——. "Plans for Work: October 1937." In *The Collected Short Prose of James Agee*, ed. Robert Fitzgerald. Boston: Houghton Mifflin, 1968.

——. "Tennessee Valley Authority." In *Film Writing and Selected Journalism*, ed. Michael Sragow, 631–646. New York: Library of America, 2005.

Agee, James, and Walker Evans. *Let Us Now Praise Famous Men*. 1941; repr. New York: Houghton-Mifflin, 2001.

Agee, Mia, with Gerald Cocklin. "Faint Lines in a Drawing of Jim." In *Remembering James Agee*, ed. David Madden. Baton Rouge: Louisiana State University Press, 1974.

Aiken, Conrad. "Poets as Reporters." *The Dial* (April 11, 1918): 351–353.

"All Stones End . . . " *Time* (October 8, 1937).

Allred, Jeff. *American Modernism and Depression Documentary*. New York: Oxford University Press, 2010.

——. "Boring from Within: James Agee and Walker Evans at Time Inc." *Criticism* 52 (2010): 41–70.

"American Storyteller." *Time* (September 6, 1952): 70ff.

Ammons, Elizabeth. "Black Anxiety About Immigration and Jessie Fauset's 'Sleeper Wakes.'" *African American Review* 42 (2008): 461–476.

Anderson, Benedict. *Imagined Communities: Reflections on the Origin and Spread of Nationalism*. Rev. ed. London: Verso, 2006.

"Annual Report of the Director of Publicity and Research for the Fiscal Year 1912." W. E. B. Du Bois Papers, University of Massachusetts Amherst Special Collections.

"Annual Report of the Director of Publicity Research for the Fiscal Year 1913." W. E. B. Du Bois Papers. Microfilm, University of Memphis. Reel 4, Slide 554.

Ardis, Ann. "Staging the Public Sphere: Magazine Dialogism and the Prosthetics of Authorship at the Turn of the Twentieth Century." In *Transatlantic Print Culture, 1880–1940*, ed. Ann Ardis and Patrick Collier, 30–47. New York: Palgrave, 2008.

Ardis, Ann, and Patrick Collier, eds. *Transatlantic Print Culture, 1880–1940: Emerging Media, Emerging Modernisms*. New York: Palgrave, 2008.

"Balance Sheet, 1913, for *The Crisis*." Microfilm of W. E. B. Du Bois Papers, University of Memphis Library. Reel 4, Slide 5-7043.

Baldasty, Gerald J. *The Commercialization of the News in the Nineteenth Century*. Madison: University of Wisconsin Press, 1992.

Baker, Carlos. *Ernest Hemingway: A Life Story*. New York: Putnam's, 1969.

——. "The Marvel Who Must Die." *Saturday Review* 34 (September 6, 1952): 10–11.

Baker, Houston. *Modernism and the Harlem Renaissance*. Chicago: University of Chicago Press, 1987.

Banning, Stephen A. "The Professionalization of Journalism: A Nineteenth-Century Beginning." *Journalism History* 24 (1998–1999): 157–163.

Barnard, Rita. *The Great Depression and the Culture of Abundance*. Cambridge: Cambridge University Press, 1995.

Barnhisel, Gregory. *Cold War Modernists: Art, Literature, and American Cultural Diplomacy*. New York: Columbia University Press, 2015.

——. *James Laughlin, New Directions, and the Re-Making of Ezra Pound*. Amherst: University of Massachusetts Press, 2005.

Batker, Carol. J. *Reforming Fictions: Native, African, and Jewish American Women's Literature and Journalism in the Progressive Era*. New York: Columbia University Press, 2000.

Beatty, Jerome, Jr. "Who Owns the Past? Hemingway vs. *Esquire*." *Saturday Review* (August 23, 1958): 9ff.

Bergreen, Laurence. *James Agee: A Life*. New York: Penguin, 1985.

Biers, Katherine. "Syncope Fever: James Weldon Johnson and the Black Phonographic Voice." *Representations* 96 (Fall 2006): 99–125.

Blackwood, Sarah. "Editing as Carework: The Gendered Labor of Public Intellectuals." *Avidly* (June 6, 2014), http://avidly.lareviewofbooks.org.

Blair, Sara. *Harlem Crossroads: Black Writers and the Photograph in the Twentieth Century*. Princeton, N.J.: Princeton University Press, 2007.

Botshon, Lisa, and Meredith Goldsmith, eds. *Middlebrow Moderns: Popular American Women Writers of the 1920s*. Boston: Northeastern University Press, 2003.

Bourdieu, Pierre. *The Rules of Art: Genesis and Structure of the Literary Field*. Trans. Susan Manuel. Stanford, Calif.: Stanford University Press, 1996.

Braddock, Jeremy. *Collecting as Modernist Practice*. Baltimore, Md.: Johns Hopkins University Press, 2013.

Breen, Melwyn. "Man, Nature and Nothing." *Saturday Night* 67 (September 13, 1952): 26.

Breit, Harvey. "Hemingway's Old Man." *The Nation* 175 (September 6, 1952): 194–195.

Brier, Evan. *A Novel Marketplace: Mass Culture, the Book Trade, and Postwar American Fiction*. Philadelphia: University of Pennsylvania Press, 2010.

Brinkley, Alan. *The Publisher: Henry Luce and His American Century*. New York: Knopf, 2010.

Brown, Tina. "The Gig Economy." *Daily Beast* (January 12, 2009), http://www.thedailybeast.com/articles/2009/01/12/the-gig-economy.html.

Bruccoli, Matthew. "A Brief Life of Fitzgerald." In F. Scott Fitzgerald, *A Life in Letters*, ed. Matthew Bruccoli, xix–xxii. New York: Simon & Schuster, 1994.

——, ed. *Hemingway and the Mechanism of Fame*. Columbia: University of South Carolina Press, 2006.

Burrows, Stuart. *A Familiar Strangeness: American Fiction and the Language of Photography, 1839–1945*. Athens: University of Georgia Press, 2008.

——. "'Losing the Whole in the Parts': Identity in *The Professor's House*." *Arizona Quarterly* 64, no. 4 (2008): 21–48.

Bush, Ronald. "T. S. Eliot and Modernism at the Present Time." In *T. S. Eliot: The Modernist in History*, ed. Ronald Bush, 191–204. Cambridge: Cambridge University Press, 1991.

Butcher, Fanny. "Willa Cather Tells Purpose of New Novel." *Chicago Tribune* (September 12, 1925). Reprinted in *Willa Cather: The Contemporary Reviews*, ed. Margaret Anne O'Connor, 237–238. Cambridge: Cambridge University Press, 2001.

Canby, Henry Seidel. "An Unforgettable Picture of Man Against the Sea and Man Against Fate." *Book of the Month Club News* (August 1952): 2–3.

Carlston, Eric G. "Modern Literature Under Surveillance: American Writers, State Espionage, and the Cultural Cold War." *American Literary History* 22, no. 3 (2010): 615–625.

Carroll, Anne Elizabeth. *Word, Image, and the New Negro: Representation and Identity in the Harlem Renaissance*. Bloomington: Indiana University Press, 2005.

Castronovo, Russ. "Beauty Along the Color Line: Lynching, Aesthetics, and the *Crisis*." *PMLA* 121, no. 5 (2006): 1443–1459.

Cather, Willa. *Alexander's Bridge.* 1912; repr. New York: Houghton, 1922.

——. "Ardessa." In *Stories, Poems, and Other Writings*, 167–184.

——. "Escapism." In *On Writing*, 18–29.

——. "Miss Jewett." In *Not Under Forty*, 76–95. New York: Knopf, 1936.

——. *My Ántonia.* 1918; repr. Lincoln: University Nebraska Press, 1994.

——. "My First Novels (There Were Two)." In *On Writing*, 91–97.

——. "The Novel Démeublé." In *Not Under Forty*, 43–51. New York: Knopf, 1936.

——. *O Pioneers!* 1913; repr. Lincoln: University of Nebraska Press, 1992.

——. "On the Art of Fiction." In *On Writing*, 101–104.

——. "On *The Professor's House.*" In *On Writing*, 30–32.

——. *On Writing: Critical Studies on Writing as an Art.* New York: Knopf, 1949.

——. *The Professor's House.* 1925; repr. New York: Vintage, 1990.

——. *The Selected Letters of Willa Cather.* Ed. Andrew Jewell and Janis Stout. New York: Knopf, 2013.

——. *The Song of the Lark.* 1915; repr. Lincoln: University of Nebraska Press, 2012.

——. *Stories, Poems, and Other Writings.* New York: Library of America, 1992.

——. "When I Knew Stephen Crane." In *Stories, Poems, and Other Writings*, 932–938.

——. "The Willing Muse." In *The Collected Short Fiction*, ed. Mildred R. Bennett, 1:113–123. Lincoln: University of Nebraska Press, 1965.

——. *The World and the Parish: Willa Cather's Articles and Reviews.* Vol. 1: *1893–1902.* Ed. William Curtin. Lincoln: University of Nebraska Press, 1970.

Chalaby, Jean K. *The Invention of Journalism.* New York: St. Martin's, 1998.

Chasar, Mike. *Everyday Reading: Poetry and Popular Culture in Modern America.* New York: Columbia University Press, 2012.

Cheng, Ann. *Second Skin: Josephine Baker and the Modern Surface.* New York: Oxford, 2011.

Chesnutt, Charles. *Marrow of Tradition.* Ed. Nancy Bentley and Sandra Gunning. 1901; repr. New York: Bedford, 2002.

——. *Paul Marchand, F.M.C.* Jackson: University of Mississippi Press, 1998.

Chinitz, David E. *T. S. Eliot and the Cultural Divide.* Chicago: University of Chicago Press, 2003.

Christensen, Jerome. *America's Corporate Art: The Studio Authorship of Hollywood Pictures.* Stanford, Calif.: Stanford University Press, 2012.

Cleary, Joe. "Realism After Modernism and the Literary World-System." *Modern Language Quarterly* 73, no. 3 (2012): 255–268.

Collier, Patrick. *Modernism on Fleet Street.* Burlington, Vt.: Ashgate, 2006.

Comley, Nancy, and Robert Scholes. *Hemingway's Genders: Rereading the Hemingway Text.* New Haven, Conn.: Yale University Press, 1996.

Connor, J. D. *The Studios After the Studios: Neo-Classical Hollywood, 1970–2010.* Palo Alto, Calif.: Stanford University Press, 2015.

Coultrap-McQuin, Susan. *Doing Literary Business: American Women Writers in the Nineteenth Century.* Chapel Hill: University of North Carolina Press, 1990.

Cowley, Malcolm. *Exile's Return: A Literary Odyssey of the 1920s.* New York: Penguin, 1994.

———. "Mr. Papa and the Parricides." In *And I Worked at the Writer's Trade: Chapters of Literary History, 1918–1978,* 21–34. New York: Viking, 1963.

———. "Portrait of Mr. Papa." *Life* (January 10, 1949): 86ff.

Cramsie, Peter. *The Story of Graphic Design: From the Invention of Writing to the Birth of Digital Design.* New York: Abrams, 2010.

Culleton, Claire A., and Karen Leick, eds. *Modernism on File: Writers, Artists, and the FBI, 1920–1950.* New York: Palgrave, 2008.

Daly, Christopher B. *Covering America: A Narrative History of the Nation's Journalism.* Amherst: University of Massachusetts Press, 2012.

Davenport, Russell. "A *Life* Round Table on the Pursuit of Happiness." *Life* (July 12, 1948): 95–113.

Davis, Kenneth C. *Two-Bit Culture: The Paperbacking of America.* New York: Mariner, 1984.

Day, Elizabeth. "Is the LRB the Best Magazine in the World?" *Guardian* (March 8, 2014).

Del Ray, Jason. "As *Grantland* Grows Up, It Looks to *New York Magazine* as a Model." *Advertising Age* (January 10, 2013), http://adage.com/article/digital/grantland-grows-york-magazine-a-model/239098/.

Denning, Michael. *The Cultural Front: The Laboring of American Culture in the Twentieth Century.* London: Verso, 1997.

Dos Passos, John. "State of the Nation." *Life* (September 25, 1944).

Downs, M. Catherine. *Becoming Modern: Willa Cather's Journalism.* Selingsgrove, Penn.: Susquehanna University Press, 1999.

Du Bois, W. E. B. "Books." *The Horizon* 1, no. 4 (April 1907): 5–6.

———. *Correspondence of W. E. B. Du Bois.* Vol. 1: *1877–1934.* Ed. Herbert Aptheker. Amherst: University of Massachusetts Press, 1973.

———. "Criteria of Negro Art." In *The Emerging Thought of W. E. B. DuBois,* ed. Henry Lee Moon, 360–368.

———. "Dr. Du Bois Resigns." In *Writings,* ed. Nathan Huggins, 1259–1263. New York: Library of America, 1982.

———. *Dusk of Dawn.* 1940; repr. New York: Oxford University Press, 2007.

———. "Editing *The Crisis.*" In *The Crisis Reader: Stories Poetry, and Essays from the N.A.A.C.P.'s Crisis Magazine,* ed. Sondra Kathryn Wilson, xxvii–xxxii. New York: Modern Library, 1999.

———. "Editorial." *The Crisis* (November 1910): 10–11.

———. *The Emerging Thought of W. E. B. Du Bois: Essays and Editorials from* The Crisis, ed. Henry Lee Moon. New York: Simon and Schuster, 1972.

———. "In Black." *The Crisis* (October 1920): 263–264.

———. "Our Book Shelf." *The Crisis* (November 1925): 31.

———. "Paper." *The Crisis* (June 1920): 72.

———. "Photography." *The Crisis* (October 1923): 249–250.

——. "A Proposed Negro Journal (April 1905)." In *Against Racism: Unpublished Essays, Papers, Addresses, 1887–1961*, ed. Herbert Aptheker, 77–80. Amherst: University of Massachusetts Press, 1985.

——. "The Name 'Negro.'" In *The Emerging Thought of W. E. B. Du Bois*, ed. Henry Lee Moon, 55–57.

——. "The New *Crisis*." *The Crisis* (May 1925): 7–9.

——. "W. E. B. Du Bois to the National Association for the Advancement of Colored People" (July 11, 1930). W. E. B. Du Bois Papers (MS 312), University of Massachusetts–Amherst Special Collections.

Dubey, Madhu. *Signs and Cities: Black Literary Postmodernism*. Chicago: University of Chicago Press, 2003.

Ducille, Ann. "Blue Notes on Black Sexuality: Sex and the Texts of Jessie Fauset and Nella Larson." *Journal of the History of Sexuality* 3, no. 3 (1993): 418–444.

Earle, David M. *Re-Covering Modernism: Pulps, Paperbacks, and the Prejudice of Form*. Burlington, Vt.: Ashgate, 2009.

Edel, Leon. "A Cave of One's Own." In *Critical Essays on Willa Cather*, ed. John J. Murphy, 200–216. Boston: G. K. Hall, 1984.

Edwards, Brent Hayes. *The Practice of Diaspora: Literature, Translation, and the Rise of Black Internationalism*. Cambridge, Mass.: Harvard University Press, 2003.

Eliot, T. S. "Banquet Speech." In *Nobel Lectures, Literature 1901–1967*, ed. Horst Frenz, 433–437. Amsterdam: Elsevier, 1969.

——. *The Frontiers of Criticism*. Minneapolis: University of Minnesota Press, 1956.

——. "The Function of Criticism." In *The Selected Prose of T. S. Eliot*, ed. Frank Kermode, 68–76. New York: Harcourt Brace, 1975.

——. Introduction to *Nightwood*, by Djuna Barnes. New York: New Directions, 1937.

——. "Notes . . . from T. S. Eliot." *University of Chicago Magazine* (December 1950): 10–12.

——. *The Sacred Wood*. 1920; repr. London: Methuen, 1960.

——. *The Waste Land*, ed. Michael North. New York: Norton, 2000.

——. *The Waste Land. A Facsimile and Transcript of the Original Drafts Including the Annotations of Ezra Pound*. Ed. Valerie Eliot. New York: Harcourt Brace Jovanovich, 1971.

Elson, Robert T. *Time Inc.: The Intimate History of a Publishing Enterprise, 1923–1941*. New York: Atheneum, 1968.

English, Daylanne. *Unnatural Selections: Eugenics in American Modernism and the Harlem Renaissance*. Chapel Hill: University of North Carolina Press, 2004.

——. "W. E. B. Du Bois' Family *Crisis*." *American Literature* 72 (2000): 291–319.

English, James. *The Economy of Prestige: Prizes, Awards, and the Circulation of Cultural Value*. Cambridge, Mass.: Harvard University Press, 2008.

Esty, Jed, and Colleen Lye. "Peripheral Realisms Now." *Modern Language Quarterly* 73, no. 3 (2012): 270–290.

Farrar, John Chipman. "To an Intellectualist." In *Forgotten Shrines*, 42. New Haven, Conn.: Yale University Press, 1919.

——. "Modernist Miracle." *Time* (November 1, 1937).

Fauset, Jessie. "The Sleeper Wakes." *The Crisis* (August 1920): 168–173; (September 1920): 226–229; (October 1920): 267–274.

Fearing, Kenneth. *The Big Clock*. 1946; repr. London: Orion, 2001.

——. "Reading, Writing, the Rackets." In *New and Selected Poems*, ix–xxiv. Bloomington: Indiana University Press, 1956.

Fiedler, Leslie. "The Death of the Old Men." In *A New Fiedler Reader*, 178–188. Amherst, N.Y.: Prometheus, 1999.

Firebaugh, Joseph J. "The Vocabulary of *Time* Magazine." *American Speech* 15, no. 3 (1940): 232–242.

Fishkin, Shelly Fisher. *From Fact to Fiction: Journalism and Imaginative Writing in America*. New York: Oxford, 1985.

Fitzgerald, F. Scott. *A Life in Letters*. Ed. Matthew Bruccoli. New York: Simon & Schuster, 1994.

——. *F. Scott Fitzgerald, in His Own Time: A Miscellany*. Ed. Matthew Bruccoli and Jackson R. Bryer, 227–230. Kent, Ohio: Kent State University Press, 1971.

FitzGerald, Robert. "A Memoir." In *The Collected Short Prose of James Agee*, ed. Robert FitzGerald, 3–66. New York: Ballantine, 1970.

Flatley, Jonathan. *Affective Mapping: Melancholia and the Politics of Modernism*. Cambridge, Mass.: Harvard University Press, 2008.

——. "Like: Collecting and Collectivity." *October* 132 (2010): 71–98.

Fleissner, Jennifer. "The Biological Clock: Edith Wharton, Naturalism, and the Temporality of Womanhood." *American Literature* 78, no. 3 (2006): 519–549.

——. *Women, Compulsion, Modernity*. Chicago: University of Chicago Press, 2004.

Foley, Barbara. *Telling the Truth: The Theory and Practice of Documentary Fiction*. Ithaca, N.Y.: Cornell University Press, 1986.

Fore, Devin. *Realism After Modernism: The Rehumanization of Art and Literature*. Cambridge, Mass.: MIT Press, 2012.

"Foreign Relations: That Month." *Time* (April 23, 1963).

Foster, Frances Smith. "Genealogies of Our Concerns, Early (African) American Print Culture, and Transcending Tough Times." *ALH* 22 (2010): 368–380.

——. "A Narrative of the Interesting Origins and (Somewhat) Surprising Developments of African-American Print Culture." *ALH* (2005): 714–740.

"Free for All?" *Time* (April 28, 1923): 11.

Fried, Michael. "Art and Objecthood." In *Art and Objecthood: Essays and Reviews*, 148–172. Chicago: University of Chicago Press, 1998.

——. *Theatricality and Absorption: Painting and Beholder in the Age of Diderot*. Berkeley: University of California Press, 1980.

"From Tom to T. S." *Time* (January 2 1939): 35.

Frus, Phyllis. *The Politics and Poetics of Journalistic Narrative*. Cambridge: Cambridge University Press, 1994.

Gardiner, Harold C. "Pathetic Fallacy." *American* 87 (September 13, 1952): 569.

Gardner, Jared. *The Rise and Fall of Early American Magazine Culture*. Urbana: University of Illinois Press, 2012.

Garvey, Ellen Gruber. " 'Important, Responsible Work': Willa Cather's Office Stories and Her Necessary Editorial Career." *Studies in American Fiction* 36, no. 2 (2008): 177–196.

Gates, Jr., Henry Louis. *The Signifying Monkey: A Theory of African American Literary Criticism.* New York: Oxford University Press, 1988.

——. "The Trope of a New Negro and the Reconstruction of the Image of the Black." *Representations* 24 (Fall 1988): 129–155.

Gessen, Keith. "On *n+1*." In *The Little Magazine in Contemporary America*, ed. Ian Morris and Joanne Diaz, 38–50. Chicago: University of Chicago Press, 2015.

Gibbs, Walcott. "*Time . . . Fortune . . . Life . . . Luce.*" *New Yorker* 12, no. 41(1936): 20–25.

Gill, Brendan. "Not to Die." *New Yorker* 28 (September 6, 1952): 104.

Gingrich, Arnold. *Cast Down the Laurel.* New York: Knopf, 1935.

——. Preface to *The Armchair* Esquire. New York: Putnam, 1958.

Glass, Loren. *Authors Inc.: Literary Celebrity in the Modern United States, 1880–1980.* New York: New York University Press, 2004.

——. "#$%^&*!?: Modernism and Dirty Words." *Modernism/modernity* 14, no. 2 (2007): 209–223.

Goesser, Caroline. *Picturing the New Negro: Harlem Renaissance Print Culture and Modern Black Identity.* Lawrence: University of Kansas Press, 2007.

Gold, Matthew K., ed. *Debates in the Digital Humanities.* Minneapolis: University of Minnesota Press, 2012.

Golding, Alan. "*The Dial, The Little Review,* and the Dialogics of Modernism." *American Periodicals* 15, no. 1 (2005): 42–55.

Goodman, Paul. "Reflections on Literature as a Minor Art." In *The Paul Goodman Reader*, ed. Taylor Stoehr, 216–219. Oakland, Calif.: PM, 2001.

"Government and Newspapers." *New York Times* (May 15, 1920): 14.

Goyal, Yogita. *Romance, Diaspora, and Black Atlantic Literature.* Cambridge: Cambridge University Press, 2010.

Graff, Gerald. *Professing Literature: An Institutional History.* Chicago: University of Chicago Press, 1987.

Graham, T. Austin. *The Great American Songbooks: Musical Texts, Modernism, and the Value of Popular Culture.* New York: Oxford University Press, 2012.

Grausam, Daniel. "After the Post-al." *American Literary History* 23, no. 3 (2011): 625–642.

"The Great Trial." *Time* (July 20, 1925): 17ff.

Greenberg, Clement. "Avant-Garde and Kitsch." In *Art and Culture: The Critical Essays*, 3–21. Boston: Beacon, 1961.

Greene, Theodore P. *America's Heroes: The Changing Models of Success in American Magazines.* New York: Oxford University Press, 1970.

Guilbaut, Serge. *How New York Stole the Idea of Modern Art: Abstract Expressionism, Freedom, and the Cold War.* Trans. Arthur Goldhammer. Chicago: University of Chicago Press, 1985.

Guillory, John. *Cultural Capital: The Problem of Literary Canon Formation*. Chicago: University of Chicago Press, 1994.

——. "The Memo and Modernity." *Critical Inquiry* 31 (2004): 108–132.

Harbach, Chad. *The Art of Fielding*. New York: Little, Brown, 2011.

——. "Fielding Questions on *The Art of Fielding* [Interview with Joshua Lars Weill]." *GQ*. http://www.gq.com/story/art-fielding-chad-harbach-interview.

Hastings, Michael M. *The Last Magazine: A Novel*. New York: Blue Rider, 2014.

Hemingway, Ernest. *By-Line: Ernest Hemingway*. Ed. William White. New York: Scribners, 1967.

——. "From Ernest Hemingway to the Editors of *Life*." *Life* (August 25, 1952): 124.

——. *A Moveable Feast*. New York: Scribners, 1964.

——. *The Old Man and the Sea*. New York: Scribners, 1952.

——. *Selected Letters, 1917–1961*. Ed. Carlos Baker. New York: Scribners, 1981.

——. "The Snows of Kilimanjaro." In *The First Forty-Nine Stories*, 52–77. New York: Scribners, 1938.

"The Hemingways in Sun Valley." *Life* (January 6, 1941): 49.

Hicks, Granville. "The Case Against Willa Cather." *The English Journal* 22, no. 9 (1933): 703–710.

Hodara, Susan. "Intellectual Entrepreneurs." *Harvard Magazine* (January–February 2010): 15–18.

Howells, William Dean. "The Man of Letters as a Man of Business." In *Literature and Life*, 1–35. New York: Harper, 1902.

Hutchinson, George. *The Harlem Renaissance in Black and White*. Cambridge, Mass.: Belknap, 1995.

Hutner, Gordon. *What America Read: Taste, Class, and the Novel, 1920–1960* (Chapel Hill: University of North Carolina Press, 2009.

Hyde, Carrie, and Joseph Rezek. "Introduction: The Aesthetics of Archival Evidence." *J19: The Journal of Nineteenth-Century Americanists* 2 (2014): 155–162.

"Images, Verbal and Photographic." *Life* (September 1, 1952): 9.

"In Love and Anger." *Time* (September 26, 1960): 112.

Jackson, Bruce. "The Deceptive Anarchy of *Let Us Now Praise Famous Men*." *Antioch Review* 57, no. 1 (1999): 38–49.

Jackson, Leon. "The Talking Book and the Talking Book Historian: African American Cultures of Print—The State of the Discipline." *Book History* 13 (2010): 251–308.

Jaffe, Aaron. *Modernism and the Culture of Celebrity*. Cambridge: Cambridge University Press, 2005.

Jaillant, Lise. *Modernism, Middlebrow, and the Literary Canon: The Modern Library Series, 1916–1955*. London: Pickering and Chatto, 2014.

James, Henry. "The Future of the Novel." In *Literary Criticism: Essays on Literature, American Writers, English Writers*. New York: Library of America, 1984.

——. *Letters*. Vol. 4: *1895–1916*. Cambridge, Mass.: Belknap, 1984.

Johanningsmeier, Charles. "Determining How Readers Responded to Cather's Fiction: The Cultural Work of *The Professor's House* in *Collier's Weekly.*" *American Periodicals* 20, no. 1 (2010): 68–96.

Johnson, Abby Arthur, and Ronald Maberry Johnson. *Propaganda and Aesthetics: The Literary Politics of African-American Magazines in the Twentieth Century.* 1979; repr. Amherst: University of Massachusetts Press, 1991.

Kaplan, Richard. *Politics and the American Press: The Rise of Objectivity, 1865–1920.* Cambridge: Cambridge University Press, 2002.

——. "The Origins of Objectivity in American Journalism." In *The Routledge Companion to News and Journalism,* ed. Stuart Allen, 25–37. New York: Routledge, 2010.

Kazin, Alfred. *On Native Grounds: An Interpretation of Modern American Prose Literature.* 1942; repr. New York: Harcourt, 1970.

——. *Starting Out in the Thirties.* Boston: Little, Brown, 1962.

——. "Writing for Magazines." In *Contemporaries,* 469–474. Boston: Little, Brown, 1962.

Kenner, Hugh. *A Homemade World: The American Modernist Writers.* Baltimore, Md.: Johns Hopkins, 1975.

——. *The Invisible Poet: T. S. Eliot.* London: Allen, 1960.

Keyser, Katherine. *Playing Smart: New York Women Writers and Modern Magazine Culture.* New Brunswick, N.J.: Rutgers University Press, 2010.

Kimball, Arthur Reed. "The Invasion of Journalism." *Atlantic Monthly* 86 (July 1900): 119–125.

Kirk, Russell. *Eliot and His Age: T. S. Eliot's Moral Imagination in the Twentieth Century.* New York: Random House, 1971.

Knight, Alisha R. "To Have the Benefit of Some Special Machinery: African American Book Publishing and Bookselling, 1900–1920." In *Oxford History of Popular Print Culture.* Vol. 6: *U.S. Popular Print Culture, 1860–1920,* 437–456. Oxford: Oxford University Press, 2012.

Lahire, Bernard. "The Double Life of Writers." Trans. Gwendolyn Wells. *New Literary History* 41 (2010): 443–465.

——. *The Plural Actor.* Cambridge: Polity, 2011.

Latham, Sean. "*New Age* Scholarship: The Work of Criticism in the Age of Digital Reproduction." *New Literary History* 35, no. 3 (2004): 411–426.

Latham, Sean, and Robert Scholes. "The Rise of Periodical Studies." *PMLA* 121, no. 2 (2006): 517–531.

Leavis, F. R. *Mass Civilization and Minority Culture.* Cambridge, Mass.: Minority, 1930.

——. *New Bearings on English Poetry.* 1932; repr. Ann Arbor: University of Michigan Press, 1964.

Lee, Hermoine. *Willa Cather: A Life Saved Up.* London: Virago, 1989.

Lee, Maurice S. "Falsifiability, Confirmation Bias, and Textual Promiscuity." *J19: The Journal of Nineteenth-Century Americanists* 2 (2014): 162–171.

Leick, Karen. *Gertrude Stein and the Making of an American Celebrity.* New York: Routledge, 2009.

——. "Popular Modernism: Little Magazines and the American Daily Press." *PMLA* 123, no. 1 (2008): 125–140.

Leitch, Thomas M. "The Editor as Hero: Henry James and the New York Edition." *Henry James Review* 3, no. 1 (1981): 24–32.

Lewis, David Levering. *W. E. B Du Bois: The Biography of a Race, 1868–1919.* New York: Holt, 2000.

——. *When Harlem Was in Vogue.* New York: Penguin, 1997.

Lewis, Edith. *Willa Cather Living: A Personal Record by Edith Lewis.* New York: Knopf, 1953.

Lewis, R. W. B. "The Eccentrics' Pilgrimage." *Hudson Review* 6 (Spring 1953): 146–148.

Lofaro, Michael A., and Hugh Davis, eds. *James Agee Rediscovered: The Journals of* Let Us Now Praise Famous Men *and Other New Manuscripts.* Knoxville: University of Tennessee Press, 2005.

Love, Heather. *Feeling Backward: Loss and the Politics of Queer History.* Cambridge, Mass.: Harvard University Press, 2007.

Luce, Henry. "The American Century." *Life* (February 17, 1941): 61–65.

Luhmann, Niklas. *Observations on Modernity.* Trans. William Whobrey. Stanford, Calif.: Stanford University Press, 1998.

Lyon, Peter. *Success Story: The Life and Times of S. S. McClure.* New York: Scribners, 1963.

MacDonald, Dwight. *Against the American Grain.* New York: Random House, 1952.

——. "A Theory of Mass Culture." In *Mass Culture: The Popular Arts in America*, ed. Bernard Rosenberg and David M. White, 59–73. New York: Free Press, 1957.

MacLeish, Archibald. "The First Nine Years." In *Writing for* Fortune. New York: Time Inc., 1980.

——. *Poetry and Journalism: A Lecture Delivered at Northrop Memorial Auditorium.* The Gideon Seymour Memorial Lecture. Minneapolis: University of Minneapolis Press, 1958.

Macy, John. "Journalism." In *Civilization in the United States: An Inquiry by Thirty Americans*, ed. Harold Stearns. New York: Harcourt, Brace, and Co., 1922.

"The Man Becomes Invisible." *Life* (August 25, 1952).

Mailer, Norman. *The Armies of the Night: History as a Novel, the Novel as History.* 1968; repr. New York: Plume, 1994.

Maras, Steven. *Objectivity in Journalism.* Malden, Mass.: Polity, 2013.

Marchand, Roland. *Advertising the American Dream: Making Way for Modernity, 1920–1940.* Berkeley: University of California Press, 1985.

Marek, Jayne. *Women Editing Modernism: "Little" Magazines and Literary History.* Lexington: University of Kentucky Press, 1995.

Marshall, Kate. *Corridor: Media Architectures in American Fiction.* Minneapolis: University of Minnesota Press, 2012.

Marx, William. "Two Modernisms: T. S. Eliot and *La Nouvelle Revue Française.*" In *The International Reception of T. S. Eliot,* ed. Elisabeth Däumer and Shyamal Bagchee, 25–35. New York: Continuum, 2007.

Majeras, Elisabeth. "Determined and Bigoted Feminists: Women, Magazines, and Popular Modernism." In *Modernism,* vol. 1, ed. Astradur Eysteinsson and Vivian Liska, 619–636. Amsterdam: Johns Benjamins, 2007.

Massing, Michael, "Digital Journalism: How Good Is It?" *New York Review of Books* (June 4, 2015): 43–45.

Matthews, T. S. "T. S. Eliot Turns to Comedy." *Life* (February 1 1954): 56–64.

Maxwell, William J. *FB Eyes: How J. Edgar Hoover's Ghostreaders Framed African American Literature.* Princeton, N.J.: Princeton University Press, 2015.

McGann, Jerome. *Black Riders: The Visible Language of Modernism.* Princeton, N.J.: Princeton University Press, 1993.

——. *The Textual Condition.* Princeton, N.J.: Princeton University Press, 1991.

McGurl, Mark. *The Novel Art: Elevations of American Fiction After Henry James.* Princeton, N.J.: Princeton University Press, 2001.

——. *The Program Era: Postwar Fiction and the Rise of Creative Writing.* Cambridge, Mass.: Harvard University Press, 2009.

McHenry, Elizabeth. *Forgotten Readers: Recovering the Lost History of African American Literary Societies.* Durham, N.C.: Duke University Press, 2002.

McLuhan, Marshall. *The Mechanical Bride: Folklore of Industrial Man.* New York: Vanguard, 1951.

Mellow, James R. *Ernest Hemingway: A Life Without Consequences.* New York: Houghton Mifflin, 1994.

Michaels, Walter Benn. *Our America: Nativism, Modernism, and Pluralism.* Durham, N.C.: Duke University Press, 1995.

Miller, Elizabeth Carolyn. *Slow Print: Literary Radicalism and Late Victorian Print Culture.* Stanford, Calif.: Stanford University Press, 2014.

Moody, A. D. "T. S. Eliot: The American Strain." In *Placing T. S. Eliot,* ed. Jewel Spears Brooker, 77–89. Columbia: University Missouri Press, 1991.

Moon, Henry Lee. "Introduction." In *The Emerging Thought of W. E. B. DuBois: Essays and Editorials from* The Crisis, ed. Henry Lee Moon, 11–44. New York: Simon and Schuster, 1972.

Morrisson, Mark S. *The Public Face of Modernism: Little Magazines, Audiences, and Reception, 1905–1920.* Madison: University of Wisconsin Press, 2001.

Moten, Fred. "Black Op." *PMLA* 123, no. 5 (2008): 1743–1747.

——. *In the Break: The Aesthetics of the Black Radical Tradition.* Minneapolis: University of Minnesota Press, 2003.

Mott, Frank Luther. *American Journalism, a History: 1690–1960.* New York: MacMillan, 1962.

——. *A History of American Magazines.* Vol. 4: *1885–1905.* Cambridge, Mass.: Belknap, 1957.

——. *A History of American Magazines*. Vol. 5: *1905–1930*. Cambridge, Mass.: Belknap, 1968.

Murray, F. H. M. "Headlines." *The Horizon* 1, no. 4 (April 1907): 22–24.

——. "Magazinelets." *The Horizon* (April 1908): 22–23.

Nadell, Martha Jane. *Enter the New Negroes: Images of Race in American Culture*. Cambridge: Harvard University Press, 2004.

Nathan, George Jean. "The Magazine in the Making." *Bookman* (1911): 414–417.

Nealon, Christopher. "Affect-Genealogy: Feeling and Affiliation in Willa Cather." *American Literature* 69, no. 1 (1997): 5–37.

"The Negro in Art: How Shall the Negro be Portrayed? A Symposium." *The Crisis* (March 1926): 219–220.

Ngai, Sianne. *Our Aesthetic Categories: Zany, Cute, Interesting*. Cambridge, Mass.: Harvard University Press, 2012.

North, Michael. *Camera Works: Photography and the Twentieth-Century Word*. Oxford: Oxford University Press, 2005.

——. *Reading 1922: A Return to the Scene of the Modern*. New York: Oxford University Press, 1999.

Ohmann, Richard. *Selling Culture: Magazines, Markets, and Class*. London: Verso, 1995.

Osterling, Anders. "Presentation Speech." In *Nobel Lectures, Literature 1901–1967*, ed. Horst Frenz, 431–433. Amsterdam: Elsevier, 1969.

Ovington, Mary. *The Shadow*. New York: Harcourt, 1920.

"People." *Time* (December 13, 1963).

P. S. J. " 'The Old Man' and the Book." *Publishers' Weekly* 162 (September 13, 1952): 1011.

Pink, Daniel H. *Free Agent Nation: The Future of Working for Yourself*. New York: Warner, 2001.

Poirier, Richard. "The Difficulties of Modernism and the Modernism of Difficulty." *Images and Ideas in American Culture*, ed. Arthur Edelstein, 125–140. Hanover, N.H.: Brandeis University Press, 1979.

Pound, Ezra. *ABC of Reading*. 1934; repr. New York: New Directions, 2010.

——. *The Letters of Ezra Pound, 1907–1941*. New York: Faber and Faber, 1951.

——. "Small Magazines." *The English Journal* 19, no. 9 (November 1930): 689–704.

Prescott, Orville. "Books of the Times." *New York Times* (August 28, 1952): 21.

Pressman, Jessica. "The Aesthetic of Bookishness in Twenty-First-Century Literature." *Michigan Quarterly Review* (Fall 2009): 465–483.

Pulitzer, Joseph. "The College of Journalism." *North American Review* (May 1904): 641–680.

Rabinowitz, Paula. *American Pulp: How Paperbacks Brought Modernism to Main Street*. Princeton, N.J.: Princeton University Press, 2015.

——. "Voyeurism and Class Consciousness: James Agee and Walker Evans, *Let Us Now Praise Famous Men*." *Cultural Critique* 21 (1992): 143–170.

Radway, Janice A. *A Feeling for Books: The Book-of-the-Month Club, Literary Taste, and Middle-Class Desire*. Chapel Hill: University of North Carolina Press, 1997.

Raeburn, John. *Fame Became of Him: Hemingway as Public Writer.* Bloomington: Indiana University Press, 1984.

Rainey, Lawrence. *Institutions of Modernism: Literary Elites and Public Culture.* New Haven, Conn.: Yale University Press, 1998.

——. *Revisiting* The Waste Land. New Haven, Conn.: Yale University Press, 2005.

Rando, David. *Modernist Fiction and the News: Representing Experience in the Early Twentieth Century.* London: Palgrave, 2011.

Rascoe, Burton. "Shreds and Tatters." *Newsweek* (April 3, 1939): 40.

Reed, T. V. "Unimagined Existence and the Fiction of the Real: Postmodern Realism in *Let Us Now Praise Famous Men.*" *Representations* 24 (1988): 156–176.

"Reflections." *Time* (March 6, 1950): 22ff.

"A Regressive Avant-Garde." *n+1* (Summer 2004), http://nplusonemag.com /issue-1/the-intellectual-situation/regressive-avant-garde/.

Reymond, Rhonda L. "Looking In: Albert A. Smith's Use of *Repoussoir* in Cover Illustrations for *The Crisis* and *Opportunity.*" *American Periodicals* 20, no. 2 (2010): 216–240.

Richards, I. A. *Principles of Literary Criticism.* 1926; repr. New York: Routledge, 2001.

Robertson, Michael. *Stephen Crane, Journalism, and the Making of Modern Literature.* New York: Columbia University Press, 1997.

Ross, Andrew. "The Mental Labor Problem." *Social Text* 18, no. 2 (2000): 1–31.

Rubin, Joan Shelley. *The Making of Middlebrow Culture.* Chapel Hill: University of North Carolina Press, 1992.

Russell, John. *Reciprocities in the Nonfiction Novel.* Athens: University of Georgia Press, 2000.

Ryley, Robert M. "Introduction." In *Complete Poems of Kenneth Fearing.* Orono, Maine: National Poetry Foundation, 1994.

Sawaya, Francesca. *Modern Women, Modern Work: Domesticity, Professionalism, and American Writing, 1890–1950.* Philadelphia: University of Pennsylvania Press, 2004.

Schatz, Thomas. *The Genius of the System: Hollywood Filmmaking in the Studio Era.* New York: Holt, 1988.

Schivelbusch, Wolfgang. *The Railway Journey: The Industrialization of Time and Space in the Twentieth Century.* Berkeley: University of California Press, 2014.

Schneirov, Matthew. *The Dream of a New Social Order: Popular Magazines in America, 1893–1914.* New York: Columbia University Press, 1994.

Schnitzer, Deborah. *The Pictorial in Modernist Fiction from Stephen Crane to Ernest Hemingway.* Ann Arbor, Mich.: UMI Research Press, 1988.

Scholes, Robert, and Clifford Wulfman. *Modernism in the Magazines: An Introduction.* New Haven, Conn.: Yale University Press, 2010.

Schudson, Michael. *Discovering the News: A Social History of American Newspapers.* New York: Basic Books, 1981.

——. "News, Politics, Nation," *American Historical Review* 107, no. 2 (April 2002): 481–492.

———. *The Sociology of News.* 2nd ed. New York: Norton, 2003.

Schuman, Edwin Llewellyn. *Practical Journalism: A Complete Manual on the Best Newspaper Methods.* New York: D. Appleton, 1910.

Schwartz, Delmore. "T. S. Eliot as International Hero." *Partisan Review* 12, no. 2 (1945): 199–206.

Sedgwick, Eve Kosofsky. "Willa Cather and Others." In *Tendencies.* Durham, N.C.: Duke University Press, 1993.

Seltzer, Mark. *Bodies and Machines.* New York: Routledge, 1992.

"Shantih Shantih Shantih." *Time* (March 6, 1923): 12.

Shirky, Clay. *Here Comes Everybody: The Power of Organizing Without Organizations.* New York: Penguin, 2009.

Smith, Henry Nash. "The Scribbling Women and the Cosmic Success Story." *Critical Inquiry* 1, no. 1 (1979): 47–70.

Smith, Shawn Michelle. *Photography on the Color Line: W. E. B. Du Bois, Race, and Visual Culture.* Durham, N.C.: Duke University Press, 2004.

Spiegel, Alan. *James Agee and the Legend of Himself: A Critical Study.* Columbia: University of Missouri, 1998.

Steffens, Lincoln. *Autobiography of Lincoln Steffens.* New York: Houghton, 1931.

Stein, Gertrude. "Off We All Went to See Germany." *Life* (August 6, 1945): 54ff.

Stewart, Garret. "Painted Readers, Narrative Regress." *Narrative* 11, no. 2 (2003): 125–176.

Stouck, David. "Historical Essay." In *O Pioneers!,* 283–303. Lincoln: University of Nebraska Press, 1992.

Strychacz, Thomas. *Hemingway's Theaters of Masculinity.* Baton Rouge: Louisiana State University Press, 2003.

———. *Modernism, Mass Culture, and Professionalism.* Cambridge: Cambridge University Press, 1993.

Sundquist, Eric. "Introduction." In the *Oxford W. E. B. Du Bois Reader,* ed. Eric Sundquist. New York: Oxford University Press, 1996.

Svensson, Ove G. "Ernest Hemingway and the Nobel Prize for Literature." *Hemingway Review* 27 (2008): 118–122.

Szalay, Michael. "HBO's Flexible Gold." *Representations* 1, no. 126 (2014): 112–134.

———. *New Deal Modernism: American Literature and the Invention of the Welfare State.* Durham, N.C.: Duke University Press, 2000.

Tiffany, Daniel. *My Silver Planet: A Secret History of Poetry and Kitsch.* Baltimore, Md.: Johns Hopkins University Press, 2014.

Trilling, Lionel. *Beyond Culture.* New York: Viking, 1965.

———. "Hemingway and His Critics." *Partisan Review* 6 (Winter 1939): 52–60.

Turner, Catherine. *Marketing Modernism Between the Two World Wars.* Amherst: University of Massachusetts Press, 2003.

Tzara, Tristan. *Seven Dada Manifestos and Lampisteries.* Trans. Barbara Wright. Surrey: One World, 2011.

Untermeyer, Louis. "Delusion vs. Dogma." *Freeman* (January 7, 1923): 453.

Urgo, Joseph A. "Willa Cather's Political Apprenticeship at *McClure's* Magazine." In *Willa Cather's New York: New Essays on Cather in the City*, ed. Merril Macguire Skaggs, 60–74. Madison, N.J.: Farleigh Dickinson University Press, 2000.

Vanderlan, Robert. *Intellectuals Incorporated: Politics, Art, and Ideas Inside Henry Luce's Media Empire*. Philadelphia: University of Pennsylvania Press, 2012.

Virno, Paolo. *A Grammar of the Multitude*. Trans. Isabella Bertoletti, James Cascaito, and Andrea Casson. Los Angeles: Semiotext[e], 2004.

Vismann, Cornelia. *Files: The Law and Media Technology*. Trans. Geoffrey Winthrop-Young. Stanford, Calif.: Stanford University Press, 2008.

Walkowitz, Rebecca. *Cosmopolitan Style: Modernism Beyond the Nation*. New York: Columbia University Press, 2007.

Wall, Cheryl A. *Women of the Harlem Renaissance*. Bloomington: Indiana University Press, 1995.

Wallace, David Foster. *Both Flesh and Not: Essays*. New York: Little, Brown, 2012.

Weeks, Edward. "Hemingway at His Best." *Atlantic* 190 (September 1952): 72.

White, Horace. "The School of Journalism." *North American Review* (January 1904): 25–32.

Whitehead, Colson. "Interview with Nancy Smith." *The Rumpus* (July 17, 2012), http://therumpus.net/2012/07/the-rumpus-interview-with-colson-whitehead/.

——. *John Henry Days*. New York: Doubleday, 2001.

Whyte, William H. "How to Back Into a *Fortune* Story." In *Writing for* Fortune, 189–194. New York: Time Inc., 1980.

——. *The Organization Man*. 1956; repr. Philadelphia: University of Pennsylvania Press, 2002.

Wicke, Jennifer. *Advertising Fictions: Literature, Advertisement, and Social Reading*. New York: Columbia University Press, 1988.

Wiener, Jon. *How We Forgot About the Cold War: A Historical Journey Across America*. Berkeley: University of California Press, 2012.

Wilson, Christopher P. *The Labor of Words: Literary Professionalism in the Progressive Era*. Athens: University of Georgia Press, 1985.

Wilson, Harold S. *McClure's Magazine and the Muckrakers*. Princeton, N.J.: Princeton University Press, 1970.

Winfield, Betty Houchin, ed. *Journalism 1908: The Birth of a Profession*. Columbia: University of Missouri Press, 2008.

Wood, James. "Human, All Too Human." *New Republic* (August 30, 2001): 28.

——. "Virtual Prose." *New Republic* (August 6, 2001): 30–34.

Woodress, James. "The Pre-Eminent Magazine Genius: S. S. McClure." In *Essays Mostly on Periodical Publishing in America*, ed. James Woodress, 171–192. Durham, N.C.: Duke University Press, 1973.

——. *Willa Cather: A Literary Life*. Lincoln: University of Nebraska Press, 1989.

Writers at Work: The Paris Review *Interviews, Second Series*. New York: Viking, 1963.

Yarborough, Richard. "Violence, Manhood, and Black Heroism: The Wilmington Riot in Two Turn-of-the-Century African American Novels." In *Democracy Betrayed: The Wilmington Race Riot of 1898 and Its Legacy*, ed. David S. Cecelski and Timothy B. Tyson, 225–252. Chapel Hill: University of North Carolina Press, 1998.

Yates, Norris. "The Vocabulary of *Time* Magazine Revisited." *American Speech* 56, no. 1 (1981): 53–63.

Zurier, Rebecca. *Art for the Masses: A Radical Magazine and Its Graphics, 1911–1917.* Philadelphia: Temple University Press, 1988.